# MARVELL: THE WRITER IN PUBLIC LIFE

LONGMAN MEDIEVAL AND RENAISSANCE LIBRARY

General Editors:
CHARLOTTE BREWER, Hertford College, Oxford
N. H. KEEBLE, University of Stirling

Published Titles:

*Shakespeare's Mouldy Tales: Recurrent Plot Motifs in Shakespearian Drama*
Leah Scragg

*The Fabliau in English*
John Hines

*English Medieval Mystics: Games of Faith*
Marion Glasscoe

*Speaking Pictures: English Emblem Books and Renaissance Culture*
Michael Bath

*The Classical Legacy in Renaissance Poetry*
Robin Sowerby

*Regaining Paradise Lost*
Thomas N. Corns

*English and Italian Literature from Dante to Shakespeare: A Study of Source, Analogue and Divergence*
Robin Kirkpatrick

*Shakespeare's Alternative Tales*
Leah Scragg

*The Gawain-Poet*
Ad Putter

*Donne's Religious Writing: A Discourse of Feigned Devotion*
P. M. Oliver

*Images of Faith in English Literature 700–1500: An Introduction*
Dee Dyas

*Courtliness and Literature in Medieval England*
David Burnley

*Wyatt, Surrey and Early Tudor Poetry*
Elizabeth Heale

*A New Introduction to Chaucer*
Derek Brewer

*Marvell: The Writer in Public Life*
Annabel Patterson

Annabel Patterson

# MARVELL: THE WRITER IN PUBLIC LIFE

LONGMAN

*An imprint of* PEARSON EDUCATION

Harlow, England · London · New York · Reading, Massachusetts · San Francisco · Toronto · Don Mills, Ontario · Sydney
Tokyo · Singapore · Hong Kong · Seoul · Taipei · Cape Town · Madrid · Mexico City · Amsterdam · Munich · Paris · Milan

**Pearson Education Limited**
Edinburgh Gate
Harlow
Essex CM20 2JE
England
and Associated Companies throughout the world

*Visit us on the World Wide Web at:*
www.pearsoned-ema.com

First published 2000

ISBN 0-582-35676-8 CSD
ISBN 0-582-35675-X PPR

**British Library Cataloguing-in-Publication Data**

A catalogue record for this book is available from the British Library

**Library of Congress Cataloging-in-Publication Data**

A catalog record for this book is available from the Library of Congress

Set by 35 in 10.5/12pt Mono Bembo

Printed and bound by CPI Antony Rowe, Eastbourne
Transferred to digital print on demand, 2008

# Contents

# List of illustrations

# Author's acknowledgements

For the opportunity to reintroduce this book to the public, I thank Neil Keeble, the editor responsible for Renaissance titles in the Longman Medieval and Renaissance Library series, and a wise adviser to boot. For the idea to do so, I am grateful to Tom Healy, who in his Longman Critical Reader considered the original, published in 1978, as then inaugurating a new phase of Marvell studies. For wary enthusiasm and learned friendship, I have been able to draw on my team of editors for the Yale edition of Marvell's prose, Martin Dzelzainis, Neil Keeble again, Nigel Smith and Nicholas von Maltzahn; and, until his sudden death in the winter of 1998, on Jeremy Maule, who was an amazing source of Marvell lore and biographical tips, and one of the most generous scholars I have ever known.

# Publisher's acknowledgements

The publishers would like to thank the following for permission to reproduce copyright material:

National Portrait Gallery for Illustration 1; Hull City Museums and Art Gallery for Illustration 2; Birmingham Museum and Art Gallery for Illustration 5; and the Scottish National Portrait Gallery for Illustration 6.

# Introduction

Twenty years ago, I began the earlier version of this study of Andrew Marvell by quoting what he himself wrote as an introduction to the *Second Part* of the *Rehearsal Transpros'd*. It seems even more appropriate now:

> Those that take upon themselves to be Writers, are moved to it either by Ambition or Charity: imagining that they shall do therein something to make themselves famous, or that they can communicate something that may be delightful and profitable to mankind. But therefore it is either way an envious and dangerous imployment. For, how well soever it be intended, the World will have some pretence to suspect, that the Author hath both too good a conceit of [her] own sufficiency, and that by undertaking to teach them, [s]he implicitly accuses their ignorance. So that not to Write at all is much the safer course of life:[1]

No one was more alert than Marvell to the moral and professional hazards of the writer's trade; and as someone who practised concealment whenever he could, he would have been doubly amused to hear his own words produced to justify not merely another book about himself, but a reappearance of an older book, on the grounds that it still has something important to tell us. It is impossible to explain this revised edition of *Marvell and the Civic Crown*, originally published by Princeton University Press in 1978, without making claims for its usefulness that by Marvell's standards are self-promotional.

Nevertheless (and this is a favourite conjunction in Marvell's own rhetorical strategy), the *Second Part* of the *Rehearsal Transpros'd* was indeed written, and written out of his urgent concern for justice to the Nonconformists during the intolerant 1670s; and I wrote the first version of this book driven by a desire to see justice done to Marvell himself. I wanted to show how unreasonable it was to assume that Marvell either wasted or lost his unique talents when he turned from woods and meadows to political subjects; to prove that he was just as witty in his political satires as in *The Garden*, just as 'literary' in the

*Rehearsal Transpros'd* and his other pamphlets in defence of toleration as he was in *The Coronet* or *On Mr. Milton's Paradise Lost*; and that for him poetics and politics were not incompatible but logically inextricable and mutually exhilarating. I wanted, also, to put Marvell back together again, and to exhibit, as far as was possible with so reticent a person, the internal structure of his beliefs, his practices and his psyche.

This poet with too many personae, as Rosalie Colie called him,[2] has often been pulled apart, though from the best of motives, by other writers with axes to grind. Like his own *Unfortunate Lover*, or rather the Lover's mother, his reputation seems to have been 'split against the Stone,/In a Cesarian Section'. The oldest image of Marvell was part of the creation of a Whig 'canon' by figures such as John Toland, Marvell's nephew William Popple, Thomas Hollis and editors of successive volumes of *Poems on Affairs of State*. To this movement belong Thomas 'Hesiod' Cooke's two-volume edition of Marvell's poetry in 1726, whose preface declared: 'My design in this is to draw a pattern for all freeborn Englishmen in the life of a worthy patriot, whose every action has truly merited to him, with Aristides, the surname of the "Just"'. This tradition is still reflected in Wordsworth's early sonnet, written about 1802, on the 'Great Men' that England, in contrast to France, had produced: 'The Later Sydney, Marvel, Harrington,/Young Vane, and others who call'd Milton Friend'.[3] But as Wordsworth would change his commitments, so would literary criticism, which became increasingly uncomfortable with the idea that value in the writings of the past could be attributed on the basis of something so tendentious and non-universal as a political ideology. The desire to write about Marvell exclusively as a poet rather than a political figure was visible throughout the nineteenth century and prominent in the first two decades of the twentieth. Its most influential expression was by T. S. Eliot.

Eliot solved the problem of Marvell's diversity by simply declaring that 'of all [his] verse, which is itself not a great quantity, the really valuable part consists of a very few poems',[4] and by proceeding to base his enormously influential judgements on the *Nymph complaining, To his Coy Mistress* and the *Horatian Ode*, each of which met his New Critical criteria. In 1966, J. B. Leishman's *The Art of Marvell's Poetry* carried to perfection the mandate given by Eliot and H. G. Grierson forty years earlier, situating Marvell in a 'metaphysical' mode (to be found in individual poems, or even in individual lines and images) in which he could be distinguished from Carew, Crashaw, Cowley, Cleveland and above all Donne only by the finest of critical sensibilities. Even when the whole man was treated, as in Legouis's great biography, first published in French in 1928 but translated into English in 1965, the book's subtitle, *Poet, Puritan, Patriot*, created alternative rather than interdependent categories. Legouis initiated the assumption that by entering Cromwell's service and committing himself to a life of political action, Marvell abandoned the intellectual delicacy which was his greatest strength, and that everything he later wrote was more or less clumsy in consequence.

Since the 1960s, as New Criticism gradually lost its dominant position, a rather marked split developed. Some readers rediscovered the Marvell of the Whig tradition, while others moved him into a world of theoretical play and meta-literary (as distinct from Metaphysical) sophistication. Making the second choice in 1970 were Donald Freedman and Rosalie Colie, among others. Making the first choice early was John M. Wallace (significantly a historian), later Warren Chernaik and most recently Patsy Griffin.[5]

The politics/literature dialectic thus represented established the terms of everything that followed in the next two decades. It appears that we still need to bring the two sides of the dialectic together, if Marvell's canon and reputation are to be made whole. To that end, *Marvell and the Civic Crown* has been re-titled and revised, with a student audience particularly in mind. Rather than increasing the weight of footnotes by citing scholarship accumulated in the interim, some of which is acknowledged in the Bibliography, I have simplified the system of reference and omitted the more esoteric aspects of the traditions Marvell was trained in. A British Council booklet (1994) taught me to write more economically about my favourite author, and some of its sentences have been 'transpros'd' into this book. And other new material has been added, especially on the *Short Historical Essay touching General Councils*, which, I was late to realize, was one of Marvell's most important and influential prose pamphlets, and on the *Account of the Growth of Popery*, equally influential in the century following his death, and the progenitor of a new genre, 'secret history'. Another new ingredient is an Appendix transcribing the texts of the *Second* and *Third Advices to the Painter*, as preserved in the 'Popple' manuscript of Marvell's poetry in the Bodleian Library. Given that my fourth chapter consists largely of an argument that these *are* poems by Marvell, that the 'Popple' manuscript is steadily increasing in authority, and that, although other sections of it have been made available in facsimile, these have not, it seemed useful to print them here in the form authorized by Marvell's own family.[6]

I have preserved my determination not to write extensively about the most frequently anthologized poems, and retained for this version only those readings which still seem the most independent and innovative; but the new version has become, if anything, *more* literary. More attention has been paid, particularly, to Marvell's grammar as a primary tool of the fine intellectual distinctions he made, in both poetry and prose. A new chapter on the devotional poems, which came first in the *Miscellaneous Poems* of 1681, provides a different kind of tie between his private life as a poet and his public life as a polemicist in church affairs. Believing that classical rhetoric was not esoteric to Marvell's contemporaries, but the very stuff of their education, I have retained a good many of the technical terms that help to explain how educated Marvell was in rhetorical and genre theory. But the governing principle behind the book remains the same: that Marvell should be honored, not implicitly disparaged or censored by the anthology principle, for having developed strong commitments – even though there will be many readers who cannot share his admiration for Oliver Cromwell, his scepticism about the Restoration monarchy, or the importance of abstruse arguments about Nonconformity.

There is another aspect of Marvell's work emphasized herein that requires special introduction. He had a habit of borrowing other men's words, a habit which has, since it was first discovered, been variously interpreted. The pamphleteers who replied to the *Rehearsal Transpros'd* not surprisingly regarded Marvell's borrowings from John Owen as a sign of incompetence: 'The worthy Author, that he might not seem a Plagiary, doth with much modesty call his Book, *The Rehearsal*, willing to intimate, that, whatever may be accounted any thing in it, was taken from others'.[7] Modern critics and editors have discovered local imitations of Cleveland, Waller, Jonson, Donne, Thomas May, Mildmay Fane, St Amant, Hermann Hugo, Henry Hawkins, Crashaw, Cowley and a host of less convincing likenesses. For J. B. Leishman, Marvell did not so much borrow as share, using a common and fashionable fund of conceits and topoi; and essays on individual 'sources', though often demonstrating a much more purposeful kind of imitation, have provided no general explanation of Marvell's indebtedness. For Rosalie Colie, however, the echoes we hear in *The Garden* and *Upon Appleton House* were part of Marvell's conscious strategy, a way of invoking traditions and contexts for both examination and consummation. This is just as true of the political poems where his critical impulses were supported by conviction, and what looks like imitation frequently turns out to be ideological parody. Edmund Waller was one court poet with whom Marvell seems to have carried on a long-term, one-way relationship best understood as ideological repartee. Marvell's mind, it seems, worked at all times by reflection and response. He found it easier to correct or modify other men's statements than formulate his own, to discover the ideal concept or metaphor behind its temporary aberrations, to base his differences from others upon a profound consensus of literary and political assumptions. He adjusted; and the art of adjustment that kept him writing under three radically different regimes allowed him to take what he found, in literature and politics, and literally make the best of it. But perhaps the most intriguing feature of this idiosyncrasy, this jackdaw tendency, is, as I show in Chapter 4, a habit of quoting himself.

Writing about Marvell is complicated by the fact that almost none of his poems were published during his lifetime. This means, first, that dating them has to remain hypothetical, and that all too often the question of his authorship, even, remains debatable. Marvell died in 1678, and his *Miscellaneous Poems* appeared in 1681, under the auspices of a woman who claimed to be his wife but was really only his housekeeper. The *Miscellaneous Poems* presents the poems in an order ignored or substantially altered by all modern editions, including the definitive *Poems and Letters* edited by H. M. Margoliouth and revised by Pierre Legouis. We have no way of knowing whether that order was created by Marvell himself in some more or less complete holograph manuscript, or whether separate papers were organized by his friends in what seemed to them a logical (rather than a chronological) arrangement. From time to time this book deals with the 'original' order of the 1681 volume and tries to make sense of it. One of the most interesting problems of chronology concerns *The Garden*, which Allan Pritchard has persuasively argued is a Restoration poem, echoing poems by Abraham Cowley and Katherine Philips that were published in 1668.[8] Perhaps nothing could more destabilize the assumption that Marvell's pastoral period was completely separate from (and earlier than) his political life than the discovery that this, perhaps the most famous of his lyrics, was not contemporaneous with *Upon Appleton House*, but rather with his Dutch War satires.

One of the most significant facts about the *Miscellaneous Poems* is that it was evidently intended to include the three poems on Oliver Cromwell, the *Horatian Ode*, the *First Anniversary* and the lament for Cromwell's death. But a decision to cancel these poems seems to have been made while the volume was actually in press, because even in the two copies that survive untruncated, the second half of the elegy for Cromwell (lines 185–324) is missing, and may never have been set. One extraordinarily valuable copy of the truncated version now exists in the Bodleian Library (as MS Eng. Poet. d. 49), referred to above as the 'Popple' manuscript. It contains, on extra leaves added at the back, and mostly in a single flowing hand, the full text of the three deleted 'Cromwell' poems, and the *Second* and *Third Advices to the Painter*, along with a substantial collection of shorter Restoration satires. This volume is now accepted as the one referred to by Captain Edward Thompson, the eighteenth-century editor of Marvell's works, who described in his preface receiving a manuscript belonging to Marvell's nephew William Popple, 'being a collection of his uncle Andrew Marvell's compositions [compiled] after his decease'. The significance of this manuscript in general is itself due for a new rehearsal.

For poems other than the *Advices*, I cite throughout and rely upon the scholarship of the *Poems and Letters*, edited by H. M. Margoliouth in 1927 and brought up to date by Emile Legouis in 1971. Although the two parts of the *Rehearsal Transpros'd* were edited by D. I. B. Smith for the Clarendon Press in 1971, there is as yet no complete modern edition of a collected *Works*. For the other tracts in support of toleration and the famous *Account of the Growth of Popery and Arbitrary Government*, one still has to depend on Alexander Grosart's *Complete Works*, originally published in 1875, and almost entirely innocent of annotation. But by the time 'Times winged Charriot' brings this study to the bookshops, the Yale edition of Marvell's *Prose Works* will be near completion.

In the Whig tradition of Cooke, Thompson and Alexander Grosart, editors who appreciated the importance of Marvell's prose, he was thought to have left us a precious legacy of liberalism. As Grosart put it, 'in "evil days" [he] stood forward in behalf of principles of civil and religious liberty'. The unacknowledged, taken-for-granted quotation from *Paradise Lost*, Book VII, locks Marvell and Milton together. And once we have relearned the connections between all the seemingly disparate parts of Marvell's work, we ought to be capable of recognizing his peculiar forms of heroism, which should still be worth imitating. To quote *The Unfortunate Lover* again:

> See how he nak'd and fierce does stand,
> Cuffing the Thunder with one hand;
> While with the other he does lock,
> And grapple, with the stubborn Rock:
> . . .

Who though, by the Malignant Starrs,
Forced to live in Storms and Warrs;
Yet dying leaves a Perfume here,
And Musick within every Ear:


NOTES

1.  *The Rehearsal Transpros'd and The Rehearsal Transpros'd: The Second Part*,
    ed. D. I. B. Smith (Oxford, 1971), pp. 159–60.
2.  Rosalie Colie, *'My Ecchoing Song': Andrew Marvell's Poetry of Criticism*
    (Princeton, 1970), p. 3, n. 2.
3.  Wordsworth refers to the republican Algernon Sidney, executed in
    1683, James Harrington, and Sir Henry Vane, executed in 1662 as a
    regicide.
4.  Eliot, 'Andrew Marvell', first printed in the *Times Literary Supplement*,
    31 March 1921, pp. 201–2.
5.  See the Bibliography.
6.  The reader should also consult George de F. Lord's splendidly annotated
    and partially collated edition in *Poems on Affairs of State*. A newly collated
    edition is forthcoming from Nigel Smith in the Longman Annotated
    English Poets series.
7.  Anon., *A Common-Place Book out of the Rehearsal Transpros'd* (London,
    1673), p. 1.
8.  Allan Pritchard, 'Marvell's "The Garden": A Restoration Poem?', *Stud-
    ies in English Literature* 23 (1983), pp. 371–88.

# Chapter 1

# The portraits and the life

The two most important facts about Andrew Marvell, biographically speaking, are that (despite the misleading testimony of the *Miscellaneous Poems*) he never married, and that he spent almost two decades as a Member of Parliament for Hull, from 1659, when he was thirty-eight, until his death in the summer of 1678. Hull was his home town. His family had moved there in 1624 when Marvell was three. His father, Andrew Senior, was a moderate Puritan, appointed as lecturer in Hull's Holy Trinity Church. Marvell probably attended Hull grammar school, and his return to public service for that town (though he mostly lived in London) tells us a good deal about his way of coping with the collapse of the English republican experiment in 1659–60.

So do his portraits. One of our surprises, as readers of Marvell's taut and teasing lyric poems, is coming face to face for the first time with the heavy features painted, perhaps, by Sir Peter Lely, and now in the National Portrait Gallery (Figure 1): big nose, pouchy cheeks and chin, mouth too full for a man, especially in the lower lip, the whole not so much redeemed as rendered problematic by the fine wide eyes and challenging gaze that characterize so many of Lely's portraits. George Vertue recorded in one of his notebooks that a portrait of Marvell by Lely was in the possession of the Ashley family;[1] and in *Upon Appleton House* Marvell summons an image of Lely's studio, with its 'Clothes' or canvases 'strecht to stain' (l. 444), implying that he had been there. On close inspection, this portrait, called the 'Nettleton', becomes enigmatic not only in its gaze but in its iconography. The plain white collar or 'band', the plain brown jacket and skull-cap share the 'puritan' semiotics of Lely's commonwealth style, which would be fully expressed in his portraits of Oliver Cromwell or Peter Pett. But the exuberant hair implies more courtly tendencies, while peeking out from under the stiff band is some luxurious, softer, shinier stuff, whose identification as tasselled bandstrings does little to explain away the conflicting visual message.

Figure 1    Andrew Marvell, 'Nettleton' portrait, National Portrait
Gallery, London

One would have liked to know whether Marvell had fine hands to
match his eyes, but the oval frame (characteristic of Lely's portraits of
poets)[2] excludes them from consideration.

On either side of this portrait stand, we might say, representations
of Innocence and Experience. Experience is featured in the 'Hollis'

FIGURE 2    Andrew Marvell, 'Hollis' portrait, Hull Museums

portrait (Figure 2), so called because Thomas Hollis, the late eighteenth-century Whig philanthropist, acquired it in 1763, and gave us its first formal and ideological reading: 'If Marvell's picture', he wrote, 'does not look so lively and witty as you might expect, it is from the chagrin and awe he had of the Restoration then just effected'. It 'was painted when he was forty-one; that is, in the year 1661 . . . in all the sobriety and decency of *the then departed Commonwealth*'.[3] Ideology here competes with aesthetic apology, an insight into Marvell's feelings after the death of Oliver Cromwell and the collapse of the Protectorate; but for Thomas Hollis himself, who was the devoted collector behind the first edition of Marvell's prose, this dour portrait was part of a record of integrity and commitment.

We may also, however, know what Marvell looked like as the picture of Innocence. In John L. Propert's late nineteenth-century *History of Miniature Art*, there is a reference to 'Samuel Cooper's fine portrait of Andrew Marvell',[4] along with a reproduction of a miniature said to be of Marvell, but mysteriously there attributed to Mary Beale (Figure 3). Mary Beale was born in 1633, and married in 1652. This would make her younger than Marvell by twelve years, so she can scarcely have painted Marvell as a boy. Samuel Cooper, however, was born in 1608, and had established himself as a miniature painter by 1629, when Marvell was eight years old. It is not too difficult to see this graceful child still visible in the eyes and mouth of the 'Nettleton' portrait, and nothing in the image denies Propert's identification. If this is a Cooper portrait of Marvell at, say, twelve years old, when he matriculated at Trinity College, Cambridge, its painting would be prophetic of both their careers. By 1650 Cooper's chief patron was Oliver Cromwell, who sent Cooper's images of him abroad to Dutch and French statesmen, as well as the portrait sent to Queen Christina of Sweden about which Marvell wrote a Latin poem. Cooper also painted Richard Cromwell, Thomas Fairfax, Secretary Thurlow, two of Cromwell's generals, Richard Ireton and George Fleetwood, the lawyer Sir John Maynard, who managed the impeachments of Laud and Strafford, the regicide John Carew, the Leveller leader John Lilburne, and Thomas May, translator of Lucan, who scandalized many by changing loyalties and becoming the historian of the Long Parliament.

The last image of Marvell is in fact the 'Nettleton' portrait again, copied in reverse for the engraved portrait that appeared in his posthumously published *Miscellaneous Poems* of 1681 (Figure 4). Here the face is still heavier, the hair longer and more wig-like, the plain jerkin now swathed in a cloak, the eyes warier over deep bags, the mouth sensuous no longer. If we allow this series to represent the life, a narrative of Marvell's gaze over the Revolution and the Restoration, the story, like the face, succumbs to the pull of gravity. Whatever self-contradictions were residual in the 'Nettleton' portrait (and we can perhaps imagine the 'Nectaren, and curious Peach' had once or twice reached themselves into those invisible hands), those who presented his image to a reading public in 1681 wished him to be admired for dourer, more reliable features.

Between his Hull childhood and dutiful middle age, whose record can be seen in the nearly 300 letters Marvell wrote to the Hull

FIGURE 3    Marvell as a boy, by Samuel Cooper (?), from John L.
Propert's *History of Miniature Art* (1887)

Corporation about parliamentary business, lay not quite a century of
monumental events. Marvell's response to these, or direct involvement
in them, has to be pieced together from a set of fragmentary records
and hints, some of which are his own poems. First came nine years

FIGURE 4    Andrew Marvell, frontispiece to *Miscellaneous Poems* (1681)

at Cambridge, interrupted both by his father's accidental drowning in 1641, and by his own journeys through Holland, France, Italy and Spain between 1642 and 1647. Hilton Kelliher guessed that Marvell left England soon after the outbreak of the First Civil War and returned as soon as it ended.[5] Early in 1651 he entered the employ of

Sir Thomas Fairfax as tutor to his daughter Mary, and spent the next two years at Nunappleton House, the estate in Yorkshire to which Fairfax retired after resigning his command of the parliamentary armies. In February 1653 John Milton recommended him, unsuccessfully, to John Bradshaw, President of the revolutionary Council of State, as a candidate for the Latin secretariat. In July 1653, Marvell moved to Eton to become tutor to Cromwell's prospective son-in-law, William Dutton, staying in the house of the puritan John Oxenbridge. The Dutton assignment seems to have continued through at least August 1656, when James Scudamore reported in a letter from Saumur in France the presence there of 'Mr Dutton calld by the french Le Genre du Protecteur whose Governour is one Mervill a notable English Italo-Machavillian'.[6]

Since leaving his own place of higher education, then, the only signs of Marvell's activities that have survived indicate that he had cosmopolitan manners (enough to be thought hyper-sophisticated or machiavellian) and saw himself primarily as an intellectual, one whose relation to high politics would be peripheral. In the early 1650s the connections he sought, or that were sought for him, placed him firmly apart from the king's party, although, as at least his 1649 poem to Richard Lovelace demonstrates, he had friends among the cavaliers.[7] Let us pause on that poem for a moment, not least because it has been read more than once as an expression of sympathy for the royalist cause. In fact, it merely expressed good will towards one particular royalist whose literary career has run into trouble because of his own political involvement, especially in forwarding to the Long Parliament the Kentish Petition against their proceedings; and Marvell develops that motif into a lament for the conditions of civil war culture in general.

*To his Noble Friend Mr. Richard Lovelace, upon his Poems* appeared as a commendatory poem in Lovelace's *Lucasta*, which had had difficulty with the parliamentary censors. Even after licence had been granted in February 1647/48, publication was delayed until the summer of 1649, surely because of the 'Sequestration' or temporary confiscation of Lovelace's estate to which Marvell's poem refers. That punishment for 'delinquency', or taking up arms against the parliament, had been ordered by the Long Parliament on 28 November 1648.[8] On 5 May 1649 Lovelace's name appears in the Commons Journal in a list of delinquents whose cases were to be reconsidered with a view to mitigating their fines. *Lucasta* was registered for actual publication just over a week later. These events explain the otherwise peculiar directions taken by Marvell's poem – certainly one of his earliest, but also one of his most sophisticated statements about the relations between writing and the world.

*To his Noble Friend* begins with the premise that 'our times are much degenerate' from those in which Lovelace conceived his poems: a chronology that conflates the Caroline era, so often described by court poets as a Golden Age, with the pseudo-medieval chivalry invoked by Lovelace, and both with the age of classical, Ciceronian rhetoric whose disinterested objective was social and political improvement; language in the service of the state. For this kind of 'speaking well', Marvell adopts the adjective 'ingenious', derived from the classical *ingenium*, an interesting conflation of high intelligence with cleverness or wit, from which derive both our 'genius' and 'ingenuity'. Marvell would return to this term as a problematic ideal in one of his late polemical pamphlets; but here he is concerned with the collapse of the classical ideals:

> Modest ambition studi'd only then,
> To honour not her selfe, but worthy men.
> These vertues now are banisht out of Towne,
> Our Civill Wars have lost the Civicke crowne.
> He highest builds, who with most Art destroys,
> And against others Fame his own employs.[9]

Since then, Marvell complains, 'our wits have drawne th'infection of our times'; 'Civill' and 'Civicke', though obviously related etymologically, have become antagonists; and he equates the negativity of the 'grim consistory' (the Long Parliament) and the 'yong Presbytery' (the Westminster Assembly) with the generally negative criticism supplied by the 'barbed Censurers', (ordinary readers who have translated the real hostilities of the times into trivial logomachias). A complicated series of puns connects the verdicts of these 'Word-peckers' with Lovelace's political difficulties:

> Some reading your *Lucasta*, will alledge
> You wrong'd in her the Houses Priviledge.
> Some that you under sequestration are,
> Because you write when going to the Warre.

In the first of these couplets Marvell alludes to the privilege of freedom of speech *within* the Commons, a privilege limited, however, to Members of Parliament, and denied to the rest of society specifically by the 1643 Printing Ordinance, against which Milton had delivered his famous 'speech', *Areopagitica*. In the second, he plays with the title of Lovelace's most famous poem, *To Lucasta, on going to the war*, making it serve the charge that Lovelace has confused literature and politics, as his parliamentary censors have also, of course, more ostentatiously done. This was not, however, a distinction that Marvell himself would be able to observe much longer.

There are two ways of regarding the next eight years of Marvell's career, from 1650 to Cromwell's death in 1658. By September 1657 Marvell had at last acquired a junior position in the Latin secretariat, under John Thurloe and with Milton. During this period he wrote three poems to or about Cromwell which we can date with some precision: the *Horatian Ode* on Cromwell's return from Ireland in May 1650; the *First Anniversary of the Government under O.C.*, which was advertised for sale in *Mercurius Politicus* in January 1655, but with no author's name attached; and the elegy for Cromwell's death, which occurred on 3 September 1658. He also wrote, presumably for Fairfax, three complimentary 'estate' poems, *Epigramma in Duos montes*, *Upon the Hill and Grove at Bill-borow*, and *Upon Appleton House*, all (again presumably) before he left Fairfax's employment. On the basis of this evidence it has become customary to read Milton's letter to Bradshaw as a significant dividing line, indicating for the first time Marvell's wish for some kind of political post; three years of 'detached' leisure and creative privacy are thus separated from five years of increasing commitment to Cromwell and decreasing literary significance. Not only the 'pastoral' poems but the *Horatian Ode* are thus assigned to the Fairfax period, as a time when Marvell was gracefully free of partisanship. Alternatively, the *Ode* is itself seen as the dividing line, written at the century's midpoint, when Marvell was still capable of examining dispassionately the claims of both Charles I (so recently executed) and Oliver Cromwell (so clearly the most powerful man in the state) to legitimacy and admiration.

The other way of considering Marvell's Protectorate poetry, and one I shall argue at length in the next chapter, is to see it as a whole, as a series of interdependent studies, if not exactly experiments, in the interpretation and evaluation of contemporary public figures. As an employee of both Cromwell and Fairfax, Marvell was in a position both of dependency and of peculiar privilege, as tutor to younger members of their families, a position which carried the status of intellectual superiority uneasily blended with social inferiority. As a poet, he had a medium of communication with both men which carried its own sanctions, and allowed him, in the act of evaluation, to offer advice. Furthermore, pure political chance had, as it were, offered him a subject of such classical dimensions that it is accepted even by those who would force the Protectorate poems apart. Fairfax's resignation from his generalship, and Cromwell's acceptance of leadership of the state, were not only interdependent politically but were immediately recognizable as contrasting classical archetypes of conduct. In evaluating these striking examples of political activism and contemplative retreat, Marvell offers neither of them an unquestioning advocacy. His support of Cromwell as the one strong man capable of settling the nation's divisions is heavily qualified by his dislike of Cromwell's use of violence; his respect for Fairfax, whose own position was against the execution of Charles, carries with it an equally serious reproach, that resignation at such a time was indicative of selfish weakness. By a series of calculated echoes and contrasts between the two groups of poems, Marvell created a formal but none the less urgent dialectic about the events and issues involved and, in trying to offer advice in a manner acceptable to his great subjects, he developed some intelligent modifications of traditional forms of praise.

These Protectorate poems, therefore, are vital evidence of Marvell's political poetics. They also give us two of our rare encounters with Marvell engaged in acts of self-definition, confirming that in his own eyes his own personality was split. In *Upon Appleton House* we are shown Mary Fairfax's self-indulgent tutor, whose stance, if such a word can be used of so recumbent a person, is that of the 'easie Philosopher', too lazy and too self-mocking to be simply *libertin* or truly *savant*, but who can be recalled, at least to attention, by the 'discipline' embodied in his pupil. In *The First Anniversary*, Marvell criticizes the kings of Europe for their failure to support Cromwell's crusading Protestantism, and makes for himself a strenuous commitment to write the epic of Cromwell's millennium:

> Unhappy Princes, ignorantly bred,
> By Malice some, by Errour more misled;
> If gracious Heaven to my Life give length,
> Leisure to Time, and to my Weakness Strength,
> Then shall I once with graver Accents shake
> Your Regal sloth, and your long Slumbers wake:
> Like the shrill Huntsman that prevents the East,
> Winding his Horn to Kings that chase the Beast.

(ll. 117–24)

This passage makes a significant contrast with Milton's expression, in *The Reason of Church Government*, of the literary ambitions from which he was, in the 1640s, being distracted by polemical engagement. Milton speaks of 'inward prompting', of the 'labor and intent study' which he takes to be his 'portion in this life', and of the 'strong propensity of nature' to write, all of which allow him to 'covenant' with the reader for a great work to appear in 'some few years'.[10] Marvell's disapproval of 'Regal sloth', on the contrary, is accompanied by an admission of his own 'Weakness', which, however formally proposed, is partially supported by the facts. Cromwell's epic was never written in the three years before his death, and Marvell's monumental, as distinct from occasional, impulses were deflected for over a decade.

To make an analogy with Milton, who, for all his confidence, did not complete his great work until the Restoration forced him out of public life, is to fall once again under the shadow of the politics/literature dichotomy. But when Marvell really began his own public career, as representative for Hull in Richard Cromwell's Parliament, one cannot say simply, as Milton said about himself, that he had become too active in one sphere to attend to the demands of the other. The record of his behaviour for the next twenty years is itself a record of alternating commitment and retreat and, when he moves forward, it appears he does so on both fronts. Political involvement produced, in the mid-1660s, the *Advices to the Painter*, in 1672 the *Rehearsal Transpros'd*, in 1676–77 the *Account of the Growth of Popery and Arbitrary Government*. In between these very different (and differently motivated) achievements, there is evidence of absence, withdrawal, silence.

It seems clear that Marvell entered Richard's Parliament in a mood of optimism, and with a sense of being among the reasonable majority. Despite the resistance of the anti-Protectorate group, 'it is to be hoped', he wrote in February 1658 to Downing at the Hague, 'that our justice our affection and our number which is at least two thirds will weare them out at the long runne' (*Poems and Letters*, 2: 308). He was active in committees in Richard's Parliament, and extremely so from June to December 1660 in the Convention Parliament, being appointed to thirteen, and sometimes apparently taking leadership within them. On 27 November there is an unusually full and descriptive entry in the *Journal of the House of Commons* (8: 193) showing Marvell reporting for a committee in which he might well have been particularly interested. It involved the religious climate of the universities, and their responsibility for endowing 'impropriate' rectories; and, after reporting a series of amendments to the Bill in question, 'which he read', says the journal, 'with the Coherence, in his Place', Marvell transmitted 'the desire of the said Committee, that this House would desire his Majesty, that he would be pleased to write his Letter to the Colleges in the Universities, that they would take into Consideration their respective Impropriations, and augment the Vicarages, or Curate Places, belonging thereto'.

The whole item carries a definite flavour of competence combined with respectable enthusiasm; and a concern about impropriation was to remain with Marvell long after his initial hopes for the Restoration had disappeared.

Another most significant committee for him must have been that appointed to 'settle the Militia', to work out some mechanism for controlling the army in the new conditions of peacetime. Marvell's own political views, as well as his temperamental preferences, are well expressed in a letter to his constituents in Hull written on 4 December 1660, reporting indirectly on the stormy reception which had greeted the Militia Bill when it first came forward from his own committee: 'The Act for the Militia hath not been calld for of late', wrote Marvell, 'men not being forward to confirme such perpetuall & exorbitant powrs by a law as it would be in danger if that Bill should be carryed on. Tis better to trust his Majesty's moderation & that the Commissioners if they act extravagantly as in some Countyes should be liable to actions at law', (*Poems and Letters*, 2: 7–8). What role he had played in the initial 'forwarding' is not clear; but Marvell's position was now, and was to remain, opposed to a standing army, symbolic of violent intervention in the state, and therefore symbolically inconsistent with the new 'moderation' expressed in Charles's Declaration of Breda. Though events had in the past required and would again require Marvell to accept 'forward' behaviour in others and in himself, 'moderation' and its concomitant term 'modesty' were to remain his better values.

One such event has a special value for this study in that it signifies the reciprocity of Marvell's literary and political beliefs. In Marvell's connection with Milton there is more than friendship and certainly more than some points of analogy between their respective careers. In December 1660 Marvell spoke in the House of Commons in defence of Milton, an act which must have required considerable courage, since a few days earlier he had reported to Hull that the bodies of the chief regicides were to be publicly dishonored. Parliamentary history records that 'the famous Mr. Milton having now laid long in Custody of the Serjeant at Arms, was released by Order of the House. Soon after Mr. Andrew Marvel complained that the Serjeant had exacted £150. Fees of Mr. Milton', a sum obviously in excess of what might have been expected. Others seconded the protest and, notwithstanding the assertion of Sir Heneage Finch 'That Milton was Latin Secretary to Cromwell, and deserved hanging', the matter was referred to the Committee of Privileges and resolved somewhat more in Milton's favour.[11]

However, in the first years of the Restoration Parliament, the records (and the gaps in the records) present a very different picture. In those difficult months when the religious settlement was being negotiated, the bishops restored to the Lords, and the Nonconforming ministers ejected from their pulpits, Marvell made no speeches, although he was later to comment bitterly on those events in the *Third Advice to the Painter*. Instead, he was chiefly remarkable for his quarrel with Thomas Clifford in the House, which nearly resulted in his expulsion for breach of privilege. On 20 March 1662 the Speaker reported that 'he had examined the Matter of Difference between Mr. Marvell and Mr. Clifford, and found, that Mr. Marvell had given the first Provocation, that begot the Difference: And that his Opinion was, that Mr. Marvell should declare his Sorrow for being the first occasion of this Difference; and then Mr. Clifford to declare, that he was sorry for the Consequence of it: And that Mr. Clifford was willing to yield to this Determination, but that Mr. Marvell refused.'[12] The formality of the language does not conceal the heat of the incident, whose cause we do not know, nor the humiliating retreat which Marvell was forced to make when summoned with Clifford before the House, which, upon receiving their apologies, withdrew the breach-of-privilege charge. Less than two months later, on 8 May 1662, Marvell informed the Hull Trinity House of his decision to go abroad[13] and, although recalled from Holland by the fear of losing his seat, he soon found occasion for a further and longer absence to accompany the Earl of Carlisle on his embassy to Russia and Sweden. He did not return to his seat in the House until February 1665, three years after his departure and one month before the Second Dutch War was officially declared.

This pattern was to be repeated. From late 1665 to early 1668 Marvell clearly found himself excited and outraged by the mismanagement of the war, the rule of the Cabal, especially of Clarendon, and the financial impasse between king and Parliament. He was appointed to several major committees of public inquiry, notably that directed to inquire into the 'miscarriages' of the war,[14] and he made speeches on issues connected with those acts of mismanagement and chicanery. He also discovered a new connection between political and literary activity, which was more direct and certainly more dangerous than the role of poet–counsellor to Cromwell and Fairfax. This was the authorship of secretly printed satirical poems that attacked the government's conduct of the Dutch War and eventually recommended a complete change in the ministry.

In late 1666 and 1667, partly in response to Edmund Waller's ill-timed panegyric on the Battle of Lowestoft, there appeared a series of *Advices to the Painter*, which will be discussed in detail in Chapter 4. There seems to have been a vigorous Opposition underground press, which managed, in defiance of rigorous censorship, to print and circulate such pamphlets, sometimes in Westminster itself. This form of publication was intended to influence policy, to apply pressure, not only to the king, to whom some of the *Advices* were formally addressed, but in Parliament; circulation, it appears, was timed to coincide with crucial parliamentary sessions. In this situation, an Opposition Member who also happened to be a writer of talent could, if he avoided discovery, perform an invaluable double function. Inside knowledge could, in effect, create an outspoken but anonymous lobby for positions which could only be held discreetly in the House. It is noticeable that when the temper of the Commons was for putting most of the blame for the war onto Clarendon, a position argued with violence in the *Second* and *Third Advices* and the *Last Instructions*, Marvell spoke three or four times in the House against impeachment, perhaps to dissociate himself publicly from the satires. Later, when Clarendon had fled the country, Marvell sat on the committee appointed to arrange for his banishment. However, in the spring of 1668 Marvell again committed acts of indiscretion, which marked the end of such strategic usefulness. On 15 February 1668, during the report of the committee on the miscarriages of the war, Marvell, as a member of that committee, spoke 'somewhat transportedly' on the incompetence of Arlington, Secretary of State, accusing him of having bought an office for which he had no capacity, and thereby endangering the whole fleet for want of proper naval intelligence.[15] That Marvell had partially blown his cover, and that he tried to regain it, is suggested by a letter from Arlington himself to Sir William Temple two days later, referring to the incident as the most significant, from his point of view, in the whole debate: 'The House of Commons are yet in their enquiry after miscarriages; I leave it to your other correspondents to tell you what Votes they have passed therein. But cannot forbear letting you know that Mr. Marvel hath struck hard at me, upon the Point of Intelligence . . . This Day he hath given me cause to forgive him, by being the first Man, that, in the midst of this enquiry, moved the taking into consideration of His Majesty's Speech.'[16] A few weeks later, however, there are signs that Marvell was beginning to dissociate himself in a different way from his Opposition colleagues. On 13 and 30 March Marvell attacked the proposal, favoured by the majority of the Commons, to renew the Conventicles Act preventing Nonconformists from holding religious meetings. On the second of these occasions, Marvell's was the only voice raised in opposition to the new Bill.[17] Indignation against the Cabal for misgovernment had been diverted by indignation against the Commons for their intolerance; these speeches mark the beginning of Marvell's disillusionment with the House of Commons and perhaps with his own role as cautious temporizer.

In the remaining ten years of his career as Member for Hull, although he continued to do his share of committee work and to report regularly to his constituents, Marvell made only two speeches which have been recorded, although there may have been others which have vanished without trace. On 21 November 1670 he spoke briefly on behalf of James Hayes, under prosecution for attempting to subvert the Conventicles Act,[18] a single example of that 'quintessence of arbitrary malice' which the Commons had unleashed upon the Nonconformists. However, in the same letter to William Popple in which the Conventicles Act is thus defined, Marvell made it clear that his disillusionment was caused by more than the toleration problem. The Commons have been intimidated by the king (whose new request for Supply was delivered, to Marvell's rhetoric-conscious ear, '*Stylo minaci et imperatorio*', that is, in a threatening and imperial style) and have abandoned their primary responsibility, which is to control government spending. The commissioners set up in the heat of December 1666 to inspect public accounts have been 'continually discountenanced, and treated rather as Offenders than Judges'. All of the advantages gained in the wartime crisis have been lost in cynicism and private interest, and the balance of power has shifted. 'It is also my Opinion', Marvell wrote, 'that the King was never since his coming in, nay, all Things considered, no King since the Conquest, so absolutely powerful at Home, as he is at present. Nor any Parliament, or Places, so certainly and constantly supplyed with Men of the same Temper. In such a Conjuncture, dear Will, what Probability is there of my doing any Thing to the Purpose?' (*Poems and Letters*, 2: 314–15). It was not long before Marvell's reticence in the House became common parlance. Samuel Parker, in his *Reproof* (1673), imagined him as 'fearful of speaking'. Another attack on the *Rehearsal Transpros'd* parodied Marvell's debating style: 'Mr. Speaker – I, that spoke here but once before,/ Must now speak, though I ne'er speak more.'[19] More interesting, perhaps, than these obviously hostile comments, is Marvell's apparent recognition of his own ambiguous position. Does not his silence make him complicit in the general weakness? Writing to Popple in April 1670, he comments on the spread of intimidation to the Lords, with the king in daily attendance at their debates: 'The Parliament was never so embarassed, beyond Recovery. We are all venal Cowards, except some few' (*Poems and Letters*, 2: 317).

By the middle of 1672, however, Marvell had discovered another use for his talents. The combined occasion of Samuel Parker's attacks on the Nonconformists and the king's Declaration of Indulgence offered him an opportunity to return both to the medium of print and to public statement, supported by his own strong convictions and without any of the disadvantages of overt party politics. By using a satirical exposé of Parker's style and temperament as the vehicle for a general appeal for religious toleration, Marvell was able to personalize his pamphlet, and indirectly encourage the king in what appeared to be a new lenience toward the Nonconformists on the church's left. The respectable genre of ecclesiastical debate provided formal protection and, although there were some attempts at censorship, the second impression of the *Rehearsal Transpros'd* actually went out with the licenser's permission.[20] In a few weeks it made Marvell's reputation as a writer, and gave him recognition, if not practical success. That Marvell's point had struck home is indicated by the fact that no less than six hostile answers to his pamphlet immediately appeared.[21]

Even so, in the *Second Part*, Marvell claimed to have been only an unwilling participant in the dispute, which had previously been taking place between Parker and the dissenter John Owen. It took, he wrote, a very high level of provocation on Parker's part to 'tempt [him] from that modest retiredness to which [he] had all his life hitherto been addicted' (p. 169). Although his intervention was more than justified by the dangerous implications of Parker's policies, the justice of his cause could not fully reconcile him to the methods he had been forced to use:

> Yet withall that it hath been thus far the odiousest task that ever I undertook, and has lookt to me all the while like the cruelty of a living Dissection, which, however, it may tend to publick instruction, and though I have pick'd out the most noxious Creature to be anatomiz'd, yet doth scarce excuse or recompense the offensiveness of the scent and fouling of my fingers.
>
> (p. 185)

Meanwhile, the declaration of the Third Dutch War on 17 March 1672 had initiated a new phase of activity in Parliament, in which Marvell seems to have played some part. Forced by financial necessity to recall a Parliament which had not been allowed to meet for nearly two years, Charles found himself compelled to withdraw the

Declaration of Indulgence and to accept instead a Test Bill designed to prevent Roman Catholics from holding office. As a result of the Test, Thomas Clifford resigned from his post of Treasurer and, in revenge against his all-too-flexible master, revealed to Shaftesbury (only recently made Lord Chancellor) the secret clauses in the Treaty of Dover whereby Charles had promised Louis XIV, his ally against the Dutch, his own public conversion to the Roman Catholic Church. Shaftesbury immediately went over to the Opposition in the Lords, where he was shortly joined by the Duke of Buckingham. In the Commons, the Opposition had already been strengthened by the defection of Sir William Coventry to the 'Country' party. On the Government side, the rule of the Cabal was replaced virtually by that of a single man, Thomas Osborne, the new Treasurer, shortly to be created Earl of Danby. By the summer of 1675 Marvell was remarking caustically to Popple on the formation of a new 'Episcopal Cavalier Party' (*Poems and Letters*, 2: 341), an informal allegiance between Danby, Lauderdale (who was responsible for Scotland), and the Anglican bishops. In this invigorating context, where the lines between friends and enemies could be more clearly redrawn, Marvell was apparently able to reunite his convictions and coordinate his activities on several fronts. Abandoning the Declaration of Indulgence as an empty symbol, produced moreover in highly suspicious circumstances, he continued his literary campaign for toleration on increasingly theoretical grounds. By identifying Danby and Lauderdale as the new persecutors, he was also able to realign himself with the majority in the Commons, whose strategy was, by withholding funds, to acquire some measure of control over the king's prerogative in foreign policy. An anonymous ballad, the *Charge to the Grand Inquest of England* (1674), describes the activities of the Commons at this time, focusing on the Committee of Privileges, of which Marvell was a member in 1673, and aligns the parliamentarians of the 1670s with the radicals of the 1640s in their search for parliamentary rights in the archives:

> Search the repositories of the Tower
> And your own brains to stretch your lawless power.
> Ransack your Writers, Milton, Needham, Prynne.[22]

In the list of offenders, 'Marvel, who yet wears his ears' becomes in effect a second William Prynne.

When, however, the thirteenth session of the same old Parliament was recalled in the spring of 1675 after a year's prorogation, it became clear that Danby's campaign to undermine parliamentary effectiveness was having results.[23] This was the year of the notorious Non-Resisting Bill, a new test designed to eradicate all opposition to government or church policy for the foreseeable future. Moreover, bribery of the members and conflict of interest were, if anything, on the increase. On 22 April 1675 Marvell was teller for the Yeas in a Bill to prevent MPs taking paid positions with the Government, and he reported to Popple that an attempt to impeach Danby was 'blown off at last by a great bribing' (*Poems and Letters*, 2: 342). In October, Shaftesbury and Buckingham called for a dissolution of Parliament and a new election, but instead Charles announced the notorious 'Long Prorogation', which lasted for fifteen months, during which time Louis was able to campaign without interference against the Dutch.

In 1675 the satirical *Duke of Buckingham's Litany* accused Marvell of membership in a seditious group, the Green Ribbon Club, which was supposed to have formed around Buckingham, and which met, ironically, in the King's Head Tavern. Its members reportedly included Shaftesbury, Wharton (Marvell's friend and correspondent), Blood (one of Marvell's minor heroes) and Joseph Ayloffe (later the author of the satire *Marvell's Ghost*). As the *Litany* put it:

> From changing old Friends for rascally new ones,
> From taking Wildman and Marvell for true ones
> From wearing Green Ribbons gainst him gave us blue ones,
> Libera nos domine.[24]

When the Houses met at last, in February 1677, after the Long Prorogation, the situation had changed still further for the worse. Arguing in the Lords that a prorogation for more than a year was illegal and had in effect dissolved the Parliament, the four peers, Shaftesbury, Buckingham, Salisbury and Wharton, overstepped the bounds of discretion, and were committed by Danby to the Tower, thereby becoming for Marvell the first real political heroes of the Restoration. The Lords classified as seditious a range of pamphlets questioning the validity of the Long Prorogation and, while the Commons debated how to make the king withdraw all military assistance from France, John Harrington (not to be confused with James, founder of the Rota), was 'newly committed close Prisoner', Marvell wrote to Hull, 'while he negotiated the proof of things of that nature lately done in Scotland' (*Poems and Letters*, 2: 189). Ten days later, on 27 March 1677, Marvell made his first speech in the House for seven years. Two days after that he was involved in a scuffle in the House which, in curious re-enactment of his earlier quarrel with Clifford, almost resulted in his expulsion. On both occasions he commented apologetically on his inarticulateness, observing that he had become, literally, unaccustomed to public speaking, and thereby confirming the rumours of his previous silence.

Both the speech and the fracas are worth consideration, not least because they seem to offer contradictory testimony of Marvell's state of mind. The speech was directed against a Bill for 'Securing the Protestant Religion' against the event of a Catholic succession. One might at first sight be surprised at Marvell's opposition to a Bill so entitled; but in fact it was a stratagem for protecting the succession to the Catholic James, Duke of York, by building into law provisions whereby his children would be brought up as Protestants – an education to be supervised by those villains in Marvell's moral universe, the Anglican bishops. One of the most striking characteristics of Marvell's speech, as reported, is its Solomonic emphasis on the vanity of human effort: 'if we are to intermeddle in things of this consequence, we are not to look into it so early . . . There is none yet in sight, but whose minds are in the hands of God, "who turns them like the rivers of water" . . . Whatever Prince God gives us, we must trust him . . . "Sufficient to the day is the evil thereof." ' What was required of Parliament at this point, Marvell asserted, was not better legislation against popery but personal reform. MPs should 'preserve the people in the Protestant Religion' by their own example: 'If we do not practice upon ourselves, all these Oaths and Tests are of no use; they are but Phantoms.'[25] The Bill later died a quiet death in the committee of which Marvell was himself a member; but its text was incorporated in full into his *Account of the Growth of Popery and Arbitrary Government*, where it assumes an importance quite disproportionate to other more relevant documents. This in itself might lead us to suspect that Marvell's speech on the Bill was, for him, a moment of decision, the beginning of a new mission to regenerate Parliament and to redefine his own position within it.

Marvell's near expulsion, two days later, was promoted by Sir Edward Seymour, Speaker of the House, who had been offended by what he regarded as an indecorous metaphor in Marvell's speech. When Marvell stumbled over Sir Philip Harcourt's foot, and 'seemed to give Sir Philip a box on the ear', Seymour thought it 'his duty to inform the House of it'. Although Marvell apologized for what he called a friendly tussle, he could not resist the observation that Seymour had been in breach of privilege by attacking his speech in his absence. His bold request that 'as the Speaker keeps us in order, he will keep himself in order for the future' so far cancelled the effect of his apology that he was forced to repeat it with a more expedient humility. The whole affair was an odd rumpus for a man in his fifties; even stranger was Marvell's later response to the criticism levelled at him that day. The weary protest of Sir Thomas Meres, that 'by our long sitting together, we lose, by our familiarity and acquaintances, the decencies of the House' (*JHC*, 9: 407) was retained in Marvell's memory and reappeared, in the *Account*, as part of his attack on his fellow parliamentarians:

> By this long haunting so together [the Members] are grown too so familiar among themselves, that all reverence of their own Assembly is lost, that they live together not like Parliament men, but like so many good fellows met together in a publick house to make merry. And which is yet worse, by being so thoroughly acquainted, they understand their number and party, so that the use of so publick a counsel is frustrated, there is no place for deliberation, no persuading by reason, but they can see one another's votes through both throats and cravats before they hear them.[26]

This was a Parliament which had outlived its ability for real debate. If every man knew in advance which way he was supposed to vote, and how many votes could be expected on either side of an issue, the concept of 'so publick a counsel' was nullified, and the Members might just as well have cast their votes at home. Those who believed deeply, like Marvell himself, in the value of a relevant deliberative tradition, might well (on occasion) behave with impropriety, but this remarkable echo of his own experience can hardly, in the circumstances, act as self-justification. The quotation from Sir Thomas Meres's rebuke must stand, rather, in lieu of personal confession, an admission of complicity in a decadent institution.

By Christmas of the following year, the *Account of the Growth of Popery and Arbitrary Government* had been published, anonymously and with a false Amsterdam imprint. It was, for the last time, an attempt to influence Parliament directly. Its theme was the destruction of parliamentary government in England, both by exterior coercion and interior corruption; its plea was for a regenerate (if not a new) Parliament, which would be strong enough to control the king, not only financially but in foreign policy also. The issue which had aroused the Commons during 1677 was Charles's increasingly suspicious dealings with Louis XIV of Roman Catholic France, an involvement which made the 'growth of popery' inseparable from that of 'arbitrary government' in England, and remained no less real when Charles engaged in double-dealing with Holland and France simultaneously.

Although enormously influential in the decades after Marvell's death, the *Account* had no more immediately positive effect. On May 13 Charles prorogued Parliament for ten days, a delaying tactic which had, as Marvell reminded his constituents, the same effect as a longer interruption: 'always upon Prorogation whatsoever businesse was imperfect and depending is quite cut off and if the Parliament intend to proceede againe upon it, they must resume all from the very beginning'. In a moment of candour unusual in his letters to Hull, he added: 'I doubt not but many will reflect upon this Prorogation for other reasons. But they that discourse the lest and thinke the best of it will be the wisest men and the best Subjects. God in mercy direct his Majesty always to that which may most conduce to his own and the Kingdomes happinesse' (*Poems and Letters*, 2: 234).

Marvell's last surviving letter to William Popple, written in June 1678, two months before he died, confirms the inferences about his character and motives that this chapter has collected. The letter records, in the same oblique third-person manner employed for his discussion of *Mr. Smirke*'s appearance, the public reception of the *Account*: 'There have been great Rewards offered in private, and considerable in the Gazette, to any who could inform of the Author or Printer, but not yet discovered. Three or four printed Books since have described, as near as it was proper to go, the Man being a Member of Parliament, Mr. Marvell to have been the Author; but if he had, surely he should not have escaped being questioned in Parliament, or some other Place' (*Poems and Letters*, 2: 357). This was a man, evidently, in whom discretion and indiscretion, detachment and involvement, were so inscrutably mixed that even with his own much-loved nephew he travelled *incognito*, hidden behind the protective surface of his own intelligence and wit.

But what have that intelligence and wit been doing in the arena of poetry during these last years? As one of Marvell's earliest poems, we know, was *To his Noble Friend Mr. Richard Lovelace, upon his Poems*, so one of his latest was *On Mr. Milton's Paradise Lost*, written to accompany the second edition of Milton's poem in 1674. Putting the two poems side by side shows how enormously Marvell's conception of the poet's task had grown since 1649. The two poems are almost the same length, 50 lines for Lovelace and 54 for Milton, and share the same straightforward heroic couplets; but where Marvell earlier praised his friend's 'sweet Muse' and 'fair Fortune', terms entirely appropriate to Cavalier lyric, now he invokes Milton as a 'mighty Poet', in italics, and from the beginning to the end stresses the unimaginable scale and daring of 'his vast Design'. The effect is to promote an Opposition aesthetic; a motive enhanced by Marvell's mockery of Dryden, to whose ambition to adapt Milton's poem into a rhyming opera the poem dryly alludes:[27]

> That Majesty which through thy Work doth Reign
> Draws the Devout, deterring the Profane.
> And things divine thou treatst of in such state
> As them preserves, and Thee inviolate.
> At once delight and horrour on us seize,
> Thou singst with so much gravity and ease;
> . . .
>
>                                    . . .
>
> Thy verse created like thy Theme sublime,
> In Number, Weight, and Measure, needs not Rhime.

(1: 139)

The first to identify *Paradise Lost* with the Longinian Sublime, Marvell also articulates the peculiar mixture of sensations that sublimity provokes – delight and horror – and the unique combination of talents – gravity and ease – that Milton's blank verse displays. These terms are hard won. Having expressed an earlier doubt that Milton would 'ruine' the 'sacred Truths' (as Cromwell had been able to 'ruine the great Work of Time') by reducing them to fictions, having set that aside for a greater fear that the theology of the poem would be either too abstruse or too simple ('what was easie he should render vain'), Marvell discovers the poetics of near oxymoron: gravity and ease belong together.

But as well as being hard won, in terms of his narrative of reading and rereading *Paradise Lost*, these terms are also characteristically Marvellian. In the following chapters we will see him deploying and critiquing various forms of the easy, including his own 'easie' philosophizing in the grounds of Nunappleton. We will see him investigating, with considerable gravity, what it means to be devout in poetry; and eventually we will see him creating his own mixture of gravity and levity in the pamphlets on church affairs. But here Marvell bows out of Milton's project with a self-deprecatory joke – about the infectious nature of rhyme in Restoration culture:

> I too transported by the Mode offend,
> And while I meant to Praise thee, must Commend.

And Marvell's commitment to the theory of praise as at the heart of a poet's responsibilities is the topic we take up next.

NOTES

1. George Vertue, *Notebooks* (Oxford, 1930–47), 2: 22.
2. Thomas May and Thomas Carew were both painted in ovals by Lely.
3. See Edward Thompson, ed., *The Works of Andrew Marvell*, 3 vols. (London, 1776), 1: lvii; italics added.
4. John L. Propert, *A History of Miniature Art* (London, 1887), 3: 246.
5. Hilton Kelliher, *Andrew Marvell: Poet and Politician, 1621–78* (London, 1978), p. 32. This catalogue of the tercentenary exhibition of Marvell at the British Museum brought Marvell's biography up to date, including Kelliher's own discoveries.
6. Kelliher, *Andrew Marvell*, p. 61.
7. For an up-to-date assessment of the claims of Marvell's royalism, see James Loxley, ' "Prepared at Last to Strike in with the Tyde?" Andrew Marvell and Royalist Verse', *Seventeenth Century* 10 (1995), pp. 39–62.
8. *Journal of the House of Commons*, 6: 90.
9. *The Poems and Letters of Andrew Marvell*, rev. edn, Pierre Legouis (Oxford, 1971), 1: 3.
10. Milton, *Complete Prose Works*, ed. D. M. Wolfe *et al.* (New Haven, 1953–82), 1: 806–20.
11. *Old Parliamentary History* (London, 1761), 23: 54; *Journal of the House of Commons*, 8: 209. Milton's nephew, Edward Phillips, also reported that Milton escaped punishment at the Restoration because of the intercession of Members of Parliament and the Privy Council: 'Particularly in the House of Commons, Mr. Andrew Marvell . . . acted vigorously on his behalf.' See Helen Darbishire, *The Early Lives of Milton* (London, 1932), p. 74.
12. *Journal of the House of Commons ( JHC)*, 8: 391.
13. *Poems and Letters*, 2: 37, 250. In the second of these letters Marvell spoke of 'the interest of some persons too potent for me to refuse', which allows for another interpretation of his withdrawal than embarrassment.
14. On 17 October 1667 (*JHC*, 9: 4). Marvell was also added on 25 October 1665 to the committee on the embezzlement of prize goods from the war (*JHC*, 8: 621), indicating early concern about corrupt administration, and, on 2 October 1666, to the committee appointed to investigate the Fire of London (*JHC*, 8:629, 654).
15. Anchitell Grey, *Debates of the House of Commons from the Year 1667 to the Year 1694* (London, 1769), 1:70–1.
16. *The Earl of Arlington's Letters to Sir W. Temple*, ed. Thomas Bebington, 2 vols. (London, 1701), 1: 226.
17. *The Diary of John Milward, Esq.*, ed. Caroline Robbins (Cambridge, 1938), p. 238.
18. Grey, *Debates*, 1: 294. Compare Marvell's intense comment to Popple, 18 November 1670 (*Poems and Letters*, 2: 318), that 'The Lieutenancy, having got Orders to their Mind, pick out Hays and Jekill, the innocentest of the whole Party, to shew their Power on'.

19.  Samuel Parker, *A Reproof to the Rehearsal Transprosed* (London, 1673), pp. 521–6; Edmund Hickeringill, *Gregory, Father-Greybeard, with his Vizard off* (London, 1673), p. 14.

20.  See D. I. B. Smith's account of the pamphlet's printing history, *Rehearsal Transpros'd*, xx–xxv.

21.  Henry Stubbe, *Rosemary and Bayes* (1672); *A Common-Place Book Out of the Rehearsal Transpros'd* (1673); Richard Leigh, *The Transproser Rehears'd* (1673); *S'too him Bayes* (1673); Edmund Hickeringill, *Gregory Father-Greybeard, with his Vizard off* (1673). and Parker's *Reproof to the Rehearsal Transprosed* (1673).

22.  Printed in George de F. Lord, *Poems on Affairs of State, 1660–1678*, 7 vols. (New Haven, 1963–75), 1: 220–27, with a valuable commentary.

23.  For Danby's influence, see Mark Goldie, 'Danby, the Bishops and the Whigs', in *The Politics of Religion in England*, eds. Tim Harris, Paul Seaward and Mark Goldie (Oxford: Restoration 1990), pp. 75–105.

24.  Cited in Caroline Robbins, 'A Critical Study of the Political Activities of Andrew Marvell', unpublished PhD, University of London, 1926, pp. 249–58.

25.  Grey, *Debates*, 4: 321–5.

26.  *Complete Works*, ed. A. B. Grosart (New York, 1875, repr. 1966), 4: 331.

27.  As Margoliouth explains (1: 336), Dryden's heroic opera, *The Fall of Angels and Man in Innocence*, was licensed in April 1674, but did not appear until 1677, under a new title: *The State of Innocence, and Fall of Man*. John Aubrey's comments on Milton included the statement that Milton gave Dryden 'leave to tag his verses'.

# Chapter 2

# Experiments in praise

In classical antiquity, and especially in late republican and early imperial Rome, one of the most important roles for the poet was the writing of poems of praise – in the genre of what was known as epideictic. As Marvell well knew, and had articulated in his poem to Lovelace, he 'who best could prayse, had then the greatest prayse'. Why? Because the practice of epideictic was equivalent to the expression of society's highest values of personal conduct and leadership. Marvell inherited, specifically, several models of classical praising poems; probably the most important were the odes of Horace, from which he learned the practice of *conditional* praise, or admiration mixed with advice, even alarm; and the *Sylvae* of Statius, a series of occasional poems that included political panegyric, poems in celebration of the large personal occasions of birth, marriage and death (*genethliaca*, *epithalamia* and *epicedia*), and a variety of praises of houses, country estates, or even pets, which implied the importance, goodness or charm of their owners. The implications of this precedent had been schematized in the *Poetices Libri Septem* (1561) of Julius Caesar Scaliger,[1] and Caroline poets had been practising them for a quarter of a century before Marvell entered the picture. Knowing of this tradition helps a modern reader to understand the peculiar structure of Marvell's genius. In his poems to Cromwell and Fairfax, he is constantly testing his resources, most of which are conventional, against the tendency of events to require and inspire innovation; and, as we shall see, by a process of dry allusion to the verse compliments that had been directed to Charles I by his court poets, he tried to differentiate himself from what might be seen as the mode of personal ambition and sycophancy. Throughout his career, Marvell continued to alternate between two imperatives, the social responsibility of 'speaking well' defined in the poem to Lovelace, and the other responsibility of 'speaking true', which he first defined in the *Horatian Ode*.

Marvell's poems to and about Oliver Cromwell and Sir Thomas Fairfax belong together, since both men became famous for their leadership of the parliamentary army against the king's forces; although, since Fairfax withdrew from the limelight in protest against the proceedings against the Scots and Charles himself, and Cromwell went on to become a world-famous state leader, their characterizations fell on either side of the classical divide between two types of praiseworthy behaviour: direct and usually military action (*negotium*) and stoical, contemplative retreat (*otium*). In the 1681 *Miscellaneous Poems*, the poems were to have appeared together in two related clusters, with three relating to Fairfax's estate at Nunappleton immediately preceding a much larger group concerning Cromwell, beginning with the *Horatian Ode upon Cromwel's Return from Ireland* and ending with *A Poem upon the Death of O.C.* This arrangement represents both the facts of Marvell's life – his service to Fairfax preceded his service to Cromwell – and those of his subjects – Cromwell succeeded Fairfax as Commander-in-Chief. It was, however, subverted by the last-minute precautionary decision, either by the printer Robert Boulter or some of Marvell's friends, to omit the three major poems on Cromwell;[2] and still further subverted by rearrangements of the poems by Marvell's modern editors, not to mention the critics who decided that the 'Cromwell' and 'Fairfax' poems belonged in separate camps. Putting them back together can alert us to the conceptual reverberations between them, and show that Marvell understood himself to be engaged in an interlocking series of experiments. While he partly conceived of this as a rhetorical problem (how to manage appropriate shades of praise and criticism), he also posed it as an ontological issue – of validity in historical interpretation.

## The Cromwell poems

### THE *HORATIAN ODE UPON CROMWEL'S RETURN FROM IRELAND*

The *Horatian Ode*, as its full title explains, was written to celebrate Cromwell's return in May 1650 from fighting the rebellious Irish, whom indeed he had managed to suppress with notorious brutality. In addition to the generalized debt to Horace's odes whereby Marvell identified himself with Horace's role as counsellor to Augustus, the 'Cleopatra' ode (Book 1. Poem 37), which deals with a defeated but still admirable royal enemy, is somewhere in the poem's genealogy. So too is the Statian 'return' poem, which had been a popular Caroline exercise. In late 1640, for example, the minor poets of both universities had risen to the occasion of Charles's return from Scotland,

and the superficially happy conclusion of what is sometimes called
the First Bishops' War, in which the Scots had risen against the
imposition of the Laudian prayer book. Both *Irenodia Cantabrigiensis*
and *Eucharistica Oxoniensia*, the congratulatory anthologies produced
by Cambridge and Oxford respectively, emphasized that the peace
treaty was achieved by negotiation rather than conquest, a conception most agreeable to the pacific Caroline mythology. Typical of
both collections was a poem by P. Samwayes of Trinity, Marvell's
own college. Its title emphasized that the Scottish campaign had
been settled 'non vi et armis sed lenitate' (not with force and arms
but with lenity); its strophic form is the visual equivalent of Marvell's
much discussed stanza; and its opening lines may have considerable
bearing on the opening of Marvell's own poem:

> Phoebus volentem praelia me loqui,
> Victas & urbes, & sata languida,
>    Non falce sed stricti resecta
>    Praepropero gladii furore;
> Non ante visa commonuit Dea,
> Jussitque; molli nectere carmine
>    Paci corollas . . .[3]

The opening of Marvell's poem in effect inverts this conceit, deliv-
ering a rebuke to the pacifist poet who produces 'his Numbers
languishing' in the shades of academe. The 'Muses dear' which the
'forward Youth' of 1650 is urged to forsake may include among
their meanings both the universities themselves and the spirit of
retreat from reality which they encouraged. Marvell, incidentally,
was not a contributor to *Irenodia Cantabrigiensis*.

But two other classical allusions raise the generic stakes still further.
A series of unmistakable echoes from Thomas May's translation of
Lucan's *Pharsalia*, that dark epic poem about the civil wars of Rome,
place the contest between Charles and Cromwell in the historical
shadow of that between Pompey and Julius Caesar.[4] And the much
older story recorded in Pliny's *Natural History* (Bk 28, no. 2, 6.4) of
how, when the ancient Roman Capitol was being constructed, the
discovery of a human head in the overturned soil alarmed the builders
yet was read as a portent of good, expands the Roman historical
perspective backwards towards a foundational legend. The contrasting allusions offer the audience, and Cromwell himself, a choice of
two Caesarian roles, one positive, one negative, a choice still further
complicated by the statement that Cromwell, like Olympian lightning, had blasted 'Caesar's', that is, Charles's, head through the very

laurel crown that was supposed to protect it. If one cannot have both the 'antient Rights' and the necessary revolution, the cultured, pacific, self-regarding monarch and the 'indefatigable' leader in the service of the opposite ideals, how do we choose? Indeed, *must* we choose?

Put in these terms, the question must also be answered by attention to the formal (poetic) qualities of the *Ode*, qualities which Marvell certainly chose with care. Most striking, perhaps, is the rigid control he exerts over his vocabulary, relying heavily on monosyllables, especially monosyllabic verb forms, not only to tell his story but to suggest its competing values and the demands it makes on the onlooker. By verbs of action and movement (*leave, cease, urg'd, went, rent, blast, climbe, cast, hold, break, wove, chase, clap, bow'd, fright, tam'd,*) he presents the inexorable force that Cromwell represents and its effects. By verbs of affective communication (*sing, blame, speak, plead, fear,*) he suggests the effects of 'greater Spirits' on weaker ones, including himself and the Scots. Against this stark primitivism, there stand out with startling difference his occasional Latinisms, where the values of the poem are condensed: Cromwell's 'industrious Valour', Nature's rejection of 'penetration' (two bodies occupying the same space), 'that memorable Scene' and, significantly repeated 'that memorable Hour' at the scaffold. The charge of Cromwell in the last few lines to 'March indefatigably on' in the service of Protestant imperialism speaks volumes about Marvell's own value system, in which energy, decisiveness, and sheer hard work were what separated the men from the boys. Perhaps most interesting, lexically speaking, is his ideological deployment of two seemingly weak indicators of action and constraint – *did* and *must* – which here are far from being mere intensifiers or place-holders. The poem begins by asserting that the 'forward Youth . . . *must* now forsake his Muses dear', pauses to reflect that 'Nature . . . *must* make room / Where greater Spirits come', and ends by reminding Cromwell that 'The same Arts that *did* gain / A Pow'r *must* it maintain' (italics added).

But in addition to these strategies for shaking up complacent and conventional readers, Marvell now introduces rules for the kind of poetry with which he is experimenting. To begin with, the possibilities for praise (and blame) are carefully and explicitly limited. If Cromwell is really the instrument of divine justice, then ''Tis Madness to resist or blame' actions which would normally require our condemnation. A special kind of approbation can, however, be given to Cromwell's most exemplary act so far, his sacrifice of personal privacy to take on the burdens of leadership:

And, *if we would speak true,*
Much to the Man is due.
Who, from his private Gardens, where
He liv'd reserved and austere,
. . .

                                        . . .

Could by industrious Valour climbe
To ruine the great Work of Time.

Truthful evaluation requires, especially, that the poet notice the tensions and contradictions in his subject, as well as in the society's value system. The effectiveness of these limitations is further assisted by the poem's time scheme, which keeps carefully separate facts, regrets, propositions and hopes; and this in turn makes it possible, by the use of only the most demure vocabulary, to insert the necessary warnings against excessive ambition. Cromwell is 'nor *yet* grown stiffer with Command,/But still in the Republick's hand . . . And, *what he may,* forbears/His Fame to make it theirs' (italics added).

The *Horatian Ode,* then, responds to political crisis by deft manipulation of appropriate traditions. At the same time as it alerts its audience to the difficulty of evaluating revolutionary events, especially 'if we would speak true,' it reminds them that such difficulties are not unprecedented. Horace and Lucan faced them and drew their own conclusions; the modes of classical rhetoric provide norms for locating the new experience, and formal strategies for measuring it. But there is no rigid commitment to a one-to-one system of historical analogy or a slavish reproduction of rhetorical structures, either of which would protect the audience from having to participate in the process of choice. The mixture of classical sources, the rearrangement of rhetorical expectations, provoke a lively, continuous movement between raw political fact and the possibility of categorization, between the strain of empiricism and the relaxation of system.

THE *FIRST ANNIVERSARY OF THE GOVERNMENT UNDER O.C.*

The *Horatian Ode,* we must remember, was never printed during Marvell's lifetime; the *First Anniversary of the Government under O.C.* was published anonymously. To that extent Marvell was still keeping his political cards close to his chest; and the poem itself operates in a mode of wariness mixed with enthusiasm. At first sight, one might think, and as the proponents of Marvellian detachment have suggested, it shows a simple development from choice in progress to choice complete, from a measured rhetorical stance supported by the classics to Christian determinism supported by biblical typology. However, any attempt to develop a straightforward reading of the poem as a clear alternative to the *Ode*, a 'committed' Puritan revolutionary poem which knows where it stands, is quickly defeated. Cromwell may resemble Noah or Elijah or Gideon or Jotham (sometimes by rather strange points of contact)[5] but he is also an Amphion of classical harmony, particularly as that figure had been interpreted by Horace's *Ars Poetica*. The poem seems to have no clearly visible principle of organization and, though we need not endorse Legouis' distaste for its 'ordre mi-logique, mi-chronologique'[6] it seems to work best at the local level, where the resonance of individual passages can be worked out in detail, rather than as a whole. Perhaps this was intentional. While invoking the temporal structures both of classical encomium and Christian prophecy, it also seems to subvert them in ways which can scarcely be accidental. Considered as an encomium, we find that praise of Cromwell's achievements at home and abroad *precedes* mention of his parentage and birth (*genesis*) and that a lament for his death (which turns out to be hypothetical) precedes his education (*anatrophe*) and choice of destiny (*epitedeumata*).

Considered as Christian prophecy, the poem is even more subversive, indeed explicitly so. The poet's hopes for a millennium in his own time under Cromwell's leadership are presented not as a conclusion, but toward the middle of the poem, and they are presented in the most hypothetical terms:

> Hence oft I think, if in some happy Hour
> High Grace should meet in one with highest Pow'r,
> And then a seasonable People still
> Should bend to his, as he to Heavens will,
> What we might hope, what wonderful Effect
> From such a wish'd Conjuncture might reflect.
> Sure, the mysterious Work, where none withstand,
> Would forthwith finish under such a Hand:
> Fore-shortned Time its useless Course would stay,
> And soon precipitate the latest Day.
> But a thick Cloud about that Morning lyes,
> And intercepts the Beams of Mortal eyes,
> That 'tis the most which we determine can,
> If these the Times, then this must be the Man.

(ll. 131–44)

This language is all conditional, in the grammatical sense; but as compared with the conditional praise of the *Ode*, which was merely dependent on Cromwell's fulfilling certain political responsibilities, the *Anniversary* indicates the limitations of vision. Thinking, wishing and hoping are all very well, but a 'thick Cloud' comes between the would-be prophet and his glimpses of the Apocalypse, as he considers exactly how unseasonable the people are at present:

> Men alas, as if they nothing car'd,
> Look on, all unconcern'd, or unprepar'd;
> Hence that blest Day still counterpoysed wastes,
> The Ill delaying, what th'Elected hastes;

> (ll. 149–52)

As the poem continues, then, 'the most which we determine can' is that its subject is indeed exceptional, if not superhuman. Deprived of structural guidance, its readers 'hollow far behind/Angelique Cromwell', whose legendary speed of action makes him as hard to catch as the shape of the uncertain future. But the return of the adjective 'indefatigable' from the *Ode* at l. 45 reminds us that lesser men do tire, and that speed is not mechanical but the direct correlative of human energy and effort.

In fact, the more one investigates, the more the *First Anniversary* reveals itself to be an exercise in how to avoid or alter conventional definitions and postures. The theoretical question with which the poem deals is not, as in the *Ode*, the conflicting claims of two different types of hero, two different views of what is 'right', but how to express Cromwell's uniqueness, the unprecedented position he holds in England, in Europe, in God's providential plans and, above all, in the literary imagination. Marvell is here less concerned with what traditional attitudes toward Cromwell were available to the writer than with the larger question of what, indeed, Cromwell was. Or, to put it differently, a problem in historiography and ethics has now given way to a problem in political theory, expressed as a shortage of terminology: how were the English now to define the unique position that Cromwell had achieved? What words, literally, would specify its powers and limits (if any?) Since the Protectorate was formally established a year earlier, through the 'Instrument of Government' to which the poem refers in an idealistic musical metaphor, Cromwell was not merely the supreme military commander 'still in the Republick's hand', but virtually a dictator (very much like Julius Caesar). To some it seemed clear that since he held all the powers of a king, he might as well accept the crown also, and thereby settle the problem of who would succeed him in conventional dynastic terms. Some modern readers see the *Anniversary* as an appeal to

Cromwell to do just that; and others have argued, conversely, that it casts the Protectorate, with its biblical model of the Old Testament judges behind it, as unequivocally superior to the monarchical model.[7]

The immediate occasion of Marvell's poem was not Cromwell's refusal of the crown, which had occurred in 1652 and was to be repeated in 1657. It was, rather, the first anniversary of the Instrument of Government, and also the session of the first Protectorate Parliament, which symbolized a return to some kind of constitutional government but which, between 3 September 1654 and January 1655, when Cromwell dissolved it, fought to amend the terms of the Instrument and to limit Cromwell's powers, particularly with regard to control of the army. Written late in 1654, Marvell's poem was not designed to provide symbolic sanction for the kind of rule Cromwell apparently wanted, although that inference has been drawn from his magnificent musical and architectural metaphors for the 'ruling Instrument'. Rather he is concerned to investigate the historical significance, the internal paradoxes, and indeed even the disadvantages, of that rule, subjecting the conventions normally associated with rulers to the scrupulous pressure of his own intelligence.

The central paradox of the Protectorate was, of course, implicit in the title of the Protector, a title with no constitutional precedent whose beneficent significance, some clearly felt, was merely a cover for despotism. Why, in any case, if Cromwell was only the servant of his country, did he need a title at all? In Milton's *Second Defence of the English People*, published earlier in 1654, there is an elaborate rationalization of the title in terms of a republican ethos:

> Your deeds surpass all degrees, not only of admiration, but surely of titles too ... But since it is, not indeed worthy, but expedient for even the greatest capacities to be bounded and confined by some sort of human dignity ... you assumed a certain title very like that of Father of your country. You suffered and allowed yourself, not indeed to be borne aloft, but to come down so many degrees from the heights and be forced into a definite rank, so to speak, for the public good.

The name of Protector, Milton asserts, though an inadequate expression or devaluation of Cromwell's natural superiority, is nevertheless better than the title he has recently refused:

> The name of king you spurned from your greater eminence, and rightly so. For if when you became so great a figure, you were captivated by the title which as a private citizen you were able to send under the yoke and

reduce to nothing, you would be doing almost the same thing as if, when you had subjugated some tribe of idolaters with the help of the true God, you were to worship the gods that you had conquered.[8]

In June of 1654 Milton had entrusted Marvell with the delivery of a complimentary copy of the *Second Defence* to John Bradshaw, and Marvell reported in a letter how the gift had been received, adding his own accolade. 'I shall now studie it', he wrote, 'even to the getting of it by Heart: esteeming it according to my poor Judgement . . . as the most compendious Scale, for so much, to the Height of the Roman eloquence' (2: 306). It looks as though Marvell had so far succeeded in getting the *Second Defence* by heart that he incorporated this central paradox of the Protectorate into his own poem. Commenting, as in the *Ode*, on the great man's sacrifice of privacy to the demands of public life, he wrote:

> For all delight of Life thou then didst lose,
> When to Command, thou didst thy self Depose;
> Resigning up thy Privacy so dear,
> To turn the headstrong Peoples Charioteer;
> For to be Cromwell was a greater thing,
> Then ought below, or yet above a King:
> Therefore thou rather didst thy Self depress,
> Yielding to Rule, because it made thee Less.
>
> (ll. 221–8)

But perhaps because of the contraction required by the verse, Marvell's version of the paradox is truly ambiguous where Milton's is not. While a literal understanding of what is neither below nor above kingship would seem to be kingship itself, this is clearly not what Marvell means. Nor does he praise the solution of the term 'Protector'. Rather, the idea of what it is 'to be Cromwell' remains inscrutable, tilted slightly toward the idea of a selfhood for which all political titles are irrelevant.

Nothing could be more unlike the propagandist tactics of George Wither, whose poem *The Protector . . . Briefly illustrating the Supereminency of that Dignity; and Rationally demonstrating, that the Title of Protector . . . is the most Honorable of all Titles* (1655) allows, to say the least, no possibility of misunderstanding. Wither reduces the constitutional paradox to bluntly expedient terms:

> Why by the name of King, should we now call him,
> Which is below the Honours, that befall him;

And makes him to be rather less than great,
(As in himself) and rather worse then better
As to his People . . .
It will deprive him ev'n of that Defence
Which seems intended; and, will him expose
To all the purposed Cavils of his Foes.

(p. 31)

The difference is not just that Marvell's obliqueness allows for a more high-minded interpretation of Cromwell's motives, though that may be relevant. It is rather that the problem of what it is 'to be Cromwell', in a constitutional sense, is more significant than any available verbal formulation.

In the case of Wither's time-serving poem on the Protectorate, Marvell was merely competing with (though he may have preceded) another Cromwellian wannabe. But in other parts of the poem, he reveals an alertness to Caroline panegyric that results in a sort of poetic repartee. Edmund Waller, for instance, had been one of Charles I's most assiduous panegyricists, and he would continue in that role at the Restoration, turning his hand to support Charles II and the Duke of York in the Second Dutch War. In the 1630s he had undertaken, rather oddly, to justify the renovation of St Paul's cathedral, commissioned by Charles and Archbishop Laud, against the attacks of the Puritans, who interpreted the project as a consolidation of conservative, even reactionary, Anglican polity.[9] In *Upon his Majesties repairing of Paul's*, Waller's rhetorical strategy was to praise the modesty of Charles in merely improving a structure begun by James I, therefore removing the charge of innovation in church affairs:

Ambition rather would effect the fame
Of some new structure; to have borne her name.
Two distant vertues in one act we finde,
The modesty, and greatnesse of his minde;
Which not content to be above the rage
And injury of all impairing age,
In its own worth secure, doth higher clime,
And things half swallow'd from the jaws of time
Reduce; an earnest of his grand designe,
To frame no new Church, but the old refine:[10]

It is accepted[11] that Marvell responded to this claim by developing the metaphor of the building of the Temple, a favourite Puritan metaphor for liturgical and organizational reform of the English church as an institution, rather than a building.

In 1644, for example, Milton had incorporated into *Areopagitica* an appeal against those who resisted, by censorship, diversity of opinion:

> as if, while the Temple of the Lord was building, some cutting, some squaring the marble, others hewing the cedars, there should be a sort of irrationall men who could not consider there must be many schisms and many dissections made in the quarry and in the timber, ere the house of God can be built. And when every stone is laid artfully together, it cannot be united into a continuity, it can but be contiguous in this world . . . nay rather the perfection consists in this, that out of many moderat varieties and brotherly dissimilitudes that are not vastly disproportional arises the goodly and the gracefull symmetry that commends the whole pile and structure. Let us therefore be more considerat builders, more wise in spirituall architecture, when great reformation is expected.[12]

Marvell's reproach of kings who 'neither build the Temple in their dayes,/Nor Matter for succeeding Founders raise' (ll. 33–4) is both a specific response to Waller's praise of those conservative rulers who, like Charles, do not move forward the Protestant Reformation, who 'frame no new Church, but the old refine', and an adjustment of Milton's more idealistic metaphor. Whereas Milton suggests that the harmony of the building comes from the diversity of opinion itself, Marvell translates this into a more exact architectural metaphor. It is the internal stresses and strains of a building that keep it together, but they require both an architect to arrange them, and one dominant architectural element to lock them into place. It was only when Cromwell as Amphion struck the magical musical chord that harmony was possible, first ensuring that 'the Temples rear'd their Columns high', and then turning to secular or political reconstruction:

> The Commonwealth then first together came,
> And each one enter'd in the willing Frame;
> All other Matter yields, and may be rul'd;
> But who the Minds of stubborn Men can build?
> No Quarry bears a Stone so hardly wrought,
> Nor with such labour from its Center brought;
> None to be sunk in the Foundation bends,
> Each in the House the highest Place contends,
> And each the Hand that lays him will direct,
> And some fall back upon the Architect;
> Yet all compos'd by his attractive Song,
> Into the Animated City throng.
> The Common-wealth does through their Centers all

Draw the Circumf'rence of the publique Wall;
The crossest Spirits here do take their part,
Fast'ning the Contignation which they thwart;
. . .

But the most Equal still sustein the Height,
And they as Pillars keep the Work upright;
While the resistance of opposed Minds,
The Fabrick as with Arches stronger binds,
Which on the basis of a Senate free,
Knit by the Roofs Protecting weight agree.

(ll. 75–98)

Thus the downward pressure of Cromwell's authoritarian behaviour on the new constitution has the effect of converting all the centrifugal pressures (of ambition and resistance) into solidity and permanence. Marvell's reference to 'the most Equal' as the supporting element implies his preference for a *more* egalitarian system than had previously been in place, and for genuinely parliamentary government; nevertheless, Marvell drew a clear line between his own concept of 'most Equal' (an equivocation a little like Eve's ambition to be 'more Equal' in *Paradise Lost*) and the claims of the Levellers and other protest groups who campaigned for a radical egalitarianism that Cromwell and the other grandees had never envisaged. To carry that message – "Tis not a Freedome . . . where All command;/Nor Tyranny, where One does them withstand,' (ll. 279–80) – the Old Testament fable of the trees seeking a ruler (Judges 9: 8–9) was appropriated and slightly redesigned.

In terms of Marvell's own thought and character, this account of the building of the new regime is clearly one of the most important passages in the *Anniversary*, and perhaps in his canon as a whole. Politically, Marvell's adjustments are precise, locating his opinions on the Puritan side, but accepting a more authoritarian model of the 'Architect' than Milton ever could. In literary practice he is equally exact, for by making his ideological correction of Waller within the same symbolic construct, hugely expanded, he asserts the permanence and accepts the sanctions of the great architectural metaphor.

Another riposte to Caroline poetry occurs at the poem's striking conclusion. One of the poets who specialized in idolizing the royal family, often to the point of near blasphemy, was Robert Herrick. Herrick's *To the King, to Cure the Evill*, had invoked the biblical story of the miracle of Bethesda:

To find Bethesda, and an Angell there,
Stirring the waters I am come; and here
. . .

                                                . . .

I kneele for help; O! lay that hand on me,
Adored Caesar! and my Faith is such,
I shall be heal'd, if that my King but touch.[13]

With the same precision that he used in adapting the temple-building
image, Marvell appropriated Herrick's metaphor of healing for the
last lines of his poem, which are addressed directly to Cromwell. In
so doing he finally explained the point of the 'anniversary' genre he
has chosen. Whereas Herrick's poem had conflated the angel who
stirred the waters of Bethesda with Christ and both with the 'Caesar'
to whom his poem is addressed, Marvell restricts his praise. Cromwell
is to be recognized merely as 'the Angel of our Commonweal', *not* as
Christ, and his healing is specifically attributed not to the sacramental
powers by which kings were supposed to heal the King's Evil, but to
those disturbing aspects of his character and authority that were so
difficult to assimilate to conventional thought. It is because he comes
'Troubling the Waters' that he can heal the sickness in the commonwealth, rather than in the individual; and if he comes 'yearly' like the
angel, other anniversaries will follow.

    In the context of echoes like these we may better understand
Marvell's peculiar treatment of Cromwell's coaching accident, an
event which occupies the centre of the poem; that is to say, the
poem is in dialogue with other published comments on the accident.
Like George Wither's *Vaticinium Causuale* (1654), Marvell rebuts
various hostile responses to the incident, which certainly had satiric
potential. The six runaway horses, which had been a gift from the
Duke of Holstein, were all too convenient a metaphor for the three
kingdoms Cromwell was trying to manage; and *A Jolt on Michaelmas
Day*, which drew the obvious analogy with Phaeton but suggested
that Cromwell had been saved for the hangman's cart, represented
the direction of contemporary lampoons. Wither's response was to
congratulate the Protector upon his escape, to replace Phaeton with
Hippolytus, and to interpret Cromwell's lucky escape as a sign of his
special relationship with Providence, which had nevertheless given
him due warning of his mortality. His poem draws these construc-
tions in a tone of pompous didacticism. Marvell's response is to
replace ambitious Phaeton with Elijah, who also drove a chariot, but
safely, and up to heaven; and by concentrating not on the escape but
the danger, he produces a radical innovation in poetic strategy.

Preservation from danger (or recovery from sickness) of a public figure was in itself a recognized subject for poetry, producing *soteria*, as in Statius' congratulation to Rutilius Gallicus (*Sylvae*, 1: 4), and all too many imitations by Caroline poets. Apart from the university anthologies, Marvell would probably have been aware of Waller's *Of the danger his Majesty (being Prince) escaped in the rode at St Andere* (1645). The purpose of *soteria*, to define value by exploring its near loss, requires or at least justifies the use of hyperbole. Nature's lament for the death of Orpheus, which is imported from Ovid into both Waller's and Marvell's poems, is only excessive because it is not needed, because a death of equal significance has in fact been averted. It indicates the extravagance of relief. There is, however, a peculiar development in Marvell's poem, which goes far beyond anything similar in Waller. The poet becomes trapped in his own fiction, and begins to describe Cromwell's death as if it had actually occurred. *Soteria* becomes *epicedion*, elegy. It only 'seem'd' that 'Earth did from the Center tear', but the effects on human institutions were less retractable, because the tenses have changed:

> Justice obstructed lay, and Reason fool'd;
> Courage disheartned, and Religion cool'd.

In the analogy with Elijah, the sense of deliverance disappears entirely from view, to be imaginatively replaced by another kind of escape altogether, an apotheosis:

> But thee triumphant hence the firy Carr,
> And firy Steeds had born out of the Warr,
> From the low World, and thankless Men above,
> Unto the Kingdom blest of Peace and Love:
> We only mourn'd our selves, in thine Ascent,
> Whom thou hadst left beneath with Mantle rent.

> (ll. 215–20)

Fiction has taken over, but only, paradoxically, to insist on another kind of truth. The 'elegy' enforces dramatic recognition of Cromwell's human status, the fragility of his regime, the problem of the succession. Its realism, Marvell tells us, is essential to the validity of the whole poem:

> Let this one Sorrow interweave among
> The other Glories of our yearly Song.
> . . .

So shall the Tears we on past Grief employ,
Still as they trickle, glitter in our Joy.
*So with more Modesty we may be True,*
*And speak as of the Dead the Praises due.*

(ll. 181–8; italics added)

As the *Ode* had insisted that 'if we would speak true' we would have to acknowledge Cromwell's willing sacrifice of privacy to the demands of leadership, so the *Anniversary* insists that a fair view of the Protector requires our imagining what life would be like without him. Only from the perspective of fictive bereavement can the poet achieve 'modesty' in his praise – a term that Marvell continually used to denote an acceptable stance, and that seems to combine sobriety of tone with an unself-serving agenda.

*A POEM UPON THE DEATH OF O.C.*

If the first (and only) Anniversary for Cromwell questions the Anniversary's success in defining the unique, *A Poem upon the death of O.C.* seems to sound a deliberate retreat. Far from adjusting or arguing with conventions, Marvell seems to have fallen back into one of the best defined and most luxurious, the classical *epicedion* with its well-marked conventions. A simple chronology presents the prior circumstances and causes of Cromwell's death (his grief for his daughter), the natural and supernatural portents, the date (coincidentally that of the battle of Dunbar), and the response of his survivors. To them is given the task of enumerating his cardinal virtues as modified by a Christian–Stoical tradition; and giving the lament of what is 'no more', in language imitative both of Virgil's description of the heroic underworld and of Milton's pastoral elegy for Lycidas / Edward King. The poem concludes with three different but equally conventional passages of consolation: Cromwell's immortality in the imagination and 'martiall Verse' of 'th' English Souldier'; a Christian heaven for Cromwell himself, where he can meet face to face the biblical types (Moses, Joshua, and David) he now resembles; and a political reincarnation in his successor, for 'Richard yet, where his great parent led,/Beats on the rugged track' (ll. 305–6). Our after-knowledge of Richard's inadequacies as a solution to the constitutional problem perhaps distorts our view of the last lines and makes them seem unduly fatuous; but Marvell has made no effort here to distinguish himself from poetic tradition at its most obedient.

What are we to make of this apparent collapse of critical intelligence into the swaddling bands of convention? The poem has been largely dismissed by both schools of criticism on the grounds of the same assumption, that Marvell's devotion to Cromwell had by this time become the dominant motive. The literary critic, as represented by Legouis, compares the elegy unfavourably with the hard formalism of the *Ode*, and discovers to its credit only pathos;[14] the political analyst is likely to grant it only a personal status, which does not justify a major evaluation.[15] But there is no need to assume that Marvell was unable to write a public poem on Cromwell's death because a political force had become a friend, nor that feeling is incompatible with speculation. There is evidence in the elegy that Marvell found Cromwell's death as significant as his rule, and that the conventionality of his response was a deliberate response to his understanding of it. A remarkable series of echoes link the *Ode* and the elegy in an argument about historical evaluation and perspectivalism.

In all the attention given to Marvell's use of Lucan in the *Ode*, nobody seems to have noticed that the famous passage describing Caesar as lightning is preceded by a description of Pompey as a majestic but decayed oak. In Thomas May's translation, firmly established as the source of many phrases and attitudes in the *Ode*, the passage reads:

> one in yeares was growne,
> And long accustomde to a peacefull gowne
> Had now forgot the Souldier: . . .
> . . . new strength he sought not out,
> Relying on his ancient fortunes fame,
> And stood the shadow of a glorious name.
> As an old lofty Oake, that heretofore
> Great Conquerours spoiles, and sacred Trophyes bore,
> Stands firme by his owne weight, his roote now dead,
> And through the Aire his naked boughes does spread,
> And with his trunke, not leaves, a shadow makes:
> Hee though each blast of Easterne winde him shakes,
> And round about well rooted Trees doe grow,
> Is onely honour'd;[16]

Marvell must have had this passage close at hand when, after an opening which emphasizes the peacefulness of Cromwell's last years, he describes his appearance in death:

> Yet dwelt that greatnesse in his shape decay'd,
> That still though dead, greater than death he lay'd;

Not much unlike the sacred oak, which shoots
To Heav'n its branches, and through earth its roots:
Whose spacious boughs are hung with trophies round,
And honour'd wreaths have oft the victour crown'd.
When angry Jove darts lightning through the aire,
At mortalls sins, nor his own plant will spare;
(It groanes, and bruises all below that stood
So many yeares the shelter of the wood.)

(ll. 259–68)

Marvell has here combined the Pompeian oak, honoured but decayed, with the Caesarian lightning to give a double resonance to Cromwell's death. Once the lightning himself, blasting Caesar's head through his laurels, Cromwell has now become subject to the the natural cycles of change and vulnerable to Jove's bolt. Even the phrase 'nor his own plant will spare' derives from Lucan's subsequent description of the Caesarian lightning ('Not Joves own Temple spares it') which not only helps to substantiate the source but emphasizes the deliberate synthesis which Marvell's allusions achieve.

The elegy, then, returns via Lucan to a concept of time and history essentially repetitive, a view denied by the *Anniversary* in its attempt to grapple with the man of the moment. While it corrects the vision of the *Anniversary*, this passage also uses the fallen oak to expand and support one of the *Anniversary*'s major theoretical positions:

The tree ere while foreshortned to our view,
When fall'n shews taller yet than as it grew:
So shall his praise to after times encrease,
When truth shall be allow'd, and faction cease,
And his own shadows with him fall; the eye
Detracts from objects than itself more high:
But when death takes them from that envy'd seate,
Seeing how little, we confess how greate.

(ll. 269–76)

The point of the hypothetical elegy in the *Anniversary* was that praise cannot function properly, truthfully, in the biased view of the moment. In the real elegy, Marvell's image of the fallen tree diagrams this previously elliptical statement. The tree, being now on our level, and the finished career, being now immune from envy and prejudice, can be accurately measured; and the proverbial generosity of statements about the dead is revealed, paradoxically, as truly historical objectivity.

Cromwell's submission to natural law, the end of his unique trajectory, the final speed trap, allows him, in the elegy, to appear as a figure no longer antipathetic to Charles. His 'last Act' recalls the 'Royal Actor' of the 'Tragick Scaffold'. Action gives way to 'gentle Passions'. His military victories are expressed as the victories of prayer. Awkward questions likely to be raised with respect to the cardinal virtues are resolved by the substitution of Friendship for Justice; while the fusion of military and spiritual values permits Cromwell to find a place, however pre-eminent, in the structure of Christian legend. None of this makes the return to convention intrinsically better, of course. *Upon the death of O.C.* competes effectively neither with the strenuous mental activity of the earlier Cromwell poems nor with the voluptuous emotional activity of an elegy, like Milton's *Lycidas*, written to explore the very meaning of mourning. But the return to conservatism in form is at least strategic, the result of a decision to re-absorb Cromwell into the known patterns of human experience. It looks forward to the fully strategic conservatism of the *Rehearsal Transpros'd*, where Marvell could accept, as the next cycle, 'his present Majesties happy Restauration'. Nor did that later conviction that 'all things happen in their best and proper time, without any need of our officiousness'[17] imply the rejection of Cromwell's phenomenal activity, since that had already been absorbed into a formal pattern of interdependent modes of experience.

## The Fairfax poems

If the major 'Cromwell' poems seem occasionally to adopt a defensive tone about their subject's reputation, about the potentially threatening side of his forceful character, this is another reason for reading them alongside the three poems in which Marvell attempted to assess the character of Thomas Fairfax, and to explain his premature retirement. That there was, in fact, a dialectical relationship between the two sets of poems is made clear by deliberate echo. Consider these interlocking couplets, the first from the *Horatian Ode*:

> So restless Cromwel could not cease
> In the inglorious Arts of Peace

and, from *Upon Appleton House*, the matching but contrasting description of Fairfax:

> Who, when retired here to Peace,
> His warlike Studies could not cease.

In this dialectic, 'inglorious' is never cancelled. And, despite the apparent symmetry, we learn that Fairfax's warlike studies at Nunappleton consisted in simulating military formations in his flowerbeds.

Beyond this, contemporary documents betray the possibility that Fairfax's retirement, as much as Cromwell's government, was open to interpretation in a distinctly unfavourable light. Rumours that Lady Fairfax made all her husband's decisions (off the battlefield) centred on the fact that his refusal to participate in the king's trial at Westminster was announced in his absence, from the gallery, by herself.[18] Fairfax's apparent inaction between Charles's trial and execution gave rise to another discreditable legend, that he had been kept foolishly praying with Colonel Harrison, on Cromwell's instructions, until the execution was over, thereby losing his chance for a last-minute rescue.[19] These rumours point in caricature to an interpretation of Fairfax as politically indecisive and not exactly astute. Clarendon remarked, in his definitive manner, upon 'the drowsy, dull Presbyterian humour of Fairfax; who wished nothing that Cromwell did, and yet contributed to bring it all to pass'.[20]

Perhaps the most revealing testimony of all is a poetical comment on the execution of Charles written in Fairfax's own commonplace book.

> Oh Lett that Day from time be blotted quitt
> And lett beleefe of't in next Age be waved
> In deeper silence th'Act Concealed might
> Soe that the King-doms Credit might be save'd
> But if the Power devine permited this
> His Will's the Law and we must acquiesse.[21]

Beside such dreary religious passivity, Marvell's *Horatian Ode*, for all its strategic compromises, appears a model of resolution; worse still, by some standards, Fairfax's lack of control over the political situation was clearly accompanied by total helplessness in the face of English syntax. It was the author of this poem, and the owner of this ambiguous reputation, whom Marvell set out to praise; and many of the peculiarities of the Fairfax poems become, on inspection, less peculiar when seen as necessary manœuvres in the art of speaking well without stretching the truth.

### UPON APPLETON HOUSE

Marvell approached this delicate issue obliquely. The three estate poems, *Epigramma in Duos montes*, *Upon the Hill and Grove at Bill-borow* and

*Upon Appleton House* itself, all adopt the ruse of praising Fairfax's character symbolically, as reflected in some aspect of the landscape property he owned. The premise must be, of course, that retirement is not weakness (an embarrassing possibility made worse by the rumour that the strong influence of Lady Fairfax, who opposed the king's execution, was behind it), but rather a combination of strength with self-restraint. In both the *Epigramma* and *Upon the Hill and Grove* the conceit is worked out in terms of mountainous (and male) ambition versus a smoother (more feminine) mental landscape. The Latin poem was considerably less successful in this than its English counterpart because it represented Fairfax as a split personality, half Amos Cliff and half Bilborough Hill; whereas in the English version he is figured only in the nicely rounded Bilborough Hill:

> See how the arched Earth does here
> Rise in a perfect Hemisphere!

The hill ascends courteously, and 'all the way it rises bends'; whereas Cromwell appears as the probable referent of the 'Mountains more unjust/Which to abrupter greatness thrust', and for whose 'excrescence ill design'd/Nature must a new Center find'.

We should remember that when Marvell probably wrote these poems he had not yet thrown in his lot with Cromwell; it may even have been that this dialectical relationship between the *Ode* and *Upon the Hill and Grove* spoke to genuine indecision as to whether discretion was not the better part of valour in the 1650s. Even so, *Upon Appleton House* seems peculiarly wary of outright praise of Fairfax, who never appears in person, his place usurped by his firmly characterized daughter. While Marvell does suggest that Fairfax's motives for retirement were idealistic if mysterious – he mentions the 'prickling leaf' of Conscience, 'which shrinks at ev'ry touch' – he precedes this justification by several stanzas that develop the idea of Fairfax's commitment to gardening into something remarkably close to a reproach. England itself is presented as a greater garden ('that dear and happy Isle/The Garden of the World ere while') that Fairfax has abandoned for Nunappleton:

> And yet their [sic] walks one on the Sod
> Who, had it pleased him and God,
> Might once have made our Gardens spring
> Fresh as his own and flourishing.

(ll. 345–8)

'But he *preferred* . . .' Marvell continues, his private gardens, which were, of course, precisely what he had praised Cromwell for abandoning.

The main strategy for *forgiving* Fairfax for this preference, we might say, is to locate it among traditionally sanctioned forms of retreat. It has long been recognized that in its stress on the 'sober Frame' and unpretentious architecture of Nunappleton House, the poem belongs among those estate poems deriving from Martial and Horace that celebrate modesty and frugality rather than conspicuous consumption. In its classical and neo-classical forms, this genre has been succinctly described as depending, both for its images and its sanction, on 'the wholesome moderation of rural living, the possibility of contentment with a small, choice acquaintance, and on the continuation of familial and cultural traditions in a place and manner untouched by the shifting fads of the city'.[22] This neoclassical context of Appleton House is further reinforced by allusions to Aeneas' stooping to enter Evander's world, and to Romulus' 'bee-like cell'. But the praise of the contemplative life, whether pagan or Christian, is peculiarly distorted in this poem by two other models of *otium*, neither of which are presented as admirable: the 25-stanza excursus on the convent that once occupied the estate, and the 35 stanzas during which the poet–tutor usurps his patron's function as the contemplative man observing the beauties of his property. The first of these is immediately recognizable as anti-monastic satire, a genre that gained new respectability as a result of the English Reformation and the dissolution of the monasteries. The rhetoric, the sensuality, the self-indulgence of the 'Suttle Nunns' who practise idolatry and goodness knows what else readily invite both stigmatization and destruction. The temptation expressed in the nun's speech identifies itself as a type of poetry, the 'sucreries devotes' of a highly affective and feminized devotion which had developed under the influence of the Pléiade in France: 'So through the mortal fruit we boyl/The Sugars uncorrupting Oyl' (ll. 173–4). For national and ethical reasons, therefore, we are clearly supposed to admire the rescue of Isabella Thwaites from the nuns' clutches by Fairfax's ancestor William Fairfax, and the ethical conclusion, when it comes ('Twas no Religious House till now') comes pat.

But if this kind of contemplative life is supposed to stand for an abuse which the Protestant and sober Fairfax will clearly avoid, we are not presented with a clearly admirable alternative. On the contrary, the second model of *otium* practised by the poet–tutor seems to be equally self-indulgent, and it too has a continental source: the 'solitude' poems of Théophile and Saint-Amant, a genre defined by the undirected and self-amusing play of ideas over a natural environment.[23] Like the subject of Saint-Amant's *Le Contemplateur*, the poet–tutor conjures out of the landscape an irresponsible mixture of analogues, and refuses to limit himself to images proper to the meditative state. Like Fairfax, he plays at making mental warfare, perceiving the mowing as a 'Massacre' of grass, the call of birds frightened by the death of the rail (quail) as 'Death-Trumpets' at a military funeral, and the hayfield itself 'A Camp of Battail newly fought . . . quilted ore with Bodies slain'. 'Bloody Thestylis', who seizes on the dead bird with triumph, may derive her name from Virgil's second Eclogue, but the mode in which she operates is far from pastoral. Ironically, it is her brutal literalism that breaks the illusion that only we and the poet know his thoughts, and that alerts us to his unruly imaginative processes. 'He call'd us Israelites', she cries, snatching up the wounded rail:

> But now, to make his saying true,
> Rails rain for Quails, for Manna Dew.
>
> (ll. 407–8)

'To make his saying true' is clearly a significant idiom in a praising poem; and Thestylis is, among other reproaches, questioning the poet–tutor's qualifications to give his experience a biblical flavour.

When he leaves the meadows for the woods, the idea of the Ark has no more authority for this poet than that of a pagan temple, whose 'Corinthean Porticoes' grow in as 'loose an order' as his mental images; and the misuse of Noah, first Carpenter, type of the active and regenerative life, contrasts with the *First Anniversary*, where even the patriarch's errors serve as metaphors for Cromwell's states-manship. In this undiscriminating intellect, 'What Rome, Greece, Palestine, ere said' is reduced to a single 'light Mosaick', with the pun on the Mosaic writings somewhat shockingly undermined by the adjective. One does not think of Moses as a light authority. Similarly, Saint-Amant's emphasis on the pleasures of solitude is caricatured as a fully libertine sensuality and laziness. 'Languishing with ease', 'On Pallets swoln of Velvet Moss', the 'easie Philosopher' merely thinks he is thinking. His claims to universal knowledge and penetration of 'Natures mystick Book', sometimes taken so gravely, exaggerate to the point of folly Saint-Amant's already dubi-ous claims:

> Tantost faisant agir mes sens
> Sur des sujets de moindre estoffe,

De marche en autre je descens
Dans les termes du Philosofe:
Nature n'a point de secret
Que d'un soin libre, mais discret,
Ma curiosité ne sonde,
Ses cabinets me sont ouvers,
Et dans ma recherche profonde
Je loge en moy tout l'Univers.[24]

The solipsism of this condition is further admitted in the stanza
which contains Marvell's best-known echo of Saint-Amant. In *La
Solitude* Saint-Amant had observed of a river:

Le Soleil s'y fait si bien voir,
Y contemplant son beau visage,
Qu'on est quelque temps a scavoir
Si c'est luy mesme, ou son image.[25]

It is important to realize that Fairfax himself had translated this
poem, with extreme literalness, in his commonplace book.[26] In ironic
imitation of his patron, Marvell turns the river on his patron's estate
into a 'Chrystal Mirrour slick':

Where all things gaze themselves, and doubt
If they be in it or without.
And for his shade which therein shines,
Narcissus like, the Sun too pines.

(ll. 637–40)

But Marvell has *added* the reminder of Narcissus, and so transformed
Saint-Amant's conceit into another admission of human self-pleasuring.
    What is missing from *Upon Appleton House*, however, is any positive
figure of English Protestant contemplation, such as had already been
clearly defined by Fairfax's own brother-in-law, Mildmay Fane, whose
*Otia Sacra* (1648) had defined, efficiently if without brilliance, a
merger between Virgilian and Horatian pastoral and Christian contemplation of Nature. In *To Retiredness*, Fane had indeed set out a
programme for the proper use of solitude:

For so my Thoughts by this retreat
Grow stronger like contracted heat.
Whether on Nature's Book I muse
Or else some other writes on't, use
To spend the time in, every line,

Is not excentrick, but Divine;
And though all others downward tend,
These look to heaven, and ascend
From whence they came; where pointed hie
They ravish into Mysterie,
To see the footsteps here are trod
Of mercy by a Gracious God.[27]

The absence of this 'beatior ille' from Marvell's poem is surely strategic. In the inferential space between the nuns and the tutor he exists as a possibility only, a possibility indicated in the crucial and warning lines, themselves an allusion to Fane:

Thrice happy he who, *not mistook*,
Hath read in Natures mystick Book. (italics added)

His audience is thereby obliquely directed, not to the pursuit of 'thrice-great Hermes', but to the threefold happiness (*beatus, beatior, beatissimus*) which results when Stoicism, mysticism and Christianity are properly blended.

There remains, of course, the last phase of the poem, where the praise of Fairfax is fulfilled in (as his estate is entailed on) his daughter. Praise of a man by his descendants is the counterpart of praise by his ancestry, enlarged by the knowledge that the family virtues have been preserved by his paternal care. Mary Fairfax not only exemplifies Fairfax's 'Discipline severe' but in her modesty, both natural and philosophical, must surely demonstrate his. When Nature offers her the river as a looking-glass, it immediately repents of its error, and the 'Wood about her draws a Skreen' in acknowledgement that she is no Narcissus:

For She, to higher Beauties rais'd,
Disdains to be for lesser prais'd.
She counts her Beauty to converse
In all the Languages as hers;
Nor yet in those her self imployes
But for the Wisdome, not the Noyse;
Nor yet that Wisdome would affect,
But as'tis Heavens Dialect.

(ll. 705–12)

We are given in this stanza another Fairfax who flies her own praise, but in so doing begs none of the questions attached to her father's modesty. As her use of solitude is unambiguously devotional, so the force of her personality ensures that no one will ever suspect her of escapism. Shaming the poet–tutor out of his self-indulgent laziness, she acts like a military commander reviewing her slack troops. 'Loose Nature, in respect/ To her, it self doth recollect'. Dialectically, she belongs with Cromwell, as a figure who will leave her private gardens to fulfil her dynastic obligations; what actually happened to Mary after her reckless marriage to the Duke of Buckingham only underlines the problem of validation, the temporal and cognitive limitations of true praise in the human perspective.

It should not be forgotten that in *Musicks Empire*, also addressed to a patron who 'flies the Musick of his praise', Marvell identified the major alternative to secular epideictic. In turning from evaluating 'Mens Triumphs' to the unquestionable validity of 'Heavens Hallelujahs', he pointed to *Bermudas*, *The Coronet* and *On a Drop of Dew*, and to the problems of devotional poetics, the subject of Chapter 3.

NOTES

1. For the history of epideictic from Plato to the Renaissance, and a summary of its topics, see O. B. Hardison, *The Enduring Monument: A Study of the Idea of Praise in Renaissance Literary Theory and Practice* (Chapel Hill, NC, 1962), pp. 26–42.
2. For more detail, see my 'Miscellaneous Marvell', in *The Political Identity of Andrew Marvell*, ed. Conal Condren and A. D. Cousins (Aldershot, 1990), pp. 188–212.
3. P. Samwayes, 'De rebus in Scotia . . .' in *Irenodia Cantabrigiensis* (Cambridge, 1641), Ir, v: 'Phoebus spoke to me as I was hoping for battles and conquered cities, and crops languishing, cut down not by the scythe but by the rage of the too-hasty sword; a goddess not seen before advised and instructed me to weave the garlands of peace in a soft song.'
4. For the extensive bibliography that deals with Marvell's use of Roman texts in the *Ode*, the reader is referred to *Poems and Letters*, 1: 294–303. See also Blair Worden, 'Andrew Marvell, Oliver Cromwell and the Horatian Ode', in *Politics of Discourse*, eds. Kevin Sharpe and Steven Zwicker (Berkeley, Los Angeles and London, 1987), pp. 362–76.
5. For a detailed discussion of Marvell's use of biblical typology in this poem, see *Marvell and the Civic Crown*, pp. 82–6.
6. Pierre Legouis, *André Marvell* (Paris, 1928), p. 193.
7. See J. A. Mazzeo, 'Cromwell as Davidic King', in *Reason and the Imagination* (New York, 1962), pp. 183–208; John M. Wallace, 'Andrew Marvell and Cromwell's Kingship', *ELH* 30 (1963), 209–35; *Destiny his Choice: The Loyalism of Andrew Marvell* (Cambridge, 1968), pp. 106–40.

Contrast Steven Zwicker, 'Models of Governance in Marvell's "The
First Anniversary"', *Criticism* 16 (1974), 1–12.

8.  Milton, *Complete Prose Works*, ed. D. M. Wolfe *et al.* (New Haven,
    1953–82), 4.i: 672.

9.  See Warren Chernaik, *The Poetry of Limitation* (New Haven, 1968),
    p. 41, n. 23.

10. Edmund Waller, *Workes* (London, 1645), p. 4.

11. See Ruth Nevo, *The Dial of Virtue: A Study of Poems on Affairs of State
    in the Seventeenth Century* (Princeton, 1963), pp. 20–7, 74–118.

12. Milton, *Complete Prose Works*, 2: 555.

13. Herrick, *Poetical Works*, ed. L. C. Martin (Oxford, 1956), pp. 61–2.

14. Legouis, *André Marvell*, p. 215.

15. John M. Wallace, *Destiny his Choice: The Loyalism of Andrew Marvell*
    (Cambridge, 1968), p. 143.

16. Thomas May, *Lucan's Pharsalia* (London, 1627), A3.

17. *The Rehearsal Transpros'd and The Rehearsal Transpros'd: The Second
    Part*, ed. D. I. B. Smith (Oxford, 1971), p. 135.

18. C. R. Markham, *A Life of the Great Lord Fairfax* (London, 1870),
    p. 349.

19. As recorded in Richard Perinchieffe's *Life and Death of Charles the First*
    (London, 1693), pp. 219–20. Markham, *A Life* (p. 351), rejected this
    story partly on the grounds that it represented Fairfax as a 'born idiot'.
    For a kinder view of Fairfax, see Patsy Griffin, *The Modest Ambition of
    Andrew Marvell* (Newark and London, 1995), pp. 56–74.

20. Edward Hyde, first earl of Clarendon, *The History of the Rebellion and
    Civil Wars in England* (Oxford, 1702–04), 2: 66.

21. Bodleian MS Fairfax 40, p. 600.

22. By M.-S. Røstvig, *The Happy Man: Studies in the Metamorphoses of a
    Classical Ideal 1400–1708* (Oslo, 1954), p. 90; G. R. Hibbard, 'The
    Country House Poem of the Seventeenth Century', *Journal of Warburg
    and Courtauld Institute* 19 (1956), 159–74.

23. See Terence Cave, *Devotional Poetry in France, c. 1570–1613* (Cam-
    bridge, 1969), pp. 244–66.

24. Saint-Amant, *Le Contemplateur*, in *Œuvres* (Rouen, 1638), pp. 18–19:
    'Meanwhile, agitating my senses on subjects of lesser substance I descend
    progressively into philosophical terms. Nature has no secret which,
    with generous but careful attention, I cannot fathom. Her cabinets are
    open to me, and in my profound research I contain within myself the
    entire Universe'.

25. Saint-Amant, *Œuvres*, p. 12: 'The sun can there so well be seen,
    contemplating his fair face, that it take some time to be sure whether
    it is himself or his image [in the water]'.

26. Bodleian MS Fairfax 40, pp. 562–53.

27. Mildmay Fane, *Otia Sacra* (London, 1648), pp. 173–4.

# Chapter 3

# Devotional poetry

Marvell himself provided a neat transition between devotional poetry and the idea of praise in a poem elusively entitled *Epitaph upon* – , a poem that thematizes modesty as anonymity:

> Enough: and leave the rest to Fame.
> 'Tis to commend her but to name.
> Courtship, which living she declin'd,
> When dead to offer were unkind.
> Where never any could speak ill,
> Who would officious Praises spill?
> Nor can the truest Wit or Friend,
> Without Detracting, her commend.
> To say she liv'd a Virgin chast,
> In this Age loose and all unlac't;
> Nor was, when Vice is so allow'd,
> Of Virtue or asham'd, or proud;
> That her Soul was on Heaven so bent
> No Minute but it came and went;
> That ready her last Debt to pay
> She summ'd her Life up ev'ry day;
> Modest as Morn; as Mid-day bright;
> Gentle as Ev'ning; cool as Night;
> 'Tis true: but all so weakly said;
> 'Twere more Significant, She's Dead.[1]

Starting from the initial conceit, that the mere naming of an unnamed lady is her truest praise, the poem develops a frugal rhetoric of understatement. The concept that a chaste woman who avoided 'courtship' when alive would be offended by compliments paid to her memory is developed into the paradox that neither 'truest Wit' nor 'Friend' can define her virtues without diminishing them. Marvell's ambiguous use of 'Detracting' implies that even true praise of a woman uniquely virtuous constitutes a form of satire. The poem's own plainness and precision is true to the quiet piety it celebrates, which is conventionally enough contrasted to 'an Age loose and all unlac't' but which, in the context of Marvell's other epitaphs, all of them to members of Puritan families, may be more precisely a historical allusion to the reign of Charles II. This possibility is enhanced by the epitaph for John Trott Sr (father of the man to whom Marvell wrote a letter of consolation for the death of his son), which Margoliouth discovered in the family church at Laverstoke, and which may well be the immediate source of Marvell's opening conceit: 'If the Just are praised when they are onely named how am I surprised with a Panegyricke whilst I am telling the reader that here lyes the body of John Trott of Laverstock . . . Oct: 24. 1658' (*Poems and Letters*, 1: 339). This was, we remember, a month after the death of Oliver Cromwell. The epitaph therefore lies at the boundary of the Commonwealth; the poem straddles two modes – the poetry of secular and social praise *and* devotional or religious lyric, its values capable of identification as a minority Puritan tradition within a sexually 'loose' but politically coercive Restoration culture.

One should not, however, therefore jump to the conclusion that Marvell 'was', or was always, a Puritan, by which we mean (loosely, alas) someone to the left of the religious spectrum. One important biographical fact (or rumour) so far omitted from this story is that, as a Cambridge undergraduate, Marvell had a personal encounter with Roman Catholicism. Thomas Cooke related in his 1726 edition that soon after Marvell's arrival at Trinity College:

> his Studys were interrupted by this remarkable Accident. Some Jesuits, with whom he was then conversant, seeing in him a Genius beyond his Years, thought of Nothing less than gaining a Proselyte. And doutless their Hopes extended farther. They knew, if that Point was once obtained, he might in Time be a great Instrument towards carrying on their Cause. They used all the Arguments they could to seduce him away, which at last they did. After some Months his Father found him in a Bookseller's Shop in London, and prevailed with him to return to the College.

And Cooke's anecdote was confirmed by the later discovery of a letter from the vicar of Welton to Marvell's father, reporting on a similar experience in his own family, and asking for advice as to how to handle it.[2]

This youthful truancy, which is how Andrew Senior evidently saw it, would not be of much interest were it not for the fact that the *Miscellaneous Poems* of 1681 opens with eight devotional poems.[3] Of these, three (or four, if one counts both the English and Latin versions of *On a Drop of Dew*) have Roman Catholic antecedents or

actual sources. Yet they share the privileged space of the volume's
opening pages with *Bermudas*, whose imagined context is the flight
of Puritan settlers to the New World; and introducing all the devotional poems is *A Dialogue between the Resolved Soul, and Created
Pleasure*, whose opening lines not only celebrate a plain style of
religious experience, but might also be considered a symbolic retell-
ing of Marvell's experience: of Jesuit artful seduction countered by
paternal, Puritan restraint: 'Courage my Soul, now learn to wield/
The weight of thine immortal Shield/ . . . And shew that Nature
wants an Art/To conquer one resolved Heart'. Taken together,
however, the eight poems seem to indicate that choosing one's
religion is never so simple as the Resolved Soul's advisor believes.
Their combined subject might be described as studies in the vexed
relationship between religion and aesthetic pleasure, a problem to
which they give incompatible answers.

While we have only a slender basis on which to assign approxim-
ate dates to most of Marvell's poetry, for the devotional poems we
have no basis at all. They could belong equally to the period at
Cambridge following his return from London, c. 1640; or to his stay
at Nunappleton House, in 1651–53; or to the mid 1650s, when he
was tutoring Dutton under the eye of John Oxenbridge; or to 1672,
when he was thinking his way through the intricacies of law and
conscience in relation to *The Rehearsal Transpros'd*; or individually to
any of the above.

There is, therefore, no chronological reason *not* to begin with the
clues to his own religious stance that Marvell provided in the second
part of the *Rehearsal Transpros'd*. There he indicated that the depress-
ing history of the European churches since the Reformation might
lead, if not to relativism, at least to a moderate pragmatism. As far
back as he can remember, the 'Ecclesiasticks', as he calls the higher
clergy, have been the least interested in making 'a just and effectual
Reformation' of their churches:

> If they had, there would have been no Wicliffe, no Husse, no Luther
> in History. Or at least, upon so notable an emergency as the last, the
> Church of Rome would then in the Council of Trent have thought of
> rectifying itself in good earnest, that it might have recover'd its ancient
> character; whereas it left the same divisions much wider, and the Christian
> People of the world to suffer, Protestants under Popish Governors, Popish
> under Protestants, rather than let go any point of interested Ambition.[4]

Instead of castigating the Roman church for its irremediable decadence,
as Milton did in his church-reform pamphlets of the 1640s, Marvell

leaves open the conceptual possibility that it *could* have recovered the integrity of its 'ancient character', that is to say, its unity and unworldliness. More impartially still, he notes that its failure to do so in the face of the great schisms of the Reformation has caused as much suffering to Catholics in Protestant states as vice versa. And turning to English regulation by law of the forms of religious worship, Marvell continued:

> Even the Church of Rome, which cannot be thought the most negligent of things that concern her interest, does not, that I know of, lay any great stress upon Rituals and Ceremonials, so men agree in Doctrine, nor do I remember that they have persecuted any upon that account, but left the several Churches in the Priviledge of their own fashion.
>
> (p. 241)

By contrast, the English church seems obsessed with ceremonies or their suppression. And had not the 'Civil Magistrate', that is to say, the successive Tudor and Stuart monarchs, been persuaded by the higher clergy to intervene in a matter 'so unnecessary, so trivial, and so pernicious to the publick quiet', the English wars of religion might never have occurred:

> For had things been left in their own state of Indifferency, it is well known that the English Nation is generally neither so void of Understanding, Civility, Obedience, or Devotion, but that they would long ago have voluntarily closed and faln naturally into those reverent manners of Worship which would have sufficiently have exprest and suited with their Religion.
>
> (p. 242)

Situating himself between the Nonconformists and the High Churchmen, both of whom he suggests are intransigent, though the former more justifiably so, because they are acting according to conscience, whereas the clergy are motivated by a mixture of self-interest and expediency, Marvell identifies a new *via media* in religion, an essentially English version, in which 'reverent manners of Worship' have more status than we might have expected. Yet a few pages later we arrive at a definition of worship more clearly compatible with his epitaph to the anonymous (Puritan) lady:

> Christianity . . . aims all at that which is sincere and solid and having laid that weight upon the Conscience, which will be found sufficient for any honest man to walk under, it hath not pressed and loaded men further with the burthen of Ritual and Ceremonial traditions and Impositions.
>
> (p. 246)

Again, a certain amused pragmatism accompanies the traditional Reformation language, and grounds it in mundane experience: 'most Creatures know when they have their just load, nor can you make them go if you add more' (p. 246).

Devotional poetry, we might say, is in this period largely concerned with the vexed relation between Conscience and Ritual, inner and outer, soul and body, religious beliefs and religious practices. As devotion, it must privilege the first element in each of those pairs; as poetry, it is tied to the second. Like Donne and Herbert, Marvell was intrigued by this paradox. Unlike them, he experimented with a whole range of different solutions to the paradox, solutions which themselves can be recognized as having different confessional allegiances, different positions along the religious spectrum. Four of them, as I have said, have Jesuit or Roman Catholic connections. Kitty Scoular Datta discovered that the source for the *Dialogue between the Soul and Body* was the Jesuit Hermann Hugo's Latin emblem book, *Pia Desideria*, first published in Antwerp in 1624, and astonishingly successful, with translations into French, Flemish, German and Spanish.[5] Likewise, Rosalie Colie discovered that Marvell's two versions of *On a drop of Dew*, one in English, one in Latin, contained echoes of Henry Hawkins' symbolic essay on 'The Deaw' in *Parthenia Sacra*, another Jesuit emblem book.[6] As a model, Hawkins' work was more loaded with political significance than Hugo's, since it was published in English, one of a series of works designed for the English Catholic market during the reign of Henrietta Maria that implicitly conflated her with the worship of the Virgin Mary. In addition, *Eyes and Tears* was more distantly influenced by the dozens of 'Holy Weeper' or 'tear' poems generated by the Council of Trent's emphasis on penance, and on the figure of Mary Magdalene. What do these connections mean? Are the poems relics of Marvell's youthful flirtation with the Jesuits? Or are they a more mature commentary on the deep appeal of the Counter-Reformation to those in the English church who still yearned for images, music, certain kinds of mysticism and asceticism, and perhaps a feminized and tender religious culture?

These questions are hard to answer definitively, because Marvell plays his religious cards, like his political ones, extremely close to his chest. His modern readers can disagree absolutely about what he was up to. My own contribution to these debates is to suggest that the poems that directly derive from Counter-Reformation sources are posited on the tricky idea of sublimation – that is to say, allowing the experience of religion to be deeply, even sensually, pleasurable, but requiring that pleasure to be explicitly transcended. *The Garden* is not explicitly a devotional poem and was not so located in the *Miscellaneous Poems*, but its structure helps to explain Marvell's religious psychology. The soul in *The Garden* willingly withdraws from 'pleasures less' to 'a green Thought', and then casts 'the Bodies Vest aside', in preparation for 'longer flight'. But the process of sublimation starts in – indeed, depends on – a physical environment whose attributes require description by the following adjectives: 'delicious', 'am'rous', 'wond'rous' and 'Luscious'. We might think we were back in the world of the subtle nuns of Nunappleton, were it not for the corrective phrases of the final stanza, with its '*industrious* Bee' and its 'sweet and *wholsome* Hours' (italics added).

### ON A DROP OF DEW

This hypothesis is developed with greater discipline in the two poems on the dew, though the English version is still more precise intellectually than its Latin companion. In fact, as Colie pointed out, a comparison of the poem with its 'source' in Hawkins reveals that discipline is one of the poem's central imperatives. The metaphor that Marvell, following Hawkins, has chosen to intimate the soul is as nearly beyond the carnal as an image can be – a drop of water, related to the tears which make us human, for, as his *Eyes and Tears* reminds us, 'only humane Eyes can weep'. But whereas Hawkins' essay described the dew as 'the verie teares of Nature, dissolved & soft through tendernes',[7] Marvell carefully explains that the natural dewdrop 'Shines with a mournful Light; *Like* its *own* Tear', explaining through that small but careful 'like' that the pathetic fallacy is a merely human addition. The drop of dew is, moreover, purer, more perfectly spherical, than a tear as it lies in the curved petal of a rose, and unlike human tears, is not to be wiped away but rather reabsorbed. But Hawkins' dew is first a symbol of the Virgin and then of her Son, 'to which the Church alluding sayth: Let him ascend into the Virgins womb like Deaw therin' (p. 64). Marvell's dewdrop, though eminently real, natural, visible, is delicately restricted in significance. It is only our way of *imagining* the attributes of the soul.

The structure of the English version, especially, is elegant in the extreme, enhancing the intellectual discipline of the exercise. Eighteen lines, beginning with an invitation to visualize ('See how the Orient Dew'), set out the precarious acts of self-definition, reflection, world-rejection and aspiration that we can pretend the dewdrop engaged in:

For the clear Region where 'twas born
  Round in itself incloses:
  And in its little Globes Extent,
Frames as it can its native Element.
  How it the purple flow'r does slight,
    Scarce touching where it lyes,
. . .

                 . . .

  Restless it roules and unsecure,
    Trembling lest it grow impure:
  Till the warm Sun pitty it's Pain
And to the Skies exhale it back again.

(Poems and Letters, 1: 12–13)

These are followed by eighteen lines applying these characteristics, scrupulously but wittily, to the invisible and almost inconceivable: 'So the Soul, that Drop, that Ray . . . could it within the humane flow'r be seen', would be seen to behave in the same manner, shunning 'the sweat leaves and blossoms green' of its earthly environment. Why are *these* adjectives reversed from normal expectation? Perhaps to prevent too easy a slippage from vehicle to tenor. 'Recollecting its own Light' is a characteristic Marvellian pun, combining a psychological idea of remembrance with a concept from physics – the concentration of light by a watery lens. The poem begins to comment on its *own* activity, for which the dew can stand as an emblem. It, too, 'does, in its pure and circling thoughts, *express*/The greater Heaven in an Heaven less', and it, too, is 'wound' in a 'Figure' which Marvell designates, surprisingly, as 'coy'. If 'coy' means sexual shyness (as in *To his Coy Mistress*), then Marvell's own 'Figure' of the soul is equally inhibited. And, he continues, the desires of this soul, and this figure, for full comprehension must necessarily be expressed as a series of paradoxes. Seen from below (our perspective) both the soul and its figurative expression are 'dark' (incomprehensible):

  Dark beneath, but bright above:
  Here disdaining, there in Love.
How loose and easie hence to go:
How girt and ready to ascend.
Moving but on a point below,
It all about does upward bend.

Adjectives that we have seen before in more or less negative contexts – 'loose' ('this Age loose and all unlac't') and 'easie' ('easie Philosopher', itself a contradiction in terms) – are here redeemed by their motive, which is eagerness for departure. And as Bilborough Hill complimented Fairfax by its deference ('And all the way it rises bends'), so Marvell's Soul 'all about does upward bend', a prodigious spiritual gymnastics.

Finally, Marvell rounds off the poem by extracting from Hawkins' collage of metaphors one that would serve his structural and metapoetic needs. Dew, wrote Hawkins, is 'the Manna of Nature, to vye with those Corianders, food of Pilgrims, made by Angels: with this unhappines, they could not be congealed, to make a food so much for men, as a Nectar for the plants to drink' (p. 60). Marvell's version tightens the biblical analogy:

> Such did the Manna's sacred Dew distil;
> White, and intire, though congeal'd and chill.
> Congeal'd on Earth: but does, dissolving, run
> Into the Glories of th'Almighty Sun.

Completing his series, 'See', 'So', 'Such', Marvell gives both the dewdrop and the soul what they long for; and the repeated 'congeal'd' derived from Hawkins consequently acquires structural and metaphysical status, as standing for the best that earthly art can do.

If one gives this poem the theoretical space it deserves in Marvell's canon, and especially if one wonders why he wrote it twice, once in the Roman language, it suggests that Marvell remained, temperamentally and aesthetically, sympathetic to the old religion, while politically he threw in his lot with those toward the other end of the ecclesiastical spectrum. On a Drop of Dew has more affiliations, perhaps, with Alexander Pope's deeply erotic Eloisa to Abelard (a male Roman Catholic poet's representation of a female conventual's unwilling sublimation of sexual desire) than it does with the sternly patriarchal religion of John Milton. On the other hand, it is far from submitting to Hawkins' luxuriant, unstructured fantasies, wherein epistemologically anything goes.

## A DIALOGUE BETWEEN THE SOUL AND BODY

The tensions inherent in On a Drop of Dew are differently configured in A Dialogue between the Soul and Body, where Marvell began virtually translating Hugo's Latin poem, which described the torments of the soul encaged in the body. Unquestionably he was attracted by the wit of Hugo's metaphors – of feet as fetters and hands as manacles, while the entire skeleton is conceived as a cage of bones. But in his second stanza he immediately declared his unique version of independence via imitation, by introducing the *other* character in the relationship – the Body, who appropriates the Soul's rhetoric of hyperbolic complaint:

> O who shall me deliver whole,
> From bonds of this Tyrannic Soul?
> Which, stretcht upright, impales me so,
> That mine own Precipice I go.
> . . .
>
>                                   . . .
> What but a Soul could have the wit
> To build me up for Sin so fit?
> So Architects do square and hew
> Green Trees that in the Forest grew.

(Poems and Letters, 1: 22–23)

That is, the Soul's very aspiration to ascend is to be understood as a torture imposed on the Body, whose consequently upright stature (that which differentiates man from the animals) is experienced as painful and dangerous. One could argue, with Datta, that Marvell is here playing 'humorous havoc with a Jesuit poet', and reasserting his Puritan leanings (p. 246); or alternatively, that if the Soul's argument stands for a Counter-Reformation unworldliness such as the dew-drop symbolized, the Body's stands for the predicament of the young man dragged back from London to continue his studies in Puritan Cambridge. But if the Body identifies with all things 'Green', a Marvellian term of positive value, it acknowledges the Soul the owner of 'wit', which the poem undoubtedly celebrates, finding its source in Hugo. Even though the Body has the last word (and four extra lines) it is impossible to choose *between* these alternatives. We have to give credit to both antagonists, not least for the extraordinary entente they perpetually maintain.

## BERMUDAS

One of the loveliest poems Marvell wrote was a comment on the relation between religious controversy and the settlement of the New World. *Bermudas* may have been written in 1653 in the house of John Oxenbridge, himself a former minister to the Bermudas, but its meanings extend far beyond a particular friend or patron. Here the focus is not on the metaphysical versus the physical, but rather on contrasting styles of worship, and the translation of pleasure in the world into acceptable devotion. Deftly, with a single phrase, 'Safe from the . . . Prelat's rage', Marvell intimates a historical context for his poem, though not a very precise one, chronologically speaking. The protagonists in *Bermudas*, the 'we' of the poem, singing in an 'English boat', are evidently a group of Puritan refugees from ecclesiastical repression. We have to remember that in *Upon Appleton House* Marvell saw himself looking, in the woodland temple, 'like some great Prelate of the Grove' (l. 592), that is to say, an Anglican bishop. Yet these puritans are neither committed to the 'discipline severe' that corrects the poet–tutor's excesses nor opposed to natural delights. Having begun their song with a clear statement of their redirection of praise to a spiritual, not a secular, patron ('What should we do but sing *his* Praise'), they fill it with a medley of phrases taken from or reminiscent of the Psalms, particularly those devoted to praise and thanksgiving rather than penitence and self-flagellation:

> He gave us this eternal Spring,
> Which here enamells every thing;
> And sends the Fowl's to us in care,
> On daily Visits through the Air.
> . . .
>
>                                   . . .
> He makes the Figs our mouths to meet;
> And throws the Melons at our feet.

(Poems and Letters, 1: 18)

This vision of a natural bounty more generous than any real-life settlers in the New World were likely to experience resembles the earthly paradise that Marvell conjured up for himself in *The Garden*, where the fruits of the earth behaved with equal abandon. Here, however, the real agent of their forwardness is God himself.

And, given what we have seen of Marvell's responses to Edmund Waller in the *First Anniversary*, it is less surprising to learn that *Bermudas* is also a riposte to Waller's *Battle of the Summer Islands*, a minor epic account of the settlement in the Bermudas which was entirely secular, royalist and amorous in tone.[8] All of Marvell's echoes of Waller take issue with these values. The whales, whose slaughter was the main subject of Waller's poem, reappear in Marvell's as 'the huge Sea-Monsters' from whom God protects his psalmists, as he did in Psalm 74: 14: 'Thou breakest the heads of leviathan in pieces'. Where Waller's earthly paradise has 'Orange trees which golden fruit do bear', rivalling the apples of the Hesperides, Marvell's God 'hangs in shades the Orange bright,/Like Golden Lamps in a green Night', allowing recollection of Psalm 119: 105: 'Thy word is a lamp unto my feet'. Where Waller's admiration for the Bermudan cedars is expressed in terms of secular imperialism ('The lofty Cedar, which to heaven aspires,/The Prince of trees . . . Such as might Pallaces for Kings adorne') Marvell invokes, as does Psalm 104: 16, the cedars of Lebanon, from which Solomon built the Temple. It is the conclusion we expect, therefore, when *Bermudas* finally makes the translation from physical to spiritual riches, and its arriving (or departing) settlers '*rather* boast/The Gospels Pearl upon our Coast' than any previous item in the catalogue of bounty.

But there is another layer of meaning to *Bermudas*, expressed in the four lines that close the frame of the poem. 'Thus sang they', wrote Marvell, 'An holy and a chearful Note'. The merger of holiness with cheerfulness in the forms of devotion is not something automatically associated with Puritanism, then or now. There were extremists who disapproved of church music, set forms of prayer, and any emphasis on the poetic as distinct from the doctrinal content of Scripture. It was for their taste that the 'Geneva jigs' of the Sternhold and Hopkins psalter, with its plodding meter, had been produced, and their taste that decreed the superiority of the penitential psalms over the more exuberant ones. Even St Augustine had admitted this tendency, long before Catholic and Puritan had become terms of distinction:

> I erre out of too precise a severity: yea very fierce am I sometimes in the desire of having the melody of all pleasant Musicke, (to which David's Psalter is so often sung), banished both from mine owne ears and out of the whole Church too . . . Notwithstanding so often as I call to mind the teares I shed at the hearing of the Church-songs, in the beginning of my recovered fayth . . . I then acknowledge the great good use of this institution. *Thus floate I betweene perill of pleasure, and an approved profitable custome* . . . See now in what a perplexity I am.[9]

Marvell has his settlers, too, literally floating between peril of pleasure and an approved profitable custom, but resolves the perplexity with his own editorial comment. The holy *and* cheerful notes of *Bermudas* are an acceptable compromise between the Resolved Soul and Created Pleasure, rather than a victory of the former over the latter.

## THE CORONET

If we wished to return to the question of where Marvell himself stood on 'those reverent manners of Worship' he discussed in his prose tracts, each of which had their equivalent in devotional poetry, *On a Drop of Dew* might be placed somewhere to the right, between ordinary Anglicanism and an ecstatic or at least monastic Catholicism, and *Bermudas* somewhere between that same theoretical centre and one of the more rigorous forms of Non-conformity, with the *Dialogue between the Soul and Body* squarely in the centre. *The Coronet*, however, cannot be placed with confidence at any point on that imaginary line. It is formally and generically related both to Donne's *La Corona*, with its explanation as to how a rather ornate poetry can constitute a worthy 'crown of prayer and praise', and to Herbert's *A Wreath*, a chain-link structure of repeated words, which ends by offering to 'give,/For this poore wreath . . . a crown of praise'. Both models had been available in print since 1633. More autobiographical than either, *The Coronet* is confessionally opaque; whereas Donne's circlet of sonnets had adapted the Catholic rosaries or 'lady's psalters' for Protestant use, and Herbert's was presumably governed by the Anglican structure of *The Temple* as a whole.

*The Coronet* seems to be a poem which deliberately abandons the poise, balance or compromise of the three discussed hitherto. It recreates instead the problem of Christian eloquence in all its Augustinian perplexity. In place of the assured status of biblical echoes, we are given highly ambiguous metaphors which may and probably do mean several things at once; and instead of the neat stanzas of the *Dialogue* or the directed couplets of *Bermudas* or even the confident symmetry of *On a Drop of Dew*, *The Coronet* consists of two long verse paragraphs of uneven length and unobvious rhyme patterns. Two winding sentences, the first running through eighteen lines, the second comprising the last eight lines of the poem, represent the poet's rejected past and his projected future, which will depend on divine intervention. Throughout, a convoluted syntax deliberately entangles the reader.

We can still, however, sort out its threads. A brief introduction presents the past as a 'long, too long' period of sin, represented as the construction of a crown of thorns for his Saviour's head. There follows his conversion from secular poetry (tributes for shepherdesses) to devotion, the weaving of 'Garlands to redress that Wrong' from the very materials of the old abuse. The flowers (not fruits) he gathers for the new task are surely the flowers of rhetoric. But even as he works on this new coronet, he discovers a third, unintentional construction:

> Alas I find the Serpent old,
> That twining in his speckled breast,
> About the flow'rs disguis'd does fold,
> With wreaths of Fame and Interest.

(Poems and Letters, 1: 14–15)

The result of this discovery is a shift from nominative to vocative mode, from narrative to dramatic; the poet appeals to God to save him from his own complexity, to destroy his 'curious frame' along with the serpent of impure motivation. And he concludes with a new hypothesis, that the products of this destruction will somehow 'crown [his] Feet, that could not crown [his] Head'. A third (or is it a fourth?) coronet has mysteriously been woven. The curious frame resembles the coy figure of *On a Drop of Dew* in being multi-referential. Is it the rejected devotional corona, or this very autobiographical poem, or the poet's natural body? Does 'curious' recall the 'curious Peach' of *The Garden* (which itself deserves a rather long gloss) or does it imply excessive ingenuity and intricacy?

At the very end of his career, Marvell was still unwilling or unable to answer this question definitively. In the *Remarks* (1678) in defence of John Howe, in which the question of ceremonies and conformity then in dispute was partly being discussed at the level of style, Marvell reminded his opponent, Thomas Danson, that curiosity had traditionally been 'taken in many several significations'. It could either be a 'commendable exquisiteness in things considerable, and worth the labour', or an 'impertinent diligence' in insignificant or improper areas of enquiry, or, thirdly, 'a superfluous and laborious nicety; as a curious man differs from a diligent, or superstition from religion'.[10] To the end of his days, Marvell remained sensitive to the way one ideological position shades into another, often by the slippage between good intentions and 'interest'. It still remains possible, however, to reconstruct his values and to identify his characteristic vocabulary, by means of which those values were rubbed against each other, producing electricity.

NOTES

1.  *Poems and Letters*, 1: 58–9.
2.  Hilton Kelliher, *Andrew Marvell: Poet and Politician, 1621–78* (London, 1978), p. 25.
3.  The group may even consist of *nine* devotional poems, depending on how one reads *The Nymph complaining for the death of her Faun*, which immediately followed *A Dialogue between the Soul and Body*, and which has been more than once interpreted as religious allegory. See, for example, Geoffrey Hartman, '"The Nymph Complaining . . ." A Brief Allegory', *Essays in Criticism* (1968), 113–35.
4.  *The Rehearsal Transpros'd and The Rehearsal Transpros'd: The Second Part*, ed. D. I. B. Smith (Oxford, 1971), p. 240.

5.  Kitty Scoular Datta, 'New Light on Marvell's "A Dialogue between the Soul and Body"', *Renaissance Quarterly* 22 (1969), 242–55.
6.  Rosalie Colie, *'My Ecchoing Song': Andrew Marvell's Poetry of Criticism* (Princeton, 1970), pp. 115–17.
7.  Henry Hawkins, *Parthenia Sacra* (Rouen, 1633), p. 59.
8.  Edmund Waller, *Workes* (London, 1645), pp. 52–4.
9.  William Watts, *Saint Augustines Confessions translated* (London, 1631), X. 33 (italics added).
10. Marvell, *Complete Works*, ed. A. B. Grosart (repr. New York, 1966), 4: 177–8.

# Chapter 4

# Experiments in satire

Simultaneously the most controversial and the least appreciated of his poems, Marvell's satires have been treated with various combinations of wariness and distaste. Between the continued doubt as to which satires are indisputably Marvell's, and the suppressed wish that none of them were, few critics have wasted good analysis on poems at once unauthenticated and apparently unrewarding. Not even the *Last Instructions to a Painter*, which has received most attention, and of which Margoliouth remarked that 'of all the satires attributed to Marvell there is none of which one can feel less doubt' (*Poems and Letters*, 1: 346), had its authenticity confirmed by appearance in the *Miscellaneous Poems* of 1681; even the *Last Instructions* has damaged its author's reputation for delicacy of mind and sureness of touch. Still, there have been several attempts to show how that poem's effects are justified by a theory of satiric decorum, and therefore witness rather to Marvell's flexibility as a writer than to the collapse of his art in political disillusionment.[1]

This chapter extends those arguments by showing how his turn to satire was both inevitable and admirable. The concern with public standards which provoked him, in the early poem to Lovelace, to reject satire as socially destructive, led him also, in the crisis of the Second Dutch War, to regard it as socially necessary. The rhetorical training which allowed him, in the 1650s, to explore the problems of political panegyric in relation to Cromwell's Protectorate, forced him, in the years following the Restoration, to parody the propagandists of Charles's government, and to shift from conditional praise to various forms of justified blame. At the heart of both activities lie the same theoretical issues, the same questions about public values, the relationship between partisanship and objectivity, and the interdependence of aesthetic and social goals. Though Marvell's major satires have a still more direct relationship with events than do the Protectorate poems, being connected with Opposition strategy to control the Cabal and Charles II himself in fiscal and foreign policy, their pragmatic focus is not their most noticeable feature. What is most striking about them is the adoption of a new medium for satire – pictorialism, or the theory of representation in which the sister arts, poetry and painting, competed for social status. Pictorialism, as a vocabulary and set of conventions, was everywhere current in the early seventeenth century, and was normally used as a vehicle for the expression of high ideals. Its potency derived from a mixture of continental art theory and the actual commitment of Charles I and Charles II to painting as an expression of imperial court culture. It was typical of Marvell, brilliant jackdaw that he was, to appropriate this tool to the uses of political satire.

Marvell had a very few brief excursions into satire prior to the Second Dutch War. One of these was the puzzling *Fleckno, an English Priest at Rome*, which shows that Marvell's earliest concept of satire was heavily influenced by the model of John Donne, in which the deliberate awkwardness of the verse fights the pentameter couplet, and the subject intertwines the themes of bad poetry and religious tension, in both of which the narrator is made complicit. Fleckno is evidently an English Catholic studying in the college at Rome, probably pending a return mission. He is identified as a scion of the family of Lord Brooke, whose writings in favour of religious toleration were mentioned approvingly in Milton's *Areopagitica*, but he is desperately poor, and wasting his training by writing appalling verse, for which he needs a captive audience. Like Donne, who describes a similar social penance, the young satirist overstates his predicament:

> But I, who now imagin'd my self brought
> To my last Tryal, in a serious thought
> Calm'd the disorders of my youthful Breast,
> And to my Martyrdom prepared Rest.

(Poems and Letters, 1: 83)

And tempting Fleckno to break his Lenten fast by inviting the starving man to dinner, Marvell jokes that he was 'happy at once to make him Protestant,/And Silent'. The effect is neither as trenchant as Donne's exposés of late Elizabethan hypocrisy, nor genuinely amusing.

The second early satire actually involved the Dutch, and was a product of the First Dutch War conducted by the new English republic against their most threatening rival in trade and seapower. Written in the early 1650s, at a time when Marvell had not yet established personal connections with Holland, and in a mood of unabashed jingoism, it exhibits the lowest forms of the kind of insult that is based on stereotypes of national character. *The Character of Holland* contains all of the conventional interpretations of the Dutch republic – an ungenerous description of the Lowlanders' battles with the sea, demeaning references to the national diet of cheese, butter, pickled herring and beer, bad puns on 'boer' and 'Hoog', and the unwarranted accusation that the Dutch could not be trusted diplomatically. Their land is 'but th'Off-scouring of the Brittish Sand', their republic of separate states is merely 'something like Government', and their religious toleration in the service of commerce is merely a disorderly chaos:

> Sure when Religion did it self imbark,
> And from the East would Westward steer its Ark,
> It struck, and splitting on this unknown ground,
> Each one thence pillag'd the first piece he found:
> Hence Amsterdam, Turk-Christian-Pagan-Jew,
> Staple of Sects and Mint of Schisme grew;
> That Bank of Conscience, where not one so strange
> Opinion but finds Credit, and Exchange.
>
> (*Poems and Letters*, 1: 100–1)

Ironically, this nasty piece of work was republished, presumably without Marvell's consent, to serve the purposes of Government propagandists in both the Second and Third Dutch Wars, in 1665 and 1672 respectively. I say presumably without his consent; for at least by 1667 Marvell had changed his mind dramatically about the relations between England and Holland – both Protestant countries, after all, and hence more plausibly natural allies than quarrelsome neighbours.

The conduct of the Second Dutch War had, moreover, given rise to serious suspicions that it was neither necessary nor a just war in the legal sense recently defined by Hugo Grotius nor an expedient trade war that would enrich the country. Rather, it appeared to the majority in the Commons to be an excuse for extracting from them as the country's elected representatives an exorbitantly large warchest; most of which quickly vanished with very little to show for it. Charles's own speech of 24 November 1664, in which he announced his military intentions against Holland, took pains to counter 'a vile jealousy, which some ill men scatter abroad':

> that, when you have given me a noble and proportionable Supply for the support of a war, I may be induced by some evil counsellors (For they will be thought to think very respectfully of my own person) to make a sudden peace, and get all that money for my own private occasions

... Let me tell you, and you may be most confident of it, that when I am compelled to enter into a war, for the protection, honour, and benefit of my subjects, I will (God willing) not make a peace but upon the obtaining of those ends for which the war is entered into.[2]

The question of 'Supply', or funds produced by taxation by the consent of Parliament, remained a flashpoint from November 1664, when war was declared, through the spring of 1668, when the committee appointed to inquire into the 'miscarriages' (of which, as we have seen, Marvell was a member) brought in its first report. Clarendon himself, Charles's Chancellor and Chief Minister, acknowledged the strategy whereby the first unprecedented grant of £2,500,000 had been moved by Sir Robert Paston, a previously respected member of the Country party, as a way of lulling these suspicions; he also described the rage of the Commons when they learned that all the money, including the additional £1,250,000 voted at the Oxford session of 1655, had been spent with no tangible results.[3] In October 1665 the Commons appointed the first of several committees to investigate the conduct of the war, in this case to inquire into the embezzlement of prize goods taken from the Dutch, which should properly have been returned to the nation to help defray expenses. In early June 1666, largely as a result of the imprudent division of naval command between Prince Rupert and General George Monck, the Duke of Albemarle, Monck was defeated at sea, thereby cancelling the effect of the Duke of York's victory in the Battle of Lowestoft exactly a year earlier. Within a few months it became clear that the English navy was in bad shape administratively; and on 3 December Marvell wrote to Mayor Franke in Hull that the House of Commons had been busy creating commissioners 'to inspect and examine thorowly the former expense of the 2500000 [pounds], of the 1250000 [pounds], of the Militia mony, of the Prize goods &c' by a new Act which he hoped would be 'of very good service to the publick' (*Poems and Letters*, 2: 47). On 10 June 1667, symmetrically completing the pattern set by the June battles of the previous two years, the Dutch sailed up both the Thames and the Medway, and burned the English fleet at Chatham. This extraordinary disgrace, especially after the disastrous Fire of London of 1666, seemed the last nail in the coffin of English national pride and efficiency.

It was in this context that the famous series of 'Painter' poems appeared. The provocation was given by a poet with whom, as we have seen, Marvell had carried on, if not a feud, at least a long-standing ideological argument: Edmund Waller. In the spring of 1666, Waller published a poem with a long and pompous title: *Instructions to a Painter, For the Drawing of the Posture and Progress of his Majesties Forces at Sea, Under the command of His Highness Royal. Together with the Battel and Victory obtained over the Dutch, June, 3, 1655.* In this heroic poem, Waller deployed the conventions of pictorialism, specifically *ut pictura poesis*, to celebrate the war, its motives, and the conduct of its generals, especially James, Duke of York, the king's brother. Waller did not invent this idea. He was adapting to English political purposes a poem by Busenello which had celebrated a Venetian naval victory over the Turks in 1655 and was translated into English in 1658.[4] Waller abandoned any pretence of historical realism, and his painter was instructed, in his adulation of James, to replace image with concept: 'With his Extraction [high birth], and his Glorious Mind/Make the proud Sails swell, more than with the Wind' (p. 4). Waller asserted the superiority of poetry over painting, however, when it comes to representing a complex military action. Painting, being static, cannot, he claimed, interpret or select. Only poetry can 'Light and Honour to Brave Actions Yield,/Hid in the Smoak and Tumult of the Field' (p. 6). The entire argument was a mythic celebration of the courage showed by the English in the Battle of Lowestoft of June 1655, and a justification of the war in terms of ancient ideals of heroism: 'Happy! to whom this glorious Death arrives ... /For such a Cause'.

In the aftermath of this provocation, there appeared a series of parodies of Waller's poem and position, which all copied the 'Painter' device for diametrically opposite purposes. The appearance of these unlicensed, secretly printed political satires was to some extent co-ordinated with debates in the Commons on the miscarriages of the war. A *Second Advice to the Painter* was seen by Samuel Pepys on the streets shortly before Christmas 1666, and the first surviving printed text is dated 1667. It was reprinted twice in 1667, the first time very early in the year along with a new *Third Advice to the Painter*, on which Pepys commented on 20 January, the second time in a volume entitled *Directions to a Painter for Describing our Naval Business*, which added a fourth and fifth satire, but attributed the entire volume to Sir John Denham. There was an aborted attempt at a July 1667 printing of the *Second and Third Advices* by Francis 'Elephant' Smith, a notorious underground printer.[5] And then there was written the *Last Instructions to a Painter*, published apparently for the first time in *Poems on Affairs of State* (London, 1689).

How much responsibility should Marvell be assigned in the creation of this new satirical strategy? More, I believe, than is conventionally

assigned to him by most of his modern editors. The possibility that
Marvell wrote at least some of the satirical *Advices* has been in the air
for a long time. Aubrey's brief sketch of Marvell included the statement that 'The verses called The Advice to the Painter were of his
making', and Anthony à Wood, presumably on Aubrey's authority,
described the *Directions* volume, 'to which . . . tho' Sir John Denham's
name is set, yet they were then thought by many to have been
written by Andrew Marvell, Esq.'[6] James Yonge the physician, who
was in London in 1678 'in company with several parliament men',
mentioned Marvell as the 'author of some poems, Advice to the
Paynter, Miscellany, Rehersal transposed', and showed knowledge
also of *Mr. Smirke* and the *Remarks* in defence of John Howe.[7] He
seemed, in other words, to be rather well informed. And Marvell's
enemy, Sir Roger L'Estrange, implied in his attack on the *Account of
the Growth of Popery* in 1678 that at least one of the 'Painter' poems
could be laid at his door: 'By his Vein of improving the Invective
Humour, it looks in some places as if he were Transprosing the First
Painter'.[8] Of course, all of these allusions could conceivably have
been caused by knowledge of the *Last Instructions*, either in manuscript or in some illegal pamphlet publication which has completely
disappeared. Yet there remains strong internal and external evidence
that Marvell also wrote, or had a hand in, the *Second* and *Third
Advices*.

Most important, perhaps, was the testimony of Edward Thompson
who, in the preface to his 1776 edition of Marvell's works, described
how, when his three volumes were already complete, he 'was politely
complimented by Mr. Mathias [Marvell's grand-nephew] with a
manuscript volume of poems' belonging to William Popple, 'being a
collection of his uncle Andrew Marvell's compositions after his decease'.
'By this manuscript', Thompson added, 'I also find, that those two
excellent satires, entitled A Direction to a Painter concerning the
Dutch War in 1667, and published in the State Poems, . . . as Sir John
Denham's, are both of them compositions of Mr. Marvell; but as the
work is already so largely swelled out, I shall beg leave to omit them'.
The acquisition by the Bodleian Library in 1945 of what is now
taken to be the 'Popple manuscript' (MS Eng. Poet. d. 49) revealed
'those two excellent satires' to be the *Second* and *Third Advices*.

Margoliouth's original decision not to include any of the *Advices*
in his edition, despite the comments of Aubrey, Wood and Thompson,
was based primarily on cautionary and qualitative grounds: Marvell's
satirical canon was quite doubtful enough already; the *Second* and
*Third Advices*, which deal with the Dutch War directly, 'would be

more naturally assigned to some writer who took part in the naval actions'; and he thought that a 'generally consistent level of style and intelligence' linked the *Second* and *Third Advices* with the fourth and fifth, which Marvell certainly did not write (because they cover the same material as the *Last Instructions*), rather than with that poem, which was 'more the work of a learned man' (*Poems and Letters*, 1: 349). The discovery of the 'Popple' manuscript did not materially alter Margoliouth's opinion, despite his acknowledgement that it looked like a collection of Marvell's poems prepared for a new edition. But it did impress George de F. Lord, who in the late 1950s argued for the inclusion of the *Second* and *Third Advices* on the grounds of provenance, and supported his case with a certain amount of internal evidence, mostly thematic.[9]

When Pierre Legouis published his revised version of Margoliouth's edition in 1971, he supported the original decision to exclude the *Second* and *Third Advices*, remaining unconvinced by Lord's arguments. Despite his acceptance of the 'Popple' manuscript as unquestionably the one described by Thompson, who indeed had signed his name to a note in the manuscript attributing the *Second Advice* to Marvell, Legouis' edition does not reflect its textual and canonical importance. The fact that Margoliouth knew of its existence in 1952, when he himself reissued the *Poems and Letters*, is given as a precedent for the 1971 decision not to alter the canon; but we should also remember that in 1952 Margoliouth *could* not have materially altered it, since without being offered a reset edition he was confined to minor revision and whatever additional material could be inserted on 'spare pages' (*Poems and Letters*, 1: vii). He had suffered, in other words, from the same spatial (word–count) inhibition as had Thompson.

It would be strange indeed if the accidents of printing history were the determining factors in establishing Marvell's satirical achievement. And there are far better reasons for accepting Marvell's authorship of the first two satirical *Advices* than for rejecting it. Those who reject Marvell's claim are in disagreement or at a loss as to whose name should be supplied in his stead. Their arguments, moreover, are almost entirely from internal evidence. That being the case, it is odd that so little attention has been paid to the satiric programme of pictorialism which is the most distinctive feature of these poems. What most noticeably connects the *Second* and *Third Advices* to the *Last Instructions* and distinguishes all three from the other 'Painter' poems, is their rather sophisticated application of the doctrine of *ut pictura poesis* and Renaissance aesthetic theory more generally. In this respect, with all due deference to Margoliouth, all three poems may be seen as the work of a 'learned' man or men. All three poems manipulate the device of the Advice-to-the-Painter so as to make it peculiarly relevant to the contemporary political situation and the satirist's task. The very theme of these poems, it appears, is advice. The satirist's purpose is to replace the king's present advisors with other, more honest, counsel, which includes his own. The final 'advices' to the king, which appear in the *Second*, *Third* and *Last Advices*, but not, significantly, in the fourth and fifth, present the world of ideals which *ut pictura poesis* normally conjured up, the positive conduct on Charles's part which is implied and required by the previous attacks on members of his court and Privy Council. This same strategy is also employed at the end of Marvell's last political statement, the *Account of the Growth of Popery and Arbitrary Government*, and in that pamphlet it is consciously related to political theory. It enacts, in fact, the constitutional fiction expressed earlier in the *Account*, that the king's person is 'most sacred and inviolable', and that whatever criticism can be levelled against his regime, 'nothing of them all is imputed to him ... but his ministers only are accountable for all'.[10]

RENAISSANCE PICTORIALISM

The cleverness of the 'Painter' poems cannot be fully understood without some grasp of the special status held in cultural and rhetorical tradition by the doctrine of *ut pictura poesis*, a doctrine whose details had remarkable currency in seventeenth-century England. Its origins, of course, were classical. The familiar phrase from Horace's *Ars Poetica*, the *ut pictura poesis* motto itself, was taken out of context as early as the fourth century, and interpreted as a prescription that poetry and painting should imitate each other's methods. To this was assimilated the motto of Simonides, that painting is mute poetry, poetry a speaking picture, which tied the arts firmly together in what Lessing called 'the dazzling antithesis of the Greek Voltaire'.[11] In the Italian Quattrocento this relationship between the 'sister arts' was revived by a strong professional desire among painters to give painting the social status of literature, to elevate it to the ranks of the liberal arts. However, by the middle of the sixteenth century there developed for painting a theory involving both the aims and techniques of rhetoric and poetics, and from this point on the relationship became one of cross-fertilization.[12]

The doctrine was given full and clear expression in Ludovico Dolce's dialogue *L'Aretino* (1557). Dolce, who had earlier published a translation of the *Ars Poetica* (Venice, 1535), developed a fully fledged theory of Horatian decorum for painting. In discussing Invention, or the choice of an appropriate subject for a picture, Dolce gave as an example of what is unacceptable ('una sconvenevolissima invenzione') the grotesque figure described by Horace in the opening lines of the *Ars Poetica*: 'Humano capiti cervicem pictor equinam/Jungere si velit'. 'Who would not laugh at a picture in which a human head appears on the neck of a horse, or the tail of a fish below the bust of a beautiful woman'. He also undermined Horace's provision for a certain imaginative licence – 'Pictoribus atque poetis/Quidlibet audendi semper fuit aequa potestas' – by removing the implications of *quidlibet* and insisting that the freedom of genius be not abused.[13] This was perhaps the most often repeated topos of *ut pictura poesis*, which remained at all times Horatian in its general tone. Advice that might seem particularly relevant to satirists was given by Henry Peacham in his *Graphice: or the Most Auncient and Excellent Art of Drawing and Limming* (1612), where he warns his 'young Scholler' neither to waste his time nor to lose 'his eares for a libeller', by accepting the original meaning of Horace's *quidlibet audere*, 'for there be many things which as well Nature or Religion would have freed from the pencill' (p. 9). And in 1637 the *De Pictura* of Francis Du Jon, better known as Junius, translated into English the following year as *The Painting of the Ancients*, reminded the cultured audience of the early seventeenth century that Horace had prohibited the grotesque in either art:

> Now as the Artificer may not abuse the libertie of his Imaginations, by turning it unto a licentious boldnesse of fancying things abhorring from Nature; so must also a right lover of Art preferre a plaine and honest worke agreeing with Nature before any other phantastically capricious devices . . . It is then a very grosse errour to deeme with the vulgar sort that Painters as well as Poets have an unlimited libertie of devising; for if we doe but marke what Horace telleth us in the first entrance of his booke written about the Poeticall Art, wee shall confesse that neither Poets nor Painters may take such a libertie as to stuffe up their workes with all kinds of frivolous and lying conceits.
>
> (p. 43)

As secretary and curator to Thomas Howard, Earl of Arundel, the greatest of the Caroline art collectors except the king himself, Junius' words were regarded as essential reading for any cultured person interested in the arts.

A Horatian theory of decorum blends easily with idealism. Alberti, the father of Italian art theory, had qualified his advice about the use of models and precise anatomical observation by recommending a certain selectivity, an aesthetic tact which emphasizes the beautiful and suppresses unattractive features as, according to Pliny, Apelles had done in his portrait of Antigonus.[14] And during the sixteenth century *ut pictura poesis* became associated with an ideal of perfection, whether physical or moral, which it was the duty of both arts to express, and which in fact contradicted the mimetic theory to which these same critics gave lip service. Dolce said that it was the painter's duty 'not only to imitate but to surpass nature': and that where nature failed to supply models of adequate perfection he could either (1) look to classical sculpture; or (2) adjust the actual proportions of his model to some ideal scheme, as Apelles did for his famous Venus Anadyomene; or (3) abstract the best features from a number of less than perfect models, as Zeuxis of Croton did for his Venus (pp. 131–9). Other stories about ancient painters found in Pliny's *Natural History* were forced into the service of this preceptive idealism. Alexander's gift to Apelles of his favourite courtesan Campaspe (he had painted her in the nude and become enamoured in the process) became evidence of the great esteem in which monarchs held their painters; and even the competitions in skill between Zeuxis and Parrhasius, Apelles and Protogenes, shifted from illustrations of extreme realism – Zeuxis painted grapes so like the real thing that birds flew down and pecked them; Parrhasius painted a curtain over the picture so real that it deceived Zeuxis himself – to metaphors for perfectionism. One Plinean story which caused Dolce some embarrassment told how Protogenes became enraged at his failure to represent the slaver on a dog's mouth, and how by throwing a sponge at the picture in his annoyance he accidentally achieved the desired result.[15] This classical anticipation of action painting did not fit easily into a doctrine which stressed high skills and high ideals.

There were other things also which did not fit. When Michelangelo turned from the Neoplatonic beauties of the Sistine Chapel ceiling to the *terribilitas* of the Last Judgement, he himself became the great example of pictorial indecorum. Dolce pointed in displeasure to the indecencies of embracing saints, a beardless Christ, the general nakedness, and a devil clutching the testicles of one anguished sinner (p. 190). His arguments were echoed, though from a different standpoint, by Counter-Reformation theorists who eventually got the picture draped in the appropriate places; and Dolce's contrast between Raphael and Michelangelo was still current in 1662, when Roland Fréart de Chambray published his *Idée de la perfection de la peinture*. As de Chambray put it (and I cite from John Evelyn's translation of 1668, *very* close in time to the 'Painter' poems), 'we may observe in most of Raphael's Compositions a generous and free Invention, noble and Poetick; So in those of his Antagonist, a dull and rusticall heaviness; so as he never seems to have made use but of some Porter or sturdy Booby for his Modell'. Raphael is praised for his decision 'never to paint anything of Licentious ... whilst the other, on the contrary, made it his glory, publickly, to be ashamed of nothing, no, not to prophane either the most holy Places or Histories by the infamous Freedome which he assumed'.[16] In the same year as Evelyn's translation, Charles Du Fresnoy's *De Arte Graphica*, written in obvious imitation of Horace, appeared with a French translation and commentary by Roger de Piles; this too crossed the Channel, appearing in Dryden's translation of 1695 as seventeenth-century aesthetic orthodoxy:

> Painting and Poesy are two sisters, which are so alike in all things, that they mutually lend to each other both their Name and Office. One is call'd a dumb Poesy, and the other a speaking Picture. The Poets have never said anything but what they believed wou'd please the Ears. And it has been the constant endeavour of the Painters to give pleasure to the Eyes ... For both of them, that they might contribute all within their power to the sacred Honours of Religion, have rais'd themselves to Heaven, and, having found a free admission into the Palace of Jove himself, have enjoy'd the sight and conversation of the Gods ... They dive ... into all past Ages; and search their Histories, for subjects which are proper for their use: with care avoiding to treat of any but those which, by their nobleness ... have deserved to be consecrated to Eternity.[17]

And Dryden, as we shall see, had already been working on these principles in 1666, in a poem that also contributed fuel to the 'painterly' struggle for control over Restoration culture.

The only real exception to this tradition had been Leonardo da Vinci, whose *Trattato della Pittura* rigorously rejected idealism for naturalism, as it also rejected the equal sisterhood of the arts for a *paragone* or formal comparison in which painting was defined as a superior medium: superior in directness, power and truthfulness. One feature of the *paragone*, which was to have particular influence on political poetry, was Leonardo's insistence that only painting can properly represent a battle:

> If you, poet, describe a bloody battle, will it be with the air dark and murky, in the midst of frightful and death-dealing arms, mixed with thick dust that defiles the atmosphere and the frightened flight of miserable

men afraid of a horrible death? In this case, the painter will surpass you because your pen will be worn out before you describe fully what the painter with his medium can represent at once. Your tongue will be paralysed with thirst and your body with sleep and hunger, before you depict with words what the painter will show you in a moment.[18]

With this we have moved from questions of mimesis to problems of expressivism, and indeed Leonardo's later admission that neither the noise of battle nor the souls and interior life of persons could be represented on canvas became part of a discussion of even greater importance for poetry. Leonardo's position connected and contrasted with another Renaissance position, that painting was to poetry as body is to mind; this in turn connected with Pliny's statements that before Aristides Greek painting had not attempted psychological analysis, while Apelles was unique in his ability to paint things such as thunder and lightning that cannot normally be represented pictorially (xxxv, xxxvi, 96, 98).

ENGLISH PICTORIALISM

There is abundant evidence that all of these notions were current in seventeenth-century England and, significantly, that they were usually associated with the court. Richard Lovelace had included in *Lucasta* (1649) a significant comment on one of Lely's earliest royal portraits, the sombre picture of Charles I and the Duke of York, painted in 1647 when the king was a prisoner at Hampton Court. 'The amazed world', wrote Lovelace, recalling the mind/body distinction of the *paragone*, 'shall henceforth find/None but my Lilly ever drew a Minde'. Poem and picture therefore became, retrospectively, a lament for the king who had just been executed.

Lovelace himself was complimented, in one of the dedicatory poems to *Lucasta*, by a related distinction, the elegance of Cavalier verse being praised in terms of Plinean anecdote:

Poets and Painters have some near relation,
Compar'd with Fancy and Imagination;
The one paints shadowed persons (in pure kind,)
The other points the Pictures of the Mind
In purer Verse. And as rare Zeuxes fame
Shin'd till Apelles Art eclipsed the same
By a more exquisite and curious line
In Zeuxeses (with pensill far more fine,)
So have our modern Poets, late done well

Till thine appear'd (which scarce have paralel.)
They like to Zeuxes Grapes beguile the sense,
But thine do ravish the Intelligence;
Like the rare banquet of Apelles, drawn,
And covered over with most curious Lawn.

(Ar)

Abraham Cowley, in his *Poems* of 1656, commemorated the death of
Van Dyck in similarly conventional language:

Vandike is Dead; but what Bold Muse shall dare
(Though Poets in that word with Painters share)
T'expresse her sadness. Poesie must become
An Art, like Painting here, an Art that's Dumbe.
Let's all our solemn grief in silence keep,
Like some sad Picture which he made to weep,
Or those who saw't, for none his works could view
Unmov'd with the same Passions which he drew.

(p. 9)

But this poem too implicitly mourned the Caroline era and the great
Van Dyck portraits of Charles I. Even Sir William Sanderson's *Graphice*,
which was published in 1658 (the year, we remember, of Oliver
Cromwell's death) was preceded by a portrait of Charles I and a
commemorative verse to the king. Although strictly speaking not a
work of theory but a textbook on the 'Use of the Pen and Pencil',
*Graphice* occasionally reveals an idealizing bias. Repeating the story
of Zeuxis of Croton, Sanderson advises the portrait painter to gather:

from several beauties . . . a conceived Idea . . . of accomplished Pulchritude,
grace or comlinesse, according to the true rule of Symmetry. So like
the Life, (if done by Lilly) that by the Lines and Colour, a skilfull
Physiognomer (another Lilly) may by the Picture tell her fortune.

(p. 46)

This double allusion to Sir Peter Lely, who would shortly abandon
his Commonwealth style for a very different Restoration style and
clientele, paired with his partial namesake the astrologer William
Lilly, brings the old orthodoxy rather confusingly up to date.

Such elegiac and backward-looking expressions of royalist feeling
were, however, a very different matter from Waller's *Instructions to a
Painter*, which knowingly combined these by now conventional senti-
ments with an up-to-the-minute, highly provocative, political message.
Waller's poem appeared in the Stationers' Register on 1 March 1666,

and the Popple manuscript of Marvell's poetry states that the *Second Advice* was written in April, although not seen by Pepys till December. This implies an instantaneous response; and let us not forget that Marvell already had considerable practice in parodying or correcting Waller's assumptions. The *Second Advice* has been criticized for uninventive imitation of the structure of Waller's poem. In fact, its scope is much wider, but where it hews most closely to its offending model it does so in order to exploit the pictorialist tradition. Waller, for example, had thought to dignify his account of the farewell visit of Anne Hyde, Duchess of York, to the duke at Harwich by alluding to the legendary birth of Venus from the sea. Recalling that scene as conceived in antiquity by Apelles and in the Renaissance by Botticelli, the *Second Advice* contrasts classical beauty and economy with Restoration tastelessness and extravagance:

> One thrifty Ferry-boat of Mother-Pearl,
> Suffic'd of old the Cytherean Girle.
> Yet Navys are but Properties when here,
> A small Sea-mask, and built to court you, Dear;
>
> (ll. 61–4)[19]

This is followed by an insinuation that the duchess was indulging in an insincere display of marital affection. Her farewell celebrations with the duke are given a sinister ethical and historical counterpart: 'Never did Roman Mark, within the Nyle,/ So feast the fair Egyptian Crocodile'; and the painter is advised to 'spare [his] weaker art, forbear/To draw her parting Passions and each Tear'. Any reasonably alert reader would appreciate the significance of crocodile tears; but the *paragone* topos, that painting is weak on emotional representation, demanded a more educated sense of irony. Meanwhile, as I have argued in detail elsewhere, this passage is one of several in the *Advices* which contain verbal and probably intentional echoes of Marvell's earlier poems, in this instance *The Gallery* and *Upon Appleton House*.[20]

When the satirist turns to the Battle of Lowestoft itself, his intentions are further clarified by allusions to pictorial theory. The painter is asked to 'draw the Battell terribler to show/Then the last judgement was of Angelo'. The allusion to Michelangelo's 'Last Judgement' in this context is both an invocation of *terribilitas* and a statement of the poet's audacity, since that painting, itself motivated by political disillusionment following the Fall of Rome, was the most celebrated Renaissance example of stylistic irreverence and impropriety. The *Advice* also responds to the challenge of Leonardo, who had declared the poet incapable of representing 'a bloody battle . . . with the air dark and murky . . . mixed with thick dust that defiles the atmosphere and the frightened flight of miserable men afraid of a horrible death'. Waller's response has been to declare the poet superior to the painter in scenes of battle because he could discover 'Light and Honour' where the painter would show merely 'Smoak and Tumult'. The *Second Advice* asserts instead that the real nature of battle is not, in the end, accessible to any form of artful expression:

> The Noise, the Smoak, the Sweat, the Fire, the Blood
> Is not to be exprest nor understood.

> (ll. 203–4)

Neither painting nor poetry can accurately convey the horror of war to those who have not experienced it directly.

It follows that Waller's assumption of omnipresent, patriotic courage on his side is challenged by the satirist's representative English 'Gallant', who speaks his fear and rage at being dragged into a war to satisfy Chancellor Clarendon's personal ambitions. Oddly, this attack focuses first on Noah, as the father of navigation; but the oddity disappears when we recognize these lines as an echo of Marvell's *First Anniversary*, where Noah's legendary drunkenness was converted to praise of the father of viniculture. Here is the *Second Advice*:

> Noah be damn'd and all his Race accurst,
> That in Sea brine did pickle Timber first.
> What though he planted Vines! he Pines cut down,
> He taught us how to drink, and how to drown.
> He first built ships, and in the wooden Wall
> Saving but Eight, ere since indangers all.

> (ll. 131–6)

And here is the *First Anniversary*:

> Thou, and thine House, like Noahs Eight did rest,
> Left by the Warrs Flood on the Mountains crest:
> And the large Vale lay subject to thy Will,
> Which thou but as an Husbandman wouldst Till:
> And only didst for others plant the Vine
> Of Liberty, not drunken with its Wine.

> (ll. 283–8)

Given the similarity of style and subject, down to the 'Eight' members of Noah's 'House' and the shared theme of shipbuilding and viniculture, it is difficult to deny that Marvell wrote both passages;

and the connection between them grows more meaningful if we realize that the earlier allusion supported Cromwell as the saviour of his nation, the later one attacks Clarendon as its destroyer.

In addition to voicing the complaints of this generalized sailor, the *Second Advice* comes down particularly hard on those leaders of the fleet who, like William Berkeley or the 'halcyon Sandwich', had 'judg'd it safe and decent . . . to lose the Day' (ll. 189–90). In contrast to them, however, are a few brave men, such as James Ley, Earl of Marlborough, whose death drives home the unhopeful message that 'Death picks the Valiant out, the Cow'rds survive' (l. 216), and so provides one intelligible motive for the qualified pacificism of the poem.

The other motive, and the second major indecorum of the *Second Advice*, is to question the justice of the war. In response to Waller's tactless congratulations to those who were killed ('Happy! To whom this glorious Death arrives . . . / For such a Cause'), we are given an ironic summary of the supposed 'Cause' and its practical results:

> Thus having fought we know not why, as yet
> W'have done we know not what, nor what we get.
> If to espouse the Ocean all this paines
> Princes unite, and will forbid the Baines.
> If to discharge Fanaticks: this makes more;
> For all Fanatick turn when sick or poore,
> Or if the House of Commons to repay:
> Their Prize Commissions are transfer'd away.
> But for triumphant Checkstones, if, and Shell
> For Dutchesse Closet: 't has succeeded well.
> If to make Parliaments all odious: passe.
> If to reserve a Standing Force: alas.
> . . .
>
> And with four Millions vainly givn, as spent;
> And with five Millions more of detriment;
> Our Summe amounts yet only to have won
> A Bastard Orange, for Pimp Arlington.

(ll. 313–30)

A quick translation of this passage might go as follows: if you think we have been fighting to wrest control of the ocean from the Dutch, international politics forbids that; if you think it was to weaken the Nonconformists, the hardship caused by the wars will only increase their numbers; if you hoped to repay the Commons for their Supply, the loot which should have gone to repay them has been pocketed by persons unknown; but if you intended merely to enrich the Duchess

of York, you have succeeded. Other results include the destruction
of Parliament's reputation among the people and the creation of a
standing army (alas!). And the huge sums that have been spent and
the huge debts accumulated have resulted only in a marriage between
Henry Bennett, Earl of Arlington, Secretary of State, and the daughter
of Louis of Nassau, himself illegitimate son of Prince Maurice! The
financial emphasis of the passage and its parliamentary focus are, of
course, entirely appropriate to Marvell, whose concerns with these
matters are documented in Chapter 1, and who would personally
attack Arlington in the Commons on 15 February 1668.

The emphasis on the Commons is also directly connected, however, to the satirist's most daring adaptation of the pictorial tradition.
Perceiving that Waller, under the device of giving advice to the
painter, had in effect been advising the king on the war's acceptabil-
ity, the *Second Advice* concludes with its own passage of formal advice
'To the King' and a counter-recommendation. Preserving the fictional
distinction to which Charles himself had drawn attention in his
speech of 24 November 1664, between his 'own person', of which
his critics would 'be thought to think very respectfully', and the
responsibility of his 'evil counsellors', the satirist urges Charles to get
rid of his chief troublemaker Clarendon, as well as the other 'Swarms
of Insects', which, by interfering between the king and his people,
'intercept our Sunn'. Parodying Waller's allusion to Charles as Minos,
King of Crete, the *Second Advice* identifies Clarendon as the State-
Dedalus, at whose door may be laid all of the cynicism expressed
earlier in the satire, and who is therefore responsible for the failure of
*ut pictura poesis* as a medium of cultural values. The king is urged to
look upwards for his 'pattern', to 'those Kingdomes calm of Joy and
Light/Where's universall Triumphs but no Fight', and to 'let Justice
only draw' (with a neat substitution of painting for swordsmanship).
The poem's final advice is a return to the simple moral absolutes that
have disappeared in the labyrinthine structures of policy.[21]

When the *Second Advice* was reprinted in 1667 along with a *Third
Advice*, the new edition contained a feature which underlined its
purpose and conceptual context. The title page of the *Second Advice*
now carried a familiar, but also unfamiliar, Latin motto: 'Pictoribus
atque Poetis,/Quidlibet Audendi semper fuit potestas./Humano Capiti
cervicem pictor equinam,/Jungere si velit'. The two statements from
Horace's *Ars Poetica*, which in the pictorialist tradition had always
been used to support a theory of poetic or artistic decorum, were
now yoked by violence together as if to *authorize* poets and painters
who dared to portray unnatural monsters. The alternatives of daring

and self-serving decency, then, which the *Second Advice* had explored in a naval context, are revealed as being also the dialectic of the political commentator. The *Third Advice* is, in this edition, stated to be 'written by the same Hand as the former was'; and given this famous mandate, he identifies himself as a courageous iconoclast or, in Henry Peacham's terms, a 'libeller'.

The *Third Advice* was also to develop with some subtlety the idea of what it means to portray monsters. But before following that up, we need to take cognizance of two other poems which had entered the debate at this point, and may have affected the shape of the *Third Advice*. The less well known of these was Christopher Wase's *Divination*, which no longer survives in printed form, but whose appearance in another manuscript collection[22] *between* the *Second* and *Third Advice* probably accurately represents its place in the sequence. *Divination*, as its title suggests, and following William Sanderson's connection in *Graphice* between Lely and William Lilly the astrologer, also defined as a 'skilful Physiognomer', substituted for the unnamed painter of the 'Advices' the figure of Lilly, whom Wase instructed to reveal the face of the anonymous satirist who had so ungenerously betrayed his country:

> . . . I would know what hand,
> Envious of royal honor, late hath stain'd
> Valor and beauty with lamp-black defac'd,
> And what he ought to worship hath disgrac'd.
> Who draws the landscape of our woes, our wracks,
> Disasters, errors, aggravates our tax;
> What every faithful subject ought to hide
> (His country's shame) makes his delight and pride.[23]

In trying to identify this new demonic 'Angelo', who fetches his charcoal from Hell rather than from an appropriate level of political idealism, Wase is an important witness to the contemporary reception of the *Second Advice*, which he described as 'polish'd', 'well contrived and high', the work of a 'master-builder'; and, carefully rejecting a number of possibilities, *including* Sir John Denham, he supplied a 'face', an interesting ecphrasis, perhaps, of some portrait known to him, whose dark features matched the 'sober malice' he found in the poem.

The other intervention was not quite so obviously a response to the *Second Advice*, though that was clearly on its agenda. This was John Dryden's *Annus Mirabilis*, a piece of royalist propaganda which directed its attention to the two most distressing events of 1666: the division of the fleet under Monck and Prince Rupert, with its disastrous consequences in the Four Days' Battle, 3–6 June; and the Great Fire of London, 2–6 September. Dryden's poem, like Waller's, offered an intellectual challenge of irresistible proportions; for it appeared with a theoretical preface addressed to Sir Robert Howard, in which his political motives were presented in an elaborate dress of generic and rhetorical theory. 'I have chosen', wrote Dryden:

> the most heroick Subject which any Poet could desire: I have taken upon me to describe the motives, the beginning, progress, and successes of a most just and necessary War; in it the care, management, and prudence of our King; the conduct and valour of a Royal Admiral and of two incomparable Generals; the invincible courage of our Captains and Seamen, and three glorious Victories, the result of all.[24]

Dryden thus embraced Waller's programme, applying it to the second year of the war, but with considerably less grounds for his optimism.

His high-minded refusal to look at the facts was, moreover, justified by a general discussion of epic theory which Dryden merged with an idealizing pictorialism. The Virgilian images incorporated into his own poem are, Dryden asserts, the main source of the pleasure derived from heroic poetry:

> for they beget admiration, which is its proper object; as the images of the Burlesque, which is contrary to this, by the same reason beget laughter; for the one shows Nature beautified, as in the picture of a fair Woman, which we all admire; the other shows her deformed, as in that of a Lazar, or of a fool with distorted face and antique gestures, at which we cannot forbear to laugh, because it is a deviation from Nature.

(p. 46)

Consequently, Dryden proceeds, in the poem itself, to offer a neo-classical panegyric to Charles for his wisdom in dividing the fleet, to interpret Monck's narrow escape, which had included having his breeches shot off, as 'naked Valour', and to make the whole account of the fire subservient to a praise of Charles's grief for, and munificence to, his devastated London, and a prophecy of its rising anew like the phoenix from its flames. In response to the widespread rumours that the fire had been started by Roman Catholic saboteurs, he imagined that 'Ghost of Traitors from the Bridge descend,/With bold Fanatick Spectres to rejoyce' (stanza 223), implying that responsibility for arson lay rather with the Nonconformists.

Dryden's account to Sir Robert Howard of his poem's agenda was dated 10 November 1666. The poem was licensed for publication by Sir Roger L'Estrange on 22 November, and entered in the

Stationers' Register for 21 January 1667. This sequence makes it virtually certain that the poem was inspired in part by the parliamentary committee to investigate the causes of the fire, to which Marvell was appointed on 2 October (*JHC*, 8: 629, 654). If the *Second Advice* had indeed, as the Popple manuscript suggests, been written in April and circulated in manuscript since then, *Annus Mirabilis* could also be seen as a counter-proposition to the satirist's assertion that the war was neither just, necessary, nor successful. And reciprocally, if *Annus Mirabilis* had been circulating since November, it would help to explain why the *Third Advice*, reported by Pepys to be available by 20 January 1667, divides its focus between the Four Days' Battle and the Fire of London, while choosing as a spokesman for Nonconformist integrity General Monck's own wife, the Duchess of Albemarle. It is not without significance, too, that the reported appearances of *Annus Mirabilis* and the *Third Advice* closely coincide with the parliamentary debates on naval administration and the causes of the fire. On 21 January the Commons, in an unprecedented act of intervention in financial policy, set aside £380,000 of the new Supply specifically for seamen's wages; and on 22 January the committee appointed to investigate the fire made its first report to the House, 'full of manifest testimonys', as Marvell reported to Hull, that the Fire was set by 'a wicked designe' (*Poems and Letters*, 2: 53).

In this now greatly complicated situation of specific political repartee, the *Third Advice* achieved a response simultaneously to Wase's strictures and Dryden's lofty insistence that all was for the best under 'the best of Kings'. The opening invokes a particular painter, Richard Gibson, who is required to 'expresse . . . in little, how we yet do lesse', a clear warning of deflationary tactics. While the choice of Gibson, who happened to be a dwarf as well as a miniaturist, may be seen as rather a tasteless joke, it illustrates the precision with which pictorial and political knowledge is interlocked; for Gibson had begun his career as a page under Charles I, had then become Cromwell's portraitist, and was now, as official miniaturist to Charles II, assimilated into the atmosphere of the Restoration court.

Along with the invocation of Gibson goes a rejection of Sir Peter Lely as a possible artist for this project, on the grounds that 'Lilly's a Dutchman, danger in his Art:/His Pencills may intelligence impart'. At one level this is a simple warning against making secrets of state accessible to the enemy; at another it implies the traditional association between Dutch painting and excessive realism, which, as a mode of representation, could also impart 'intelligence' to the poem's audience; and at a third, it is a punning response to Wase's appeal to Lilly the astrologer to show him the face of this new and dangerous writer; for Marvell was one of the few authors reported or known to have had their portraits painted by Lely, and we have already confronted what may be Lely's representation of him.

The use, or rather the rejection, of Lely as the painter for the *Third Advice* has, however, still another dimension. As a 'Dutchman', his native tendency to realism required adjustment to the exigencies of court painting. In contrast to Van Dyck, who finished his career as the greatest of the Caroline iconographers, Lely, having painted Charles I and the Duke of York in the double portrait celebrated by Lovelace, had moved with the times. By 1651 he had painted a portrait of Cromwell, for which Cromwell had reportedly issued his own 'instructions', insisting that it be fully realistic, without flattery, even to the inclusion of 'roughnesses, pimples, warts' (Figure 5). And he was also associated with Sir Balthazar Gerbier in a proposal, never fulfilled, to decorate Whitehall with pictures celebrating the military achievements of the Revolution. By the 1660s, however, he was principal painter for the Restoration court, and of great topical interest in 1666 was his series of naval portraits commissioned by the Duke of York to commemorate the Battle of Lowestoft.[25] This great series of portraits, though far superior in realism to the more famous 'Hampton Court beauties' or other portraits of courtly compliment, is nevertheless far from the satirist's point of view; for the terms of his commission required Lely to make no distinction between William Berkeley, who had 'judgd it safe and decent . . . / To Lose the Day', and the unequivocal heroism of Christopher Myngs or Jeremy Smith. It is with a most complicated and knowing irony, then, that the *Third Advice* deploys Lely, and many of its evaluative comments on the naval commanders in the Four Days' Battle acquire a new meaning in the light of Lely's portraits. Sir John Harman, for example, is recognized as 'the great Harman chark'd almost to coale' (l. 116); but William Berkeley, 'as he long deserv'd, was shot' (l. 110).

Also in direct response to Wase, it seems, the satirist now develops, with tongue in cheek, the principle that concealment, rather than realism, is necessary to save the nation's honour:

> Ah, rather than transmit our scorn to Fame
> Draw Curtains gentle Artist o'er this Shame
> . . .
>
>                                              . . .
> And, if the thing were true, yet paint it not.

                                                (ll. 105–9)

FIGURE 5    Oliver Cromwell, by Sir Peter Lely, Birmingham City
Museums and Art Gallery

The painter is asked 'in a dark cloud' to 'cover' the defection of Sir
George Ayscue (another of Lely's subjects) and, in the episode of
General Monck's wound in the buttock, to 'Conceale, as honour
would, his Grace's Bum'. The theme of protective secrecy is sup-
ported by the historical, if mock-heroic, fog which had shielded the
English fleet from de Ruyter: 'Old Homer yet did never introduce,/
To save his Heroes, Mist of better use' (ll. 159–60).

About one-third through the poem, this pose of decorous con-cealment and mock-heroic tone are suddenly dropped. Commenting upon the bonfires and rejoicings at home after this 'empty Triumph', the satirist speaks in a new intonation of vehemence and foreboding:

> Alas: the time draws near when overturn'd
> The lying Bells shall through the tongue be burn'd
> Papers shall want to print that Lye of State,
> And our false Fires true Fires shall expiate.

(ll. 163–6)

In order to present this new, truthful view of events, as distinct from official propaganda and flattering royalist panegyric, the satirist aban-dons his own role as director of his painter's procedures. Introducing General Monck's wife, the Duchess of Albemarle, 'Paint thou but her', he says, 'and she will paint the rest'. This new persona is presented initially as one of the grotesques that the satirist's inverted Horatianism allows; 'the Monky Dutchesse', with a 'Trunk cartaliginous', a bounc-ing 'Udder', and in a most indecorous position, nailing up hangings on a horizontal ladder carried by her servants, and therefore 'In posture just of a four-footed Beast' (ll. 171–200). Yet despite this unpropitious portrait, the duchess's very coarseness has a special appropriateness to her task. Originally a common seamstress, and still a 'Presbyterian Sibyll', she is doubly an outsider whose exclusion from Cavalier and Anglican circles gives her a necessary distance, while her connection with Monck gives her credibility. She wears metaphorically 'a foule Smock, when [she] might have clean' (l. 236) because it matches her view of society. Herself a grotesque, she is at liberty to apply the 'Humano capiti cervicem' perspective of satire to her husband's col-leagues at court: 'What say I Men? nay rather Monsters: Men/Only in Bed, nor, (to my knowledge), then' (ll. 229–30).

Consequently, it is given to the duchess to express the graver part of the satirist's message. She distinguishes, for example, between the 'egregious Loyalty' of the Cavaliers who escorted Charles into a comfortable exile, and the 'true Royalists' who had struggled to make government work at home. In this she identifies herself with the Presbyterian divine Edmund Calamy ('I told George first, as Calamy did me/If the King these brought over, how 'twould be', ll. 217–18) and thus with the Nonconformist 'martyrs' expelled from their pulpits on St Bartholomew's Day, 1662, the 'ejection' which, as the duchess also points out (ll. 243–4), claimed parity with the original massacre of Huguenots on that date. And she wittily applies

the silencing, truth-concealing topos of the earlier sections of the
*Advice* to the restoration of the bishops to the House of Lords:

> The Lords House drains the Houses of the Lord
> For Bishops voices silencing the Word.

(ll. 241–2)

The duchess also provides, in her advice to her husband, the positive
norms of practical and moral conduct required of an honest naval
administrator; norms which, we are finally reminded, have a religious
base:

> Fall to thy worke there, George, as I do here:
> Cherish the valiant up, the cow'rd cashiere.
> See that the Men have Pay, & Beef, & Beere;
> Find out the cheats of the four-millioneer.
> . . .
>
>         . . .
> Looke that good Chaplains on each Ship do wait,
> Nor the Sea-Diocesse be impropriate.[26]

(ll. 325–8, 341–2)

In her analysis of Monck's earlier disaster, the duchess focuses accurately on the incompetence of Arlington in discovering the location
of the Dutch fleet:

> The Secretary that had never yet
> Intelligence but from his own gazett,
> Discovers a great secret, fit to sell:
> And pays himself for't ere he would it tell.
> He'le see the Fleet devided like his Face,
> . . .
>
>         . . .
> And through that cranny in his gristly part,
> To the Dutch chink, [his wife] intelligence may start.

(ll. 282–6, 299–300)

This passage connects subtly with the opening rejection of Sir Peter
Lely as a Dutchman, whose 'Pencills may intelligence impart'. And
by the end of the satire the duchess has been transformed, by her
own performance, from a grotesque figure with animal connotations
to a prophetess, mourning with complete conviction her vision of
the fire as the Fall of Troynovant:

> . . . Alas the Fate
> I see of England, and its utmost date.
> Those flames of theirs, at which we fondly smile,
> Kindled, like Torches, our Sepulchrall Pile.
> Warre, Fire, and Plague against us all conspire:
> We the Warre, God the Plague, Who rais'd the Fire?
> . . .
>
>                                             . . .
>
> So of first Troy, the angry Gods unpaid,
> Ras'd the foundations which themselves had lay'd.

                                                    (ll. 413–28)

The final 'advice-to-the-king' both capitalizes on this shift in the
duchess's role and clarifies its connection with the Horatian motto
on the title page. 'Pictoribus atque Poetis, Quidlibet Audendi' now
pertains directly to the problems of veracious and courageous counsel: 'What Servants will conceale, and Couns'lours *spare*/To tell, the
Painter and the Poet *dare*' (italics added), the rhyme enforcing attention
to the Horatian echo. The king is warned to avert the destruction of
his own Troy by his 'own Navy's wooden horse', and the duchess of
Albemarle is defined as a new Cassandra, who must not be ignored;
while, in a final simile, her role is compared to the mythic truth-
teller Philomela, whose tale has the same conceptual structure as *ut
pictura poesis* itself:

> So Philomel her sad embroyd'ry strung,
> And vocall silks tun'd with her Needle's tongue.
> (The Picture dumbe, in colours lowd, reveal'd
> The tragedy's of Court, so long conceal'd.)
> But, when restor'd to voice, increas'd with Wings,
> To Woods and Groves, what once she painted, sings.

                                                    (ll. 451–6)

It is difficult to do justice to the puns, paradoxes, reversals, and
condensations of this passage. The story of the enforced muteness of
Philomela, whose tongue was cut out but who nevertheless revealed
the facts of her rape in tapestry, is a most elegant illustration of the
Simonides motto that poetry is a speaking picture, painting a dumb
poetry. It also echoes the poet's earlier prophecy of a time when the
'lying Bells' of political propaganda 'shall through the tongue be
burn'd', while alluding to the Duchess of Albemarle's earlier profession
as a seamstress. Finally, Philomela's metamorphosis into the nightin-
gale, long established as a symbol of the poet, replaces painting with

poetry as the revelatory medium, and thus strengthens the impression given in the duchess's own character development that poetry, which can see beyond externals, has a closer relationship with the truth.

A final postscript to this dark conclusion may be found in Marvell's letter to William Popple, dated 21 March 1670, in which he describes how three months after his death the Duke of Albemarle's body 'yet lys in the Dark unburyed' and unhonoured by his countrymen. The duchess, true to her wifely character, died twenty days after him (*Poems and Letters*, 2: 315–16).

## THE *LAST INSTRUCTIONS TO A PAINTER*

The *Last Instructions*, which has always been accepted as Marvell's by his editors, continues and confirms the generic and strategic procedures of the *Second* and *Third Advices*. In its opening lines, it indicates that it is the *third* in a series, a point not often stressed by those who doubt Marvell's authorship of the first two:

> After two sittings, now our Lady State,
> To end her Picture, does the third time wait.
>
> (*Poems and Letters*, 1: 147)

Politically, its relationship to events is equally direct and, although no printed text earlier than 1689 survives, its function is clearly to support an Opposition campaign, in which Marvell himself took active parliamentary part, to place the blame for the war's failure on the shoulders of those actually responsible, the notable exception being, of course, Charles himself. The major event with which the *Last Instructions* was concerned was the unmitigated naval disaster of 10–12 June 1667, when the Dutch fleet easily penetrated the English defences and burned the fleet at Chatham. On 19 June Peter Pett, superintendent of the dockyard at Chatham, was brought before the Privy Council to answer charges of negligence. On 17 October Marvell was appointed to a new parliamentary committee charged with investigating the 'miscarriages' of the war (*JHC* 9: 4), and on 31 October he spoke in the House in defense of Peter Pett, who gave evidence before his committee two weeks later. At the same time, however, impeachment proceedings had been started against Clarendon, who fled the country on 29 November, before the hearings were concluded, and in December another parliamentary committee, of which Marvell was also a member, was appointed to arrange for his statutory banishment.

The *Last Instructions* was written, we may therefore surmise, to influence the debates on both sets of impeachment proceedings and, according to the 'Popple' manuscript, it was completed on 4 September 1667, a date whose very specificity must carry some weight. Marvell's intentions were clearly to remove the blame for the Chatham disaster from military administrators such as Peter Pett, whose insignificance in the political structure is demonstrated by the ironic proposition the poem makes that he had total responsibility for the entire war:

> All our miscarriages on Pett must fall:
> His Name alone seems fit to answer all.
> Whose Counsel first did this mad War beget?
> Who all Commands sold thro' the Navy? Pett.
> Who would not follow when the Dutch were bet?
> Who treated out the time at Bergen? Pett.
> Who the Dutch Fleet with Storms disabled met,
> And rifling Prizes, them neglected? Pett.
> Who with false News prevented the Gazette?
> The Fleet divided? Writ for Rupert? Pett.
> Who all our Seamen cheated of their Debt?
> And all our Prizes who did swallow? Pett.
> Who did advise no Navy out to set?
> And who the Forts left unrepair'd? Pett.
> Who to supply with Powder, did forget
> Languard, Sheerness, Gravesend, and Upnor? Pett.
> Who all our Ships expos'd in Chathams Net?
> Who should it be but the Phanatick Pett.

(ll. 767–84)

Technically a virtuoso display of rhyming ability, the passage conflates all the accusations which the *Second* and *Third Advices* had levelled against Clarendon, the two Coventrys, Sandwich, Arlington and others, and adds, like the Duchess of Albemarle, a religious motive for this absurdity. The rhetorical emphasis of the passage falls, finally, on the one word *not* previously attached to Peter Pett, but which helps to explain his scapegoating: 'Phanatick'; that is to say, Nonconformist or Puritan; a characterization of Pett that is also clearly evident, though honourably so, in Lely's commonwealth portrait.

In contrast to these absurdist propositions, the *Last Instructions* fills in the parliamentary background to the Chatham disaster by relating it to the issue of Supply. Here, too, Marvell is concerned to shift the blame from the Commons to the Cabal, who he implied had themselves caused the Commons' intransigence by proposing that the revenue needed for the war should be raised by means of a general excise tax, thereby alienating the country gentry who feared for their own estates. Moreover, the self-interest of the Country party's resistance is further exculpated by Marvell's assertion that funds already granted had not in any case been spent on the war, but on maintaining the court's luxury and debauchery; the sailors were rioting because they had been paid by tickets in lieu of money, and the fleet had been allowed to lie in disrepair:

> Mean time through all the Yards their Orders run
> To lay the Ships up, cease the Keels begun.
> The Timber rots, and useless Ax does rust,
> The unpractis'd Saw lyes bury'd in its Dust;
> The busie Hammer sleeps, the Ropes untwine;
> The Stores and Wages all are mine and thine.
> Along the Coast and Harbours they take care
> That Money lack, nor Forts be in repair.
> Long thus they could against the House conspire,
> Load them with Envy, and with Sitting tire:
> And the lov'd King, and never yet deny'd,
> Is brought to beg in publick and to chide.

(ll. 317–28)

In this formal inversion of a shipbuilding scene there lies a key to the satire's structure. The British fleet has been *unbuilt*; and in that situation there take place two parody battles, the only kinds of battle possible in such an anti-heroic world. In the first half of the poem the painter, 'wanting other', is advised to draw the parliamentary debate over the Excise as if it were a real battle. And in the second half the assault of De Ruyter on the Thames is described in all the elevated language that English conduct so lamentably failed to deserve.

In accordance with this rational, if oversimplified, political argument, the *Last Instructions* continues and develops the now familiar units of an inverted pictorialism. It lists a number of alternative styles of 'painting' appropriate to the political scene: painting without colours; signpost daubing; grotesque ale-house sketches; Indian feather paintings which, though skilful, imply both 'luxury' and primitivism; scientific enlargements of insects, as in the illustrations to Hooke's *Micrographia*; and finally, the replacement of art by accident, as in Pliny's anecdote about Protogenes and the thrown sponge. Marvell exaggerates the anger in the episode, extending it to the dog, and linking dog and painter in a crazy celebration of the unintentional:

The Painter so, long having vext his cloth,
Of his Hound's Mouth to feign the raging froth,
His desperate Pencil at the work did dart,
His Anger reacht that rage which past his Art;
Chance finisht that which Art could but begin,
And he sat smiling how his Dog did grinn.

(ll. 21–6)

By a curious coincidence, the relevance of this Plinean anecdote to
Marvell's satirical activity was later confirmed by one of the Anglican
defenders of Samuel Parker. Richard Leigh noticed Marvell's reference to the 'Sponges' of the licensers in the *Rehearsal Transpros'd*, and
remarked bitterly that:

> the Sponge has left little else visible in his Book more than what it did
> in the Figures of those two Painters, in the one of which it fortunately
> dasht the Foam of a mad Horse, and in the other, the Slaver of a weary
> Dog; the Sponges ruder Blot prevailing above all the light touches and
> tender strokes of the Pencil. And indeed for this inimitable Art of the
> Sponge, this of Expressing Slaver and Foam to the Life, I will not deny
> but this work deserves to be celebrated beyond the Pieces of either
> Painter.[27]

Later, Marvell names two other painters whose history had a
special appropriateness to his subject. In describing Lady Castlemaine's
affair with her groom, Marvell exclaims: 'Ah Painter, now could
Alexander live,/And this Campaspe thee, Apelles, give' (ll. 103–4).
But where Pliny's famous story of Alexander's gift to Apelles of his
own mistress had functioned in pictorial tradition as an elevating
example of royal generosity to painters, the fact that Castlemaine had
for seven years been Charles's far from faithful mistress was scarcely
irrelevant. A rather different function is served by Marvell's suggestion,
prior to the parliamentary section of the poem, that his painter 'rest
a little' before beginning his portrayal of the battle, 'For so too Rubens,
with affairs of State,/His lab'ring Pencil oft would recreate' (ll. 119–
20). Rubens, court painter of the Spanish Netherlands, had been
employed by the Infanta to negotiate with both England and Holland,
and became Secretary of the Spanish Netherlands. He had negotiated
under 'pretence of pictures' with Buckingham on Spain's behalf, and
in 1630 was knighted by Charles I for the diplomatic services he had
performed. This devious use of his art for political purposes made
Rubens an excellent choice for the 'painter' of the *Last Instructions*,
and an appropriate transition from the satirical portraits of the opening
section into the labyrinthine accounts of ministerial policy.

The battle of the Excise is also integrated with the theme of the grotesque announced in the opening lines of the poem, which in turn connects with the 'Humano Capiti cervicem pictor equinam,/ Jungere' motto of the *Advices*. The first portrait of the *Last Instructions* is virtually a translation of that programme, since the artist is urged to represent St Albans, ex-rake, ineffective ambassador to France, 'with Drayman's Shoulders, butchers Mien,/Member'd like Mules, with Elephantine chine' (ll. 33–34), a brilliant condensation of indecorum on both the social and ontological scales. The Duchess of York is now to be portrayed not, as in Lely's portrait of her, as gorgeously louche (Figure 6), but with 'Oyster lip . . . /Wide Mouth that Sparagus may well proclaim:/With Chanc'lor's [her father's] Belly, and so large a Rump./There, not behind the Coach, her Pages jump' (ll. 61–4). Roger Palmer, Earl of Castlemaine, carries his cuckold's horns on pilgrimage to Pasiphae's tomb, thus connecting the theme of bestiality to the Minos myth introduced by Waller. Beyond these human monsters, there are allegorical ones. In the House of Commons 'daring Seymour . . . /Had strecht the monster Patent on the Field' (ll. 257–8): but the main parliamentary battle is against 'a Monster worse than e're before/Frighted the Midwife, and the Mother tore' (ll. 131–2). With her thousand hands, hundred rows of teeth, and revolting genealogy, enriched by echoes of Milton's allegory of Sin and Death, Excise is the logical conclusion of a grotesque pictorialism.

The *Last Instructions* also develops with some subtlety the expressive claims of the *paragone*, one of which was that only poetry can represent interior reality or other abstract qualities. In the characterization of Turner, Speaker of the House, the poet needs Miltonic and Chaucerian analogues (he swells like 'squatted Toad' and is as lecherous as Chanticleer) to deal with the disparity between his attractive appearance ('Bright Hair, fair Face') and his behaviour, and the old mind/body distinction is invoked:

Dear Painter, draw this Speaker to the foot:
Where Pencil cannot, there my pen shall do't;
That may his Body, this his Mind explain:

(ll. 863–5)

And the same distinction operates during the burning of the fleet at Chatham, in the contrasting portraits of Archibald Douglas and Sir Thomas Daniel. The painter is forced to represent Daniel as a Goliath figure:

FIGURE 6    Anne Hyde, Duchess of York, by Sir Peter Lely, Scottish
National Portrait Gallery

> Paint him of Person tall, and big of bone,
> Large Limbs, like Ox, not to be kill'd but shown. . . .
> Mix a vain Terrour in his Martial look,
> And all those lines by which men are mistook.
>
> (ll. 633–4, 637–8)

Douglas, on the other hand, presents an appearance of soft, feminine
beauty, which at first deceives the eye (and the water-nymphs) by its

suitability for love rather than war. And yet it is Daniel who flees from the fire ships, and Douglas who is burned to death on his own. By denying expectations, Douglas becomes transformed by his heroism into a permanent image of value and brightness: 'His shape exact, which the bright flames infold,/Like the Sun's statue stands of burnish't Gold' (ll. 679–80). Absorbed into the venerable tradition of classical heroism by an echo of the death of Nisus and Euryalus, he makes it possible for the two arts to cooperate again in a happy moment of idealism and historical certainty:

> Fortunate Boy! If either Pencils Fame,
> Or if my Verse can propagate thy Name;
> When OEta and Alcides are forgot,
> Our English youth shall sing the valiant Scott.
>
> (ll. 693–6)

Later in his career Marvell would give him a poem all to himself.[28]

It is to this world of ideals that the poet, once more, appeals in the envoy to the king. The last lines of the satire express the hope that Charles will be able to renovate the *ut pictura poesis* tradition and rescue it from its satirical phase:

> Painter adieu, how well our Arts agree;
> Poetick Picture, Painted Poetry.
> But this great work is for our Monarch fit,
> And henceforth Charles only to Charles shall sit.
> His Master-hand the Ancients shall out-do
> Himself the Poet and the Painter too.
>
> (ll. 943–8)

The reforms which will make possible the reunification of poetry and painting, the concordance of exterior appearance with interior reality, and hence an idealized portraiture that is neither sham nor flattery, are then proposed in the final section of advice 'To the King'. These entail the replacement of most of the Privy Council, who 'about the Common Prince have rais'd a Fense', with country gentlemen who have both moral and financial independence, 'whose Courage high / Does with clear Counsels their large Souls supply' (ll. 985–6), the same men who, in an earlier phase of the poem, were responsible for defeating the general Excise tax. Like Marvell himself, they are 'to speak not forward' in the House; but when called upon in 'Countryes Cause' they represent a composite and balanced political heroism, 'in Action brave;/In giving Gen'rous, but

in Counsell Grave' (ll. 291–2), which is far more truly supportive of
the king than all the false heroics of royalist panegyric.

As in the former passage, Marvell has in the envoy managed to
state positively what the three satires imply negatively, that the Dutch
War is only the occasion of a far more serious constitutional battle
over who should control national policy. But apart from the elegant
double entendres on 'gen'rous Conscience' and 'large Souls supply',
which allude to the financial issue, the advice given to the king
remains at the level of generalization. As with the *Second* and *Third
Advices*, specific remedies for the immorality of the court, the mistakes in naval strategy, the misuse of the Supply, the collapse of
administration, the sinister diplomatic currents beneath the surface of
events, do not appear in the 'advice-to-the-king', because the world
of ideal portraiture depends on abstractions. Even monarchy itself is
finally only a symbolic relationship: 'The Country is the King'; and
without that most true of constitutional fictions it is, perhaps, not
worth supporting.

The relationship between the *Second* and *Third Advices*, then, and
the *Last Instructions* is not merely one of form, which could easily
be copied, or of identity of attitude, which could, even in its details,
be shared. It is the identity of a consistent theoretical programme,
which has a tight and timely relationship to both political and literary
events. Intelligent exploitation of the pictorial tradition supports the
impression made by coincidence of political sympathy and reference.
These characteristics are not found in the *Fourth* and *Fifth Advices*,
nor in any of the other imitations which were still to follow, despite
Marvell's declared intention to be the last.

Finally, I have argued elsewhere that Marvell's authorship of the
*Second* and *Third Advices* is confirmed by his habit of self-quotation.
The two accounts of Noah's contributions to civilization quoted
above are only one example of the way that, in the 'Painter' poems,
Marvell parodies, by echoing, his own heroic poetry of the Commonwealth era. Perhaps the most amusing of these is his rewriting
of the complaint by the kings of Europe in the *First Anniversary*
that, even if they could penetrate the armour of Cromwell's ships,
'Through *double Oak*, and lin'd with *treble Brass*/That one Man still,
although but nam'd alarms/More than all Men, all Navies, and all
Arms, (ll. 374–6) (italics added). In the *Third Advice*, in mockery of
the king's decision to divide command of the fleet between Monck
and Prince Rupert, because no one man was presumably powerful
enough for sole command, Marvell joked:

United Gen'ralls! Sure the only spell
Wherewith United Provinces to quell.
Alas, ev'n they, though shell'd in *treble Oake*
Will prove an addle Egge with *double Yolke.*

(ll. 17–20) (italics added)

This is in truth the 'sober malice' that Christopher Wase discerned in the *Second Advice*, both 'polish'd' and 'well-contrived'. But it is also the high-spiritedness we will see in Marvell's polemical pamphlets of the 1670s, which delighted Charles II as much as it succoured the Whigs and the cause of religious toleration.

NOTES

1. See, for example, Earl Miner, 'The "Poetic Picture, Painted Poetry" of *The Last Instructions to a Painter*', *Modern Philology* 63 (1966), 288–94; and Michael Gearin-Tosh, 'The Structure of Marvell's *Last Instructions to a Painter*', *Essays in Criticism* 22 (1972), 48–57.
2. William Cobbett, *Parliamentary History of England* (London, 1806–12), 4: 297.
3. Cobbett, *Parliamentary History*, 4: 303–6.
4. Giovanni Francesco Busenello, *Prospettiva del Navale Trionfo Riportato Dalla Republica Serenissima Contro il Turco* (Venice, 1656); Thomas Higgons, trans., *A Prospective of the Naval Triumph of the Venetians over the Turk* (London, 1658).
5. *Calender of State Papers Domestic*, 26 July 1667.
6. Anthony à Wood, *Athenae Oxonienses* (London, 1691), 2: 303.
7. *The Journal of James Yonge*, ed. F. N. L. Poynter (London, 1963), pp. 23, 155.
8. Sir Roger L'Estrange, *An Account of the Growth of Knavery* (London, 1678), p. 6.
9. George de F. Lord, 'Two New Poems by Marvell', *Bulletin of the New York Public Library* 62 (1958), 551–70. The only scholar to take Denham's authorship seriously was his modern editor and biographer, Brendan O. Hehir, *Harmony from Discords: A Life of Sir John Denham* (Berkeley and Los Angeles, 1968), pp. 210–29.
10. Marvell, *Complete Works*, ed. A. B. Grosart (New York, 1875; repr. 1966), 4: 249.
11. Gotthold Lessing, *Laocoön* (London, 1914), p. 4.
12. For Italian pictorial theory, see W. Rensselaer Lee, '*Ut Pictura Poesis*: The Humanistic Theory of Painting', *Art Bulletin* 22 (1940), 197–269.
13. *Dolce's 'Aretino' and Venetian Art Theory of the Cinquecento*, ed. and trans. Mark W. Roskill (New York, 1968), pp. 119–27.
14. Leon Battista Alberti, *Della Pittura* (1436).

15. For these Plinean anecdotes, see the *Natural History*, Loeb edition, xxxv–xxxvi.

16. John Evelyn, trans., *An Idea of Painting* (London, 1668), pp. 67–8.

17. John Dryden, *The Art of Painting, by C. A. Du Fresnoy . . . Ut Pictura Poesis erit – Hor. de Arte Poetica* (London, 1695), pp. 3–4.

18. Leonardo, *Treatise on Painting*, ed. and trans. A. P. McMahon (Princeton, 1956), 1: 24.

19. Pending Nigel Smith's definitive edition, the *Second* and *Third Advices* will be cited from the Popple manuscript, as transcribed in the Appendix.

20. See Annabel Patterson, 'The *Advices to a Painter* in Marvell's Canon', *Studies in English Literature* (forthcoming).

21. In the first two editions of the *Second Advice*, the sardonic passage on the motives for the war was included in the final 'advice' to the king. In the *Directions* volume, it was moved to the end of the main satire, the position that it also takes in the Popple manuscript. The effect is to remove all cynicism from the envoy, leaving it to express only conditional enthusiasm for reform.

22. Bodleian MS Eng. Poet. E4, dated about 1680.

23. Cited from George de F. Lord, *Poems on Affairs of State*, 1: 55, 63.

24. Dryden, *Works*, eds. E. N. Hooker and H. T. Swedenberg, Jr (Berkeley and Los Angeles, 1961), 1: 50.

25. See R. B. Beckett, *Lely* (London, 1951), pp. 11, 17–18.

26. These last two lines were added in the *Directions* edition (and the Popple manuscript), indicating later revision in favour of the duchess's religious sincerity. They recall Marvell's own speech in the Convention Parliament on filling impropriate livings in the universities.

27. Richard Leigh, *The Transproser Rehears'd* (Oxford, 1673), p. 131.

28. *The Loyall Scot*, a poem of the 1670s, written in the context of discussions in Parliament of a possible union between England and Scotland.

# Chapter 5

# The pamphlet wars

In the last two decades of the seventeenth century, Marvell's contemporaries began to ascribe anonymous satires to him, and from 1689 his name was used as an advertisement for editions of *Poems on Affairs of State*. This magnetic function was not, however, originally generated by his verse satires, where his authorship could only be guessed at, but by the *Rehearsal Transpros'd*, which appeared in two parts, in the autumn of 1672 and the winter of 1673–74, the second of which bore his name on the title page. This move into prose polemic quickly established his reputation as someone to be reckoned with. Gilbert Burnet's description of the two parts as 'the wittiest books that have appeared in this age',[1] Anthony à Wood's hostile admission that Marvell was 'a very celebrated wit among the Fanaticks, and the only one truly so',[2] and Dryden's conflation (in the preface to *Religio Laici*) between Marvell and Martin Marprelate, 'the first Presbyterian Scribbler, who sanctifi'd Libels and Scurrility to the use of the Good Old Cause', all tell the same story, that *The Rehearsal Transpros'd* was perceived, albeit grudgingly by his enemies, as an outstanding achievement – indeed, a breakthrough of sorts – in making polemic newly effective because amusing. Modern critics have also awarded it quite high points, either by taking its politics seriously or by paying close attention to its satirical strategies.[3] Yet perhaps the most frequently quoted passage is one in which Marvell *seems* to be espousing the position of the detached and apolitical observer (and a rather conservative one at that). Looking back in the first part of *The Rehearsal Transpros'd* at the 1640s, he sounds not unlike some revisionist historians of this period:

> Whether it were a War of Religion, or of Liberty, is not worth the labour to enquire … but upon considering all, I think the Cause was too good to have been fought for. Men ought to have trusted God; they ought and might have trusted the King [Charles I] with whole matter … The King himself being of so accurate and piercing a judgment,

would soon have felt where it stuck. For men may spare their pains
where Nature is at work, and the world will not go the faster for our
driving. Even as his present Majesties happy Restauration did itself, so all
things else happen in their best and proper time, without any need of
our officiousness.

(p. 135)

But only someone who had never read Marvell's Cromwell poems
(and the only one that had been published by this time, the *First
Anniversary*, had been published anonymously) could take this passage
at face value.

Apart from our being alert to the balancing act that Marvell was
performing in *The Rehearsal Transpros'd* with respect to his statements
about Charles I, this chapter emphasizes that to engage in church
politics, however structurally connected to affairs of state, was for
Marvell an adventure into new and dangerous territory. To concentrate only on the satirical skills or the political doctrines of *The
Rehearsal Transpros'd*, or indeed to concentrate upon it to the exclusion of the later pamphlets, is to lose sight of the enormous shift of
energy and focus that Marvell directed to his polemical prose. The
'Painter' poems, with their quickly shifting spotlight on recent events
and their galleries of sardonic portraits, are recognizably 'poems on
affairs of State'. The prose pamphlets, with the exception of the
*Account of the Growth of Popery and Arbitrary Government*, are deeply
invested in church history, policy and doctrine, and with longstanding
ideological issues. Increasingly, his commitment to ideas of toleration
and his consequent need to debate with those intolerant churchmen
who believed in enforced conformity required Marvell to do historical research into the way the church had done business in the past.
Though topical, in the sense that they speak to the predicament of
English Nonconformists under the Clarendon Code, his pamphlets
also therefore acquired a longer than topical life, and could still be
seen as pertinent whenever the issue of conformity vs. toleration
became again the centre of public attention. John Locke, for example,
owned all of Marvell's polemical pamphlets,[4] as well as the hostile
answers they spawned, and undoubtedly remembered the *Historical
Essay on General Councils* when writing his own great *Letter concerning
Toleration* in the late 1680s; and the *Essay*, as we shall see, was several
times republished in the later seventeenth and early eighteenth century,
as the more obviously literary *Rehearsal Transpros'd* was not.

And these two pamphlets, especially the first, were indeed 'literary'
– a fact that certainly explains why only they have been hitherto
granted the privilege of a modern scholarly edition. Not only did

they set a new standard of wit in theological dispute, they constituted a veritable network of intertextual relations and literary in-jokes, starting with the allusion to Buckingham's comedy *The Rehearsal*, of which John Dryden had been the primary butt. The classical satirists Horace and Juvenal, Donne's *Metempsychosis*, Davenant's *Gondibert*, Cervantes' *Don Quixote*, Butler's *Hudibras*, Hobbes's *Leviathan*, Montaigne's *Essays*, the *Cassandra* of Costes de la Calprenède, Sidney's *Arcadia*, Denham, Killigrew, Shakespeare's *Midsummer Night's Dream* and *The Merry Wives of Windsor*, John Ogilby's *Fables*, Guarini's *Il Pastor Fido*, compete for argumentative importance with Richard Hooker, Sir Francis Bacon, the Fathers of the Church, Suetonius' *Lives of the Twelve Caesars* and a vast array of historians.

But because Marvell came late to polemic, and came to it after his major experiments in satire, he discovered a procedural dilemma whereby the literary, as we understand it, came into conflict with other values. His primary qualification for engaging in this, for him, unfamiliar genre, was his irrepressible, dancing wit, which in debate with a single opponent became gladiatorial; but how was he to dispute at all about the operating terms of Christianity without himself committing an offence, without betraying the definitively Christian values – of meekness, patience and charity? Though not the first to recognize this problem – Milton had encountered it in his own pamphlets on church reform in the 1640s – Marvell engaged it with an introspective seriousness that gives his pamphlets *theoretical* importance, even today.

As always, Marvell's discovery of this permanent problem, and his gradual evolution of an acceptable rhetorical response, was the result of his commitment to public service. What caused his entry into polemics was the combined occasion of Charles's Declaration of Indulgence in March 1672, which suspended all penal laws against both Roman Catholics and Nonconformists, and the appearance of an energetic, self-appointed campaigner for enforced religious conformity, in the person of Samuel Parker. The contrast between the king's apparent intentions and the published statements of a rising member of his church establishment was striking, and any suspicions Marvell may have had about the real meaning of the royal Declaration only made Parker more of a menace. It was not that his advice was likely to influence Charles (whom it seems he only succeeded in annoying)[5] but rather that his intolerance might give fuel to the persecuting spirit in the House of Commons, which was in fact shortly to insist that the Declaration exceeded the limits of royal prerogative, and force Charles to withdraw it.

What needed to be done, therefore, was that Parker should be discredited, and his views shown to be unacceptable to any rational being. John Owen, an Independent minister, had tried to answer Parker (and indeed gave Marvell a number of strategic hints as to how he might be answered) but was partly disqualified by his role as a recognized spokesman for the Nonconformists. And so Marvell was drawn in to the dispute and not only demolished Parker's reputation but made his own. What he came to see, however, in the course of his intense exposure to Parker's style and methods, was that satire itself was a form of aggression, a version of the intolerance he despised and was attempting to refute. In Marvell's articulation of the opposite virtues as they ought to be exercised in church polity, he worked his way gradually toward a new theory of polemical style, not entirely devoid of wit, but more compatible with an ideal of moderation. Abandoning the methods of his big personal success, he moved deliberately toward a polemic which was 'not in the merry part so good as the Rehearsall Transpros'd', as he wrote to Sir Edward Harley about the reception of his next pamphlet, *Mr. Smirke, or the divine in mode* (*Poems and Letters*, 2: 346), but whose ability to cut to the heart of the deepest questions was, finally, more conducive to systemic change.

We need to set up the history of the debate into which Marvell now intervened – according to him, unwillingly. The struggle began late in the reign of Elizabeth I, when the Elizabethan church settlement began to be challenged by strong voices from the left wing of the religious spectrum, who believed that the English church retained far too many of the ceremonies of the old religion. The Admonition Controversy (named after the 'Admonition to Parliament' of 1572) had focused on relatively small abuses in the church – simony, an uneducated clergy, for example; but under the leadership of the radical Cambridge preacher Thomas Cartwright, and invigorated by the underground Marprelate pamphlets in the late 1580s, ideas of reform broadened. The Marprelate pamphlets, appearing under the pseudonym of Martin Marprelate, were a series of scandalously funny attacks on the bishops of the Elizabethan church for corruption, incompetence and intolerance. Elizabeth's wily regime was never seriously incommoded by this voluble protest, but it was unpleasant enough to have motivated two of the most influential documents in Marvell's own development. One was Richard Hooker's *Laws of Ecclesiastical Polity*, the first four books of which were published in 1593, and which established the norms of high-minded argument from first principles. The other was a monument of reasonable pragmatism.

In 1589 Francis Bacon wrote, apparently for private circulation, a pamphlet mediating between Anglicans and Puritans and calling for a cessation of hostilities. His purpose was not only to point out where each side was at fault but to emphasize what was or should be the common ground between them ('one Faith, one Baptisme, and not one Ceremonie, one Policie'), and to suggest some ground rules for the style and conduct of religious polemic conducted in the public press. Both sides were exhorted to drop the tone of abuse and mockery which had characterized the Marprelate pamphlets, and to discourse together in reason and charity:

> Indeed bitter and earnest writing is not hastily to be condemned: for men cannot contend coldly and without affection about things they hold deare and pretious. A politicke man may write from his braine without touch or sense of his heart, as in a speculation that pertaineth not unto him; but a feeling Christian will express in his words a character either of zeale or love: the latter of which as I would wish rather to be embraced, as being more fit for the times; yet is the former warranted also by great examples. But to leave all reverend and religious compassion toward evils, or indignation toward faults, to turne religion into a Comedy or Satyr, to search and rip up wounds with a laughing countenance, to intermix Scripture and Scurrility sometime in one sentence, is a thing farre from the devout reverence of a Christian, and scant beseeming the honest regard of a sober man.[6]

The significance of Bacon's protest, from a theoretical point of view, lies in its capacity to amalgamate different levels of reference. The surface of his statement is concerned with rhetorical decorum, since the polemicists have muddled their genres, treating the gravest of all subjects in the style of comedy and satire; but this issue is both included in and transcended by the criterion of Christianity itself, and the behavioural implications of the doctrines under dispute. Mockery, abuse and *ad hominem* strategies are aesthetically 'low', destructive of the public peace, and intellectually suspect, since they replace rational refutation by character assassination. Furthermore, beyond such faults, which should be apparent to any 'sober man', they are incompatible with Christian charity.

It was no coincidence that Bacon's argument was first published in 1641, at the beginning of a new outbreak of the same old arguments. The Smectymnuan Controversy of the 1640s was, at more than one level, a dispute over style. Vestments, liturgy, the episcopal hierarchy itself could be and indeed were read as language, a 'style' of Christianity now far more seriously threatened by an alternative, since the Puritan-dominated Long Parliament had virtually taken control of the country. On the left the Presbyterians, with Milton as their most memorable spokesman, stood for radical changes in the *structure* of the English church, changes which would begin with the banishment of the bishops from the House of Lords in 1642 and ended in 1646, when government of the church by bishops and archbishops was abolished. In this cause, Milton's 'vehemence', as he called it, included satire and abuse, for which, in his *Apology . . . for Smectymnuus* (1642), he provided an elaborate rhetorical and scriptural defence. On the right, the Anglican clergy were represented most eloquently by Bishop Joseph Hall, for whom 'decency' of ceremony and 'moderation' of speech were the foundations of an established church and a reasonable mind. Each set of terms had its negatives: to a Puritan, Anglican moderation was the lukewarmness rebuked in Revelations 3: 15 and Anglican decency, itself authorized by 1 Corinthians 14: 40, was a love of dress, the sign of a church still encrusted with Romish externality. To an Anglican, Puritan zeal was a form of madness, or at least bad temper. The author of *A Modest Confutation* defended Bishop Hall against Milton in terms which made explicit this exchangeability:

> Must he therefore be Luke-warm, because his zeal burns not as hot as hell? Will Grace mix with nothing but adust choler, or lowring morose peevishnesse? Cannot Grace and Nature consist? When we deny ourselves, must we deny humanity? Doth Gods Spirit now inspire Christians, as the Devill did his Priests of old, by putting them out of their wits? . . . Why else cannot a sober, modest, humble, orthodox Prelate go for a Christian among us?[7]

The balance between these rival styles was further symbolized by the use of the contradictory, side-by-side texts from Proverbs 26: 4, 5 ('Answer not a fool according to his folly, lest thou also be like unto him'.'Answer a fool according to his folly, lest he be wise in his own conceit.'). Needless to say, given his friendship with Milton, Marvell would have consulted the authorities on both sides at this stage of the dispute before beginning his own adventures in polemic. We know that he read Bacon's pamphlet, because it is quoted as an irresistible authority towards the end of the *Second Part* of *The Rehearsal Transpros'd*.

By the 1670s, the clear polarities of the Smectymnuan Controversy had become blurred. In subsequent stages of the Civil War, when the Presbyterians became the proponents of their own brand of orthodoxy, they were opposed by Independents, Levellers, and other subcultures of Puritanism. The challenge to a complex church polity by a would-be simple one was replaced by the issue of religious toleration, and the impossible search for a new structure broad enough to absorb the rapidly multiplying sectaries. Until there was once again an established church with a king at its head, polarization was impossible; and when, after twenty years of political chaos and a regicide, these conditions were fulfilled, and the Act of Uniformity drew the line between the two sides, there was naturally consider-able anxiety about reopening hostilities. The farewell sermons of the ministers ejected from their pulpits on St Bartholomew's Day (that episode lamented by the Duchess of Albemarle, we remember) were far from militant, emphasizing the duties of love, peace and patience under persecution. John Collins reminded his parishioners of St Ambrose's famous motto, 'The Arms of the Church are prayers and tears', a saying which had been used in the previous generation by the author of *Eikon Basilike* in presenting Charles I as a Christian martyr.[8] When Edmund Calamy (one of the duchess's heroes) forgot himself and preached an inflammatory sermon on the spur of the moment, he was rebuked by O. Udall in the language of Richard Hooker's preface: 'Well Master Calamy, there will come a time when three words uttered with meeknesse and charity shall receive a far more blessed reward, then three thousand Volumes written with disdainfull sharpnesse of wit, and with malicious partiality',[9] a quota-tion which, as we shall see, Marvell would later appropriate for his own side. The newly persecuted Nonconformists discovered a re-spectable spokesman in John Owen, whose response to the Clarendon Code was significantly (and accurately) entitled *A Peace-Offering in an Apology and humble Plea for Indulgence and Libertie of Conscience* (1667).

It is all the more startling, therefore, to read the preface to Samuel Parker's *Discourse of Ecclesiastical Politie* (1669), in which he set out to justify the violence of his own polemic style by an account of Non-conformist writing which is partially obsolete and certainly exaggerated, but which recalls the terminology of the Smectymnuan Controversy in an unpleasing rearrangement. He asked:

> Let any man, that is acquainted with the Wisdom and Sobriety of True Religion, tell me how 'tis possible not to be provoked to scorn and indignation against such proud, ignorant, and supercilious Hypocrites; who though they utterly defeat all the main Designs of Religion, yet boast themselves its only Friends and Patrons; signalize their Party by distinct-ive Titles and Characters of Godliness, and brand all others, howsoever

Pious and Peaceable, with bad Names, and worse Suspicions? . . . Thus the only hot fit of Zeal we find our Saviour in, was kindled by an Indignation against the Pride and Insolence of the Jews, when he whips the Buyers and Sellers out of the outward Court of the Temple . . . Now to lash these morose and churlish Zealots with smart and twingeing Satyrs is so farr from being a criminal Passion, that 'tis a Zeal of Meekness and Charity . . . If you will ever silence them, you must be as vehement as they: nothing but Zeal can encounter Zeal.

The full title of Parker's treatise explained his malevolent thesis;[10] but among the provocations it gave, the appropriation of Richard Hooker's far more irenic work, the *Laws of Ecclesiastical Polity*, which had by this time become a classic in the field, must have been high on Marvell's list. Parker's choice of style and approach therefore matched his advice to the king, whom he urged to employ his prerogative in a vigorous campaign to eradicate Nonconformity, and to employ persecution where necessary as an instrument of political stabilization.

The implications of both style and argument were immediately perceived by John Owen, who temporarily suspended his own pacifist stance, and so indicated on the title page of *Truth and Innocence Vindicated* (1669): 'Non Par[t]um studiis agimur; sed sumsimus arma, Consiliis in[n]imica tuis, Discordia Vaecors' ('We are not a little driven from our studies; but we take up arms hostile to your counsels, you crazy figure of Discord'). Owen's response to Parker's belligerence was of enormous importance for Marvell, for he perceived that the language of aggression could be turned against itself. Borrowing the mock-heroic models of Cervantes and Samuel Butler (who, not incidentally, had turned his humour against the Nonconformists), Owen created a persona for his opponent who behaves like Don Quixote, though without that elderly knight's romanticism. And why, asked Owen, did such a champion choose as his opponents such humble folk as himself? He would have been better 'to have sought out some Giant in Reason and Learning, that might have given him at least *par animo periculum*, as Alexander said in his conflict with Porus, a danger big enough to exercise his Courage, though through mistake it should in the issue have proved but a Wind-mill' (pp. 13–14). More seriously, Parker was accused of theological ignorance, or at least fatal omission. In Parker's account of human nature since the Fall there is 'neither Supposition, nor Assertion of Sin, or of a Redeemer' (p. 204), the result being 'the rudest, most imperfect and weakest Scheme of Religion' imaginable (p. 198). And he represented, Owen suggested, a clergy who were unchristian in their instincts:

It is certain, for those in particular, who take upon them ... to be Ministers of the Gospel, there are commands for meekness, patience and forbearance, given unto them. ... I know not therefore whence it is come to pass, that this sort of men do principally, if not only, stir up Magistrats and Rulers to Laws, Severities, Penalties, Coercions, Imprisonments, and the like outward means of fierce and carnal power, against those, who in anything dissent from them in Religion.

(p. 403)

## THE REHEARSAL TRANSPROS'D

There is no question but that Marvell was deeply indebted to Owen's pamphlet for the tone and method of the first part of *The Rehearsal Transpros'd*. While he adopted the standard rhetorical form for public debate, the 'animadversions' technique whereby one answers one's opponent's points one by one, Marvell added several new ingredients. His mockery of Parker as crazy Quixote, false Crusader and 'Buffoon-General to the Church of England'[11] derives directly from Owen, sometimes with specific echoes of phrase. Marvell, for example, tells his audience not to underrate Parker's crusading zeal by thinking he will 'enter the Lists where he hath but one man to combate ... Hungary, Transylvania, Bohemia, Poland, Savoy, France, the Netherlands, Denmark, Sweden, and a great part of the Church of England, and all Scotland ... may perhaps rouse our Mastiff, and make up a Danger worthy of his Courage' (p. 21). A glance back at the quotations from Owen will show where this passage originated. But, in addition to the mock-heroic strategies which Marvell developed and expanded, and which made *The Rehearsal Transpros'd* an instant success, the influence of Owen's arguments is also apparent. Like Owen, Marvell was twice provoked to comment on the irreverence of 'that most unsafe passage' in Parker's preface where a 'hot fit of zeal' was attributed to Christ (pp. 76, 144); like Owen, Marvell attacked Parker for his inability to distinguish between Grace and mere morality; and, following on Owen's initiative, Marvell developed the hypothesis that the Anglican clergy whom Parker represents have a record of propagating 'the most precipitate, brutish and sanguinary Counsels'. 'You would think the same day that they took up Divinity they divested themselves of Humanity, & so they may procure & execute a Law against the Nonconformists, that they had forgot the Gospel' (pp. 106–7). In the context of the king's Declaration of Indulgence, Marvell was able to develop Owen's criticism into a fundamental contrast between Charles and his ecclesiastical advisers:

'God be prais'd his Majesty is far of another temper' (p. 60). The effect is similar to the distinction between king and council in the satirical *Advices*; the implication is that the Declaration of Indulgence, however unconstitutional, imitated in spirit the New Dispensation. Marvell's reliance on Owen, to whose defence he came but to whom he gives no scholarly credit, did not go unnoticed. As Parker himself observed in *The Reproof to The Rehearsal Transpros'd*, 'This is very shrewd, but then it is none of your own, J. O. had it before you, and in truth you are so given to purloining, that I expect ere long to hear of you among the Advertisements at the bottom of the Gazet' (p. 28).

This substantial act of borrowing contributes to the confusions of attitude which characterize the first part of *The Rehearsal Transpros'd*. On the one hand, the need to discredit Parker has clearly directed Marvell to satiric and comic strategies which have been proven successful elsewhere. Owen, Milton, Cervantes and Butler were not really compatible models. The sustained allusion, also, to Buckingham's dramatic burlesque, *The Rehearsal*, allows Marvell to capitalize on Buckingham's deflation of Dryden (as we have seen, another enemy of the Nonconformists), while at the same time exploiting the king's fondness both for the theatre and for Buckingham himself. But the structure of Parker's 'plays' (today we might call them ploys) seems a little forced. On the other hand, Marvell seems genuinely offended by Parker's lack of 'modesty', which is from the very first page a key word in the pamphlet; he attacks him vigorously for his 'railing' style, claiming to replace it by raillery, but constantly asserting the absolute values of pacifism and restraint. The result is a radical inconsistency, which had been partially apparent in Owen's model but is fully visible in *The Rehearsal Transpros'd*. In regretting the Civil War, Marvell himself recalled St Ambrose's aphorism that the 'Arms of the Church are Prayers and Tears' (p. 135). In the very act of answering Parker, however, he had necessarily abandoned that pacifist ideal; and the more successfully he attacked Parker's personality, the closer he came to committing Parker's own offences.

One of the technical problems he faced was that the standard form for theological debate at this time was the so-called 'animadversions' method, which required one tediously to answer an opponent by following the structure of his argument, chapter by chapter, line by line. There was always the temptation, therefore, to focus on superficial mistakes or errors of taste in one's adversary's performance; and, more importantly, the animadverter had his agenda set by that adversary, something which severely limited his argumentative freedom.

Marvell tried to make comic capital out of this handicap: 'It were a wild thing for me to Squire it after this Knight, and accompany him here through all his Extravagancies against our Calvinists' (p. 32). 'Yet though I must follow his track now I am in, I hope I shall not write after his Copy'.

The last paragraph of the first *Rehearsal Transpros'd* already seems to betray uneasiness on this score. Marvell professes that he will be 'recompensed' for the labour of pursuing Parker from one disgraceful statement to another if his own polemical methods have seemed to the reader to be appropriate to the task: 'if any one that hath been formerly of another mind, shall learn by this Example, that it is not impossible to be merry and angry . . . without profaning and violating those things which are and ought to be most sacred' (p. 145). The negative syntax of this appeal is more suggestive of anxiety than satisfaction, and it leads directly into the *Second Part*, where the tensions in Marvell's polemical theory are made explicit.

The *Second Part* is not a mock-heroic pastiche. It is a fully premeditated work of epic proportions, announced by Marvell in a letter to Sir Edward Harley, in which he described being 'drawn in . . . to intermeddle in a noble and high argument'. If that is indeed an epic proposition, Marvell's remarks to Harley about the work in progress suggest an undertaking which has affinities with *Paradise Lost*, whose sublimity Marvell would praise the very next year. We have seen the connection in that poem between a high style and a theological subject:

> That Majesty which through thy Work doth Reign
> Draws the Devout, deterring the Profane.
> And things divine thou treatst of in such state
> As them preserves, and Thee inviolate.
>
> (*Poems and Letters*, 1: 138)

Similar preoccupations appear in the letter to Harley. 'I will', Marvell wrote:

> draw up an answer that shall have as much of spirit and solidity in it as my ability will afford & the age we live in will indure. I am (if I may say it with reverence) drawn in, I hope by a good Providence, to intermeddle in a noble and high argument which therefore by how much it is above my capacity I shall use the more industry not to disparage it.
>
> (*Poems and Letters*, 2: 328)

It is much to the point that Marvell's praise of Milton would focus on the blend of apparently irreconcilable opposites, 'delight and horrour', 'gravity and ease', which makes for an acceptable treatment of theological issues; for consciousness of a mixed decorum, as well as an almost obsessive concern with the problem of reverence, is everywhere apparent in Marvell's second pamphlet.

The *Second Part* begins (after a few pages of scurrilous jokes at Parker's expense) with Marvell's response to the charge that he has been disrespectful toward Parker's office as representative of the church, that he has offended against 'the Gravity of his Profession' (p. 159). What follows is a carefully sequenced apology for and defence of Marvell's satirical strategies in view of their serious intentions. He begins by stating that all writing is an 'envious and dangerous imploy-ment' because one's motives are invariably open to misinterpretation, and 'not to Write at all is much the safer course of life' – that passage I cited in the Introduction as most characteristic of Marvell's self-definition as a writer. But while all writing is dangerous, satirical writing is doubly so, since it may very likely endanger one's own reputation, but it will certainly damage that of one's victim, and hence the structure of mutual confidence on which society is based:

> For 'tis better that evil men should be left in an undisturbed possession of their repute . . . then that the Exchange and Credit of mankind should be universally shaken . . . how can the Author of an Invective, though never so truely founded, expect approbation . . . who, in a world all furnished with subjects of praise, instruction and learned inquiry, shall studiously chuse and set himself apart to comment upon the blemishes and imperfections of some particular person?
>
> (p. 161)

Furthermore, beyond the writer's duty to support societal ideals in general, there is a pressing reason why 'the Clergy certainly of all others ought to be kept and preserv'd sacred in their Reputation. For . . . few Men will or can be perswaded by his Doctrine, whose practice they conceive to be opposite' (p. 162). Marvell is construct-ing a hierarchy of reasons, from personal through social to religious, as to why one should not do what he has recently and most success-fully done.

Then, with a remarkable reversal, and a characteristic conjunc-tion, Marvell revokes all three general objections in the particular case: 'And yet *nevertheless*, and all that has been said before being granted, it may so chance that to write, and that Satyrically, and . . . this too even against a Clergyman, may be not only excusable but necessary' (p. 163) (italics added). A clergyman who leaves his pulpit to commit himself to the public press, Marvell asserts, has given up his right to sanctuary, has himself destroyed 'the Gravity of his Profession': 'In this Case . . . a Clergy-man is laid open to the Pen, of any one that knows how to manage it; and every person who has either Wit, Learning or Sobriety is licensed, if debauch'd to curb him, if erroneous to catechize him, and if foul-mouth'd and biting, to muzzle him' (p. 164). Since Parker's superiors in the church have neglected either to catechize or to curb him, to correct either his style or his doctrine, it has been left to Marvell, a 'private man' and amateur theologian, to undertake this double duty. Rhetorically, it is the 'nevertheless' at the crucial moment which reverses our expectations, and turns self-accusation into self-defence.

However, Marvell goes out of his way to emphasize that the task remains unattractive, and that he is temperamentally unsuited to the satirist's role. Forced out of a lifetime of 'modest retiredness' (p. 169), he claims a special kind of shyness: 'For I am too conscious of mine own imperfections to rake into and dilate upon the failings of other men; and though I carry always some ill Nature about me, yet it is I hope no more than is in this world necessary for a Preservative' (p. 165). Admittedly, 'modest retiredness' is an unusual description of the life of a Member of Parliament, and charitable humility is a disingenuous claim for the author of the *Last Instructions*. But, disingenuously or not, Marvell manages to give this apology a convincing tone of weariness and distaste:

> It hath been thus far the odiousest task that ever I undertook, and has look't to be all the while like the cruelty of a Living Dissection, which, however it may tend to publick instruction, and though I have pick'd out the most noxious Creature to be anatomiz'd, yet doth scarse excuse or recompence the offensiveness of the scent and fouling of my fingers.
>
> (p. 185)

Despite this clear awareness of the polemicist's dilemma, Marvell declares himself committed to finishing the unpleasant task, which he proposes to manage by a mixture of rhetorical strategies. By now fully aware of the structural problems of animadversions, Marvell invokes the metaphor of the hunt to justify his continuing in this awkward genre:

> *Yet* I will not decline the pursuit, but plod on after him in his own way, thorow thick and thin, hill or dale, over hedge and ditch wherever he leads; till I have laid hands on him, and deliver'd him bound either to Reason or Laughter, to Justice or Pity. If at any turn he gives me the least opportunity to be serious I shall gladly take it: but where he prevaricates

or is scurrilous (and where is he not?) I shall treat him *betwixt Jest and Earnest.*

(p. 187; italics added)

As Marvell was later to discover, this imaginary compromise between jest and earnest was no real solution to the fundamental clash of values defined in Bacon's *Wise and Moderate Discourse,* and he was shortly to move much closer to the Baconian position. For the moment, however, the proposal to alternate satire with rational refutation allowed Marvell to develop his critique of Parker's arguments with a new seriousness, while pausing from time to time to hit below the belt.

In the *Second Part,* the mock-heroic allusions are to a large extent replaced by the metaphor of the hunt – which in turn depends on the bestialization of Parker. Here are some examples. Parker is a diseased sheep likely to infect the whole flock:

> Yet then if our great Pastors should but exercise the Wisdom of common Shepheards, by parting with one to stop the infection of the whole Flock, when his rottenness grew notorious; or if our Clergy would but use the instinct of other creatures, and chase the blown Deer out of their Heard; such mischiefs might quickly be remedied.
>
> (p. 164)

The same passage identifies Parker also as a mad dog, 'foulmouth'd and biting', which it is Marvell's duty to muzzle, and as the traditional goat-man, a 'Satyr out of his own bounds', who ought to be hunted 'thorow the woods with hounds and horn home to his harbour' (p. 165). The figure of the mad dog deliberately recalls the Blatant Beast of Spenser's *Faerie Queene,* an image of irrational slander and detraction let loose upon the world. At the very end of his pamphlet, Marvell confirms his source and repeats the charge: 'You are a Blatant Writer and a Latrant' (p. 164). But at the same time, Marvell is able to use the hunting metaphor in reverse, as something that monarchs should avoid. By association with Nimrod, the first hunter in Christian history (Genesis 10: 8–9), whom generations of commentators had established also as the first of absolute rulers, hunting was associated with tyranny. Part of Marvell's serious strategy is to advise the king against political theory derived from the Nimrod precedent, and to warn him that 'Princes, whose dominion over mankind resembles in some measure that of man over other creatures', cannot expect to prosper, 'if by continual terrour they amaze, shatter, and hare their People, driving them into Woods, & running them upon Precipices'. Rather they should cultivate a pastoral mode of

government, for the 'wealth of a Shepheard depends upon the multitude of his flock, the goodness of their Pasture, and the Quietness
of their feeding' (p. 234).

Political meaning continues to assert itself in other sections of
Marvell's bestiary. Parker at one stage is being hunted as a whale
(p. 198); a few pages later we are shown that this connects him with
Thomas Hobbes's *Leviathan*, whose theoretical absolutism, indeed,
Parker has outdone: 'I do not see', remarks Marvell, 'but your Behe-
moth exceeds his Leviathan some foot long' (p. 214). Still later, we
perceive that the whale image signifies Parker's fatal distortion of
scale and proportion. As a whale is to a fly, so Parker's arguments
make the ceremonial issue 'at once stupendiously necessary and at
the same time despicably little' (p. 308).

It is in this context that we can understand the long quotation
from John Donne's *Progress of the Soul*, which, as Marvell must have
discovered to his delight, unites in one cynical passage all the com-
ponents of his own bestiary, and grounds them firmly, if absurdly, on
the story of the Fall. In Donne's poem, the soul, or principle of evil,
began its life cycle in a 'chast and innocent Apple', became at one
stage a lustful cock sparrow, and at another a little fish who grew up
to be 'the great Leviathan'. Contraction and expansion were repeated
in the stages of mouse and elephant, and then the soul moved into
more destructive forms, spending some time both as a dog and as a
wolf who harassed the flock of Abel, the first shepherd. Eventually,
'after this Soul had passed thorow so many Brutes, & been hunted
from post to pillar', it took refuge in a human, female form, and was
married to Cain, the first murderer (pp. 176–7).

There is, finally, a natural connection between seeing Parker
as brute, and presenting him as a reincarnation of the persecuting
Roman emperors, Nero, Caligula and Julian the Apostate. Marvell
devotes several hilarious pages to working out this analogy, which is
formally linked to the theme of brutalization by the story of Caligula's
horse, an apt metaphor for Parker the place-seeker:

> This same Caligula was he that took so great affection to Incitatus, a fleet
> and metall'd Courser, that beside a Stable of Marble, a Manger of Ivory,
> Housing-cloths of Purple, and a Poictrell of precious stones, he furnish'd
> him an house very nobly, and appointed him a family to entertain those
> who render'd visits to his Equinity and his Hinnibility ... Nay, so far
> did he carry on this humour, that 'tis said, had he not been prevented, he
> design'd to have made this race-horse Consul; as fit however for that
> Office, as his Master to be Emperor. What pity 'tis, Mr. Bayes, that you
> did not live in that fortunate age, when desert was so well rewarded and

understood, when preferments were so current! Certainly one of your
Heels and Mettle would quickly have arrived to be something more then
an Arch-Deacon.

(p. 219)

From being an emperor's horse, however, Parker grows gradually
indistinguishable from Nero in 'Savage cruelty' (p. 216), Caligula in
egomania, and Julian in mockery of the Christians. This deft application of ecclesiastical history is integrated into the formal structure
of Marvell's attack; for it serves as the subject matter or 'plot' of
'Debauchery Tolerated' and 'Persecution Recommended', two of the
six 'plays' attributed to Bayes in the overall theatrical metaphor, and
previously sketched out in the first part of *The Rehearsal Transpros'd*.

The true heart of Marvell's new profundity lies, however, in his
elaboration of the first three 'plays', the self-contradictory notions of
an 'Unlimited Magistrate', 'Public Conscience' and 'Moral Grace'.
These oxymorons were all to be found in Parker's own arguments.
To judge from Marvell's emphasis, the most dangerous of Parker's
theses, in its possible effects on the religious and political life of
England, was that an unlimited royal prerogative in ecclesiastical
matters was not only established by divine authority but actually
required for the safety of the state. As Parker himself had complained
in his *Reproof*, Marvell had initially avoided this tricky theoretical
issue, tricky, of course, because Charles II was undoubtedly paying
attention to his views; but in the new pamphlet, and the different
political circumstances of 1673, it was essential to confront it directly.
The *Declaration of Indulgence*, now withdrawn, could be recognized as
a sop to Nonconformist opinion to make more palatable Charles's
renewal of hostilities against the Protestant Dutch. The Test Act
against Catholics, passed by the Commons in reaction and suspicion,
had made an avowed Catholic of the heir presumptive, James, Duke
of York, who promptly confirmed his intentions by marrying 'the
most bigoted and francophile Catholic available',[12] the Italian Duchess of Modena. In Scotland, Lauderdale, maintaining a standing army,
was actively persecuting the Presbyterians; the Roman Catholics in
Ireland had agents at court, one of whom was discovered, as a result
of a coaching accident, to be in close contact with the Roman
Catholic Treasurer Clifford; and, perhaps as a consequence of Clifford's
resignation under the Test, rumours were circulating about the secret
clause in the Treaty of Dover whereby Charles had committed himself,
as part of his alliance with Louis XIV, to announce his own conversion, and to support his position if necessary with the assistance

of French troops. A situation which, in November 1673, drove Shaftesbury, only recently appointed Chancellor, into the Opposition, could scarcely have failed to affect Marvell; and in refuting the idea of a monarch with unlimited power over the religious life of his subjects he extended a subtle warning to Charles against any further interference in ecclesiastical matters. The issue of persecution had broadened to the point where it was possible to see a whole nation out of conformity with the religion practised at court.

Rhetorically, Marvell's refutation of Parker's central thesis is extremely subtle. His strategy is to replace his opponent's all-or-nothing approach with a set of finer distinctions, in which the sources, sanctions and uses of power are carefully separated and analysed. Similar arguments in the Cromwell poems are, perhaps deliberately, recalled. He begins, in a long elegiac passage, by reminding his audience that magistracy itself is less than an ideal institution. It 'were desirable', of course, 'that men might live in perpetual Peace, in a state of good Nature, without Law or Magistrate'; but prelapsarian society is gone for better or worse, and in its place we experience, as part of our punishment for the Fall, 'intermitting seasons of Discord, War, and publick Disturbance'. '*Nevertheless*', Marvell continues, 'it is most *certain*, that Tranquillity in Government is by all just means to be sought after' and, a moment later, 'The Power of the Magistrate does most *certainly* issue from the Divine Authority' (pp. 231–2; italics added). Without admitting any Hobbesian reasoning, some sense of causation is implicit in the placing of these arguments; the concept of divinely authorized power has already been limited by its seeming to be one of the consequences, both inevitable and unfortunate, of the Fall.

Marvell then proceeds to what he calls 'the modester Question . . . how far it is *advisable* for a Prince to exert and push the rigour of that Power which no man can deny him' (p. 233; italics added). It is in this section that he emphasizes the prudential value of clemency and moderation, going so far as to suggest that a wise patience on the ruler's part will have the effect of depoliticizing his subjects, who will out of gratitude and security themselves abrogate their constitutional rights:

> I will not say what one Prince may compass within his own time, or what a second, though surely much may be done: but it is enough if a great and durable design be accomplished in the third Life, and, supposing an hereditary succession of any three taking up still where the other left, and dealing still in that fair and tender way of management, it is

impossible but that even without reach or intention upon the Princes part, all should fall into his hand, and in so short a time the very memory or thoughts of any such thing as Publick liberty would, as it were by consent, expire and be for ever extinguish'd.

(p. 234)

This passage is in flagrant contradiction both of Marvell's private views as expressed in his letters to Popple, and of his future defence of 'Publick liberty' in the *Account of the Growth of Popery and Arbitrary Government*; it is also an ironic echo of the opening of the *First Anniversary*, where Marvell attacked the hereditary monarchs who, unlike Cromwell, fail to accomplish anything of value in a single generation, 'For one Thing never was by one King done'. In place of that 'wondrous Order and Consent' when Cromwell re-established constitutional government, anticipating the 'great Designes kept for the latter Dayes', Marvell now suggests that 'a great and durable design' to subvert the constitution might be completed, 'as it were by consent', in the reign of the third Stuart. The self-evident irony of this proposal (to anyone who had or has now access to Marvell's complete agenda) should warn us against taking literally his statement about how things happen 'in their best and proper time, without any need of our officiousness'.

In the long passage just analysed, much as in the *Horatian Ode*, seemingly insignificant parts of grammar carry a heavy conceptual load. We have moved from what 'were desirable' (the hypothetical ideal), through what is 'certain' (the harsh facts, including monarchy), to what is 'advisable' (the territory of the pragmatic and expedient). However, the argument from expediency now gives way to a more profound criterion. What is advisable in the pragmatics of power is distinguished from what is actually required of a king by the source from which his power derives. For 'as it is the Wisdom and Virtue of a Prince' to rule with moderation, 'so he hath that advantage that his safety herein is fortified by his Duty, and as being a Christian magistrate, he has the stronger obligation upon him to govern his Subjects in this Christian manner' (p. 235). Indeed, Marvell's conclusion to this argument happily unites the duties of both subject and magistrate and, translating into more acceptable terms his advice as to how 'Publick liberty' might be made obsolete, he anticipates the withering away of all laws and secular structures, not excepting monarchy itself:

[Christ] by the Gospel gave Law to Princes and Subjects, obliging all mankind to such a peaceable and gentle frame of Spirit as would be the greatest and most lasting security to Government, rendring the People tractable to Superiors, and the Magistrate not grievous in the exercise of his Dominion: And he knew very well that *without dethroning the Princes of the World at present*, yet by the constant preaching of that benevolous and amiable Doctrine . . . all opposition would be worn out, and all Princes should make place for a Christian Empire.

(p. 236) (italics added)

We find ourselves back with the millennial aspirations of the *First Anniversary*, from which have vanished all traces of prophetic timidity and shortsightedness.

This is the most important section of Marvell's advice, through Parker, to the king; but there are equally fundamental arguments addressed exclusively to the theological issues. Parker's unfitness as spokesman against the Nonconformists is proven, Marvell argues, by his failure to understand, let alone promote, the essential inwardness of Protestantism; he had even 'expounded the Fruits of the Spirit to be meer Moral virtues, and the Joy, Peace, and Faith there spoken of to be only Peaceableness, Chearfulness and Faithfulness, as if they had been no more than the three Homileticall conversable Virtues, Veritas, Comitas, and Urbanitas' (p. 265). In Parker's mind, the ceremonial differences between churches were merely a question of style, and Nonconformity was merely an irrational stubbornness. What Marvell had to do was toe a delicate line between this kind of superficiality and any overt rejection of the doctrine of things indifferent to salvation. He wished to support the position of the Nonconformists, that conscience was truly involved in their stand against the Anglican liturgy; but at the same time, in order to justify toleration, he needed to argue that ceremonial issues were not worth fighting or, more importantly, persecuting for.

In a long and carefully personalized passage, which is remarkable both for its precision and its intentional vagueness, Marvell delivered his own conclusions on the ceremonial dispute, which, he says, has drawn him in despite his own 'diffidence' about his qualifications:

Even the Church of Rome, which cannot be thought the most negligent of things that concern her interest, does not, that I know of, lay any great stress upon Rituals and Ceremonials, so men agree in Doctrine: . . . I have as much as possible disingaged my mind from all Bias and Partiality, to think how or what prudence men of so great Piety and Learning as the Guides of our Church could find out all along, it being now near an Hundred and fifty years, to press on and continue still impositions in these matters. On the Non-conformists part is plain that they have persisted in this dispute, because they have, or think they have the direct authority of Scripture on their side, and to keep themselves as remote as might be from the return of that Religion, from which they had reformed . . . But whatever design the Ecclesiastical Instruments managed, it is yet to me the greatest mysterie in the world how the Civil Magistrate could be perswaded to interess himself with all the severity of his power in a matter so unnecessary, so trvial, and so pernicious to the publick quiet. For had things been left in their own state of Indifferency, it is well known that the English Nation is generally neither so void of Understanding, Civility, Obedience, or Devotion, but that they would long ago have voluntarily closed and faln naturally into those reverent matters of Worship which would sufficiently have exprest and suited with their Religion.

(pp. 241–2)

I have cited the end of this passage before, in setting out the boundaries of Marvell's personal religious convictions. Despite his pose of 'want of capacity' or simple puzzlement, it shows Marvell moving inevitably towards the only logical conclusion – the one that Locke would fully articulate – that the magistrate should cease entirely to intervene in matters of religious belief and practice.

It is in this context that we can understand what Marvell was up to in the final section of *The Rehearsal Transpros'd*, particularly in his remarkable use of Francis Bacon's *Wise and Moderate Discourse*. He has throughout been at some pains to indicate the catholicity of his sources, to support his case that Parker's is actually the minority position by adducing authorities whom nobody could possibly accuse of Nonconformist sympathies. He cites a number of Anglican works; he cites King James I. With respect to Richard Hooker, whose authority both sides in these debates always tried to appropriate, Marvell remarked: 'it had been well that you had rather imitated the incomparable modesty and candor of Reverent Mr. Hooker in all his Writings . . . but how should you imitate him, whom . . . it seems you had never read' (pp. 303–4). No authority, however, is produced with more deliberation than Bacon, whom Marvell had threatened to quote in the first part, to refute Parker's arguments for a satirical polemic:

Nor is it worth ones while to teach him out of other Authors, and the best precedents of the kind, how he, being a Christian and a Divine, ought to have carried himself. But I cannot but remark his Insolence and how bold he makes . . . with the Memories of those great Persons there enumerated, several of whom, and particularly my Lord Verulam, I could quote to his confusion, upon a contrary and much better account.

(p. 75)

In the *Second Part*, having been challenged to make good his claims, Marvell offers several mock-anticipations of his grand denouement. A piece of folly on Parker's side about pork and Bacon has allowed him to create a form of comic suspense: 'What remains, Mr. Bayes, is to serve in your Bacon, but because I would do it to the best advantage, I shall add something else for your better and more easie digestion'; but the tone in which Bacon's *Wise and Moderate Discourse* is finally introduced is not at all flippant. Marvell's language echoes the title of the 1641 edition in its evocation of wisdom from the past:

> I the rather quote him because a wise man is as it were eternal upon earth; and he speaks so judiciously and impartially, that it seems as if these very times which we now live in had been in his present prospect.
>
> (p. 323)

So impartially, in fact, does Bacon speak that he is not to be used, like the other authorities, to bolster Marvell's case. Rather he is presented as the voice of judgement before which Marvell must plead guilty alongside his prisoner:

> Pray, Mr. Bayes let us both listen, for I assure you, before he has done, he will tell us many a wiser thing then is to be met with either in *Ecclesiastical Politie* or *Rehearsal*.
>
> (p. 323)

The passages which Marvell has selected to condemn himself as well as Parker are those in which Bacon recommended the 'virtue of Silence and Slowness to speak, commended by St. James'; in which he urged an end to the 'immodest and deformed manner of writing . . . whereby matter of Religion is handled in the stile of the Stage'; and asserted that the use of satire and mockery in religious polemic 'is a thing farre from the devout reverence of a Christian, and scant beseeming the honest regard of a sober man'. Bacon's latitudinarianism about ceremonies as things indifferent was obviously helpful to Marvell's case, as were his observations on the misuse of censorship, a point to which Marvell was to return in the *Growth of Popery and Arbitrary Government*. But the significance of Bacon's comments lay in their relevance to the problem of expression with which Marvell had been so earnestly grappling. Carefully omitting Bacon's qualified defence of 'bitter and earnest writing' when a man is inspired by genuine zeal, Marvell in effect admits his own failure to find an acceptable tone. Raillery is ultimately subject to the same criticisms as railing, not least because it may be more effective. There is,

perhaps, no viable poise 'betwixt Jest and Earnest', and the originator
of a new style of banter can only, finally, reject the whole enterprise:
'truly our sport is . . . unfit for serious Spectators. However I have
spit out your dirty Shoon' (p. 327).

## MR. SMIRKE AND THE REMARKS UPON A LATE DISINGENUOUS DISCOURSE

In the pamphlets that followed, Marvell continued his withdrawal
from satire, and moved gradually towards a style and method that
conformed more closely to the Baconian position. In the first place,
his later pamphlets present for their justification a defensive rather
than an aggressive occasion. Whereas *The Rehearsal Transpros'd* was a
piece of public execution forced upon Marvell by the negligence of
others, *Mr. Smirke: Or, The Divine in Mode* (1676) defended Herbert
Croft, Bishop of Hereford, against the only one of his three respond-
ents who answered him satirically. Similarly, Marvell's *Remarks upon
a late Disingenuous Discourse* (1678) were written in defence of John
Howe against the attack of his fellow Nonconformist, Thomas Danson.
In the case of Croft, Marvell explains how he had been drawn into
his defence by the circumstances and title under which Croft's work
appeared. Not written for publication, and intended only for circulation to Members of Parliament, Croft's pamphlet had apparently
been marketed without his consent by a 'covetous printer'. Also its
title, *The Naked Truth: Or, the True state of the Primitive Church*, along
with Croft's pseudonym, 'an Humble Moderator', sufficiently indicated
its pacific and constructive intentions, which were to look to the
agreements in belief between the different wings of the church rather
than focus on differences about vestments and ceremonies. By contrast, Francis Turner's answer to Croft was contemptuous in tone
and vicious in its recommendations. Moreover, in the case of Croft,
Marvell undoubtedly came to the rescue of someone who was in-
competent to defend himself. The preface of *The Naked Truth* presents
him as an astonishingly simple-minded person, wide open to the
charges of poor scholarship and faulty reasoning levelled against him,
a self-confessed 'weak man . . . of small ability'.

Secondly, Marvell intervened in both these later disputes on points
of theological principle. In one sense he was being more impartial
than in *The Rehearsal Transpros'd*, since *Mr. Smirke* defends an Anglican
bishop against an Anglican bishop, and his defence of John Howe
is of one Nonconformist against another. But it would be a mistake
to assume that, because his later pamphlets cannot be suspected of

alignment with any confession, the framework of his belief was weakening or, as has been suggested,[13] that he was moving under rationalist influence toward Deism. For example, in the Defence of John Howe, Marvell took issue against an uncompromising theory of predestination. Like Milton in *Paradise Lost*, he rejects the concept that Adam's Fall was itself predetermined, and that God's will directed his hand to the apple as a writing-master directs his scholar's hand. 'If the cause be not to be defended upon better terms than so', Marvell exclaims, 'what Christian but would rather wish he had never known writing master, than to subscribe to such an opinion; and that God should make an innocent creature in this manner to do a forbidden act, for which so dreadful a vengeance was to issue upon him and his posterity?'[14]

But, as his emotional response to Danson's metaphor suggests, Marvell remained deeply concerned about the act of writing itself. In *Mr. Smirke*, Marvell deftly summarizes his current theory of polemical style in any issue where the church's reputation is involved. 'The Churche's credit', he writes, 'is more interested in an ecclesiasticall drole, then in a lay chancellor':

> It is no small trust that is reposed in him to whom the bishop shall commit *omne et omnimodum suum ingenium, tam temporale quam spirituale* [absolutely all his wit, both temporal and spiritual]: and however it goes with excommunication, they should take good heed to what manner of person they delegate the keys of Laughter. It is not every man that is qualified to sustain the dignity of the Churche's jester.

All potential polemicists, therefore, should submit to a four-part qualifying examination, to determine:

> first, whether they have any sense; for without that how can any man pretend – and yet they do – to be ingenious? Then, whether they have any modesty; for without that they can only be scurrilous and impudent. Next, whether any truth; for true jests are those that do the greatest execution. And lastly, it were not amiss that they gave some account too of their Christianity; for the world has always been so uncivil as to expect something of that from the clergy, in the design and stile even of their most uncanonical writings.

> (4: 8–9)

The four principles here enunciated are in ascending order of importance. Starting with that vital classical *ingenium*, which means both intelligence and wit, the polemicist must also know how to control his wit according to the principle of modesty, which operates simultaneously in ethical and rhetorical behaviour. But even a modest wit fails if not backed up by facts, if engaged, perhaps, on a wrong cause; and, finally, the church's jesters must make it clear to their audience that they understand and indeed practise the principles of their own creed.

Similarly, in his introduction to the *Remarks*, Marvell stated that they were partially intended as an essay in 'How the unruly quill is to be managed' (4: 174). The *Remarks* are actually organized under a series of headings of 'what ought to be avoided', and so provide a negative theory of polemic. One sign that Marvell's practice has altered in accordance with his theory is that the late pamphlets show obvious strategies of depersonalization. In place of the dialogue with Parker-Bayes and the other *ad hominem* techniques of the *Rehearsal Transpros'd*, the speaker in *Mr. Smirke* deals in the third person with 'the Animadverter' or 'the Exposer'. In the *Remarks* on Danson's *Discourse* this process of depersonalization is not only extended but explained. Since the offending pamphlet appeared only under the initials T. D., implying that its author wished to remain incognito, Marvell offers to 'so far observe good manners, as to interpret them only "The Discourse," heartily wishing that there were some way of finding it guilty, without reflecting upon the Author; which I shall accordingly indeavour, that I may both preserve his, whatsoever, former reputation, and leave him a door open to ingenuity for the future' (4: 174). By the standard of this wry charity, *ad hominem* arguments are ruled out; in neither pamphlet are there any reflections upon the life of the opposing author, or upon his character, except as that is expressed in his style. It is on this issue that Marvell's wit is employed, in developing metaphors to express the 'character' both of the books he is defending and those he is defending them against.

The *Discourse*, for example, which was not satirical at all but merely pedantically technical, is personified as Parker had been, as a *miles gloriosus*, 'dreadfully accoutred and armed cap-a-pe in logic, categorical and hypothetical syllogisms, majors, minors, enthymems, antecedents, consequents, distinctions, definitions . . . terms that good Mr. Howe as a meer novice is presum'd to be unacquainted with, and so far from being able to endure the ratling of The Discourse's armour, that as those Roman legions once bragg'd, even the sweaty smell of Its armpits would be sufficient to rout him' (4: 198). More serious is a metaphor common to both *Mr. Smirke* and the *Remarks*, in which Marvell distinguishes between human and subhuman character, as expressed in language. Croft 'speaks like a man, a creature to which modesty and reason are peculiar: not like an Animadverter, that is an animal which hath nothing humane in it but a malicious grinne' (4: 22). John Howe's *Letter* is similarly, but with more justice, described as 'a manly discourse, resembling much, and expressing the humane perfection; in the harmony of language, the symmetry of parts, the strength of reason, the excellency of its end, which is so serious, that it is no defect in the similitude with man, that the Letter contains nothing in it suitable to the property of laughter' (4: 173). In this extended metaphor for style as the image of man, as man is the image of God, Marvell in effect provides the positive ideals of polemic which must replace the *Discourse*'s many faults.

However, the most important development of the later pamphlets is Marvell's discovery of a symbolic centre for the issue which he is in each case confronting, and which allows him to focus his intellectual and emotional energies with some economy. In the title of Bishop Croft's *Naked Truth* he perceived an opportunity to renovate an old Puritan trope, and make it his own credo. The personal preference for simplicity in worship which had emerged in the *Rehearsal Transpros'd* is now enlarged into a complete persona, Andreas Rivetus, whose name is both an anagram for *Res nuda veritas*, the naked truth itself, and a hint at his own 'Andrew'.

Similarly, Marvell took issue with Danson's title, and his claim to speak 'De Causa Dei':

Who would have thought that T. D. should have become the defender of the faith, or that the cause of God were so forlorn, as to be reduced to the necessity of such a champion? . . . The cause of God! Turn, I beseech you, Its whole book over, and show me anything of that decorum with which that should have been managed. What is there to be found of that gravity, humility, meekness, piety or charity requisite to so glorious a presence? (graces wherewith God usually assists those that undertake His quarrel?)

(4: 234)

The image of a false Crusader, occurring incidentally in Marvell's responses to Parker and Turner, has now become central, thanks to Danson's own presumption. It has also now become completely clear in Marvell's mind that the cause of God must not be undertaken in a militant manner, that the cross and the sword are indeed opposed symbols, and that the pen, when engaged in the service of the cross, must not be used as a sword. Even St Peter's defence of Christ, despite its personal heroism, is to be rejected, as it was by Christ himself: 'our Savior though [it was] done in His defence, rebuked him; adding, "They that take the sword, shall perish by the sword"; . . . and the taking of the pen hath seldom better success, if handled in the same manner' (4: 174).

It is now possible to see the whole process by which Marvell worked out his own response to the dilemma of the Christian polemicist. Starting with Owen's handy model and the experience of his own satires, the last lines of the *Rehearsal Transpros'd* and the opening defence of its sequel showed him growing self-conscious about the disparity between jest and earnest, when the only way to separate them was to alternate them. By the end of the *Second Part*, Marvell seemed to have rejected his own mixture of jest and earnest for a wiser and more moderate discourse, and the opening of *Mr. Smirke* offered a set of positive criteria for the church's jester. Although *Mr. Smirke* itself retained a satirical title and sometimes the tone of satire, it was noticeably more restrained, less 'literary' (and hence, alas, less readable) than either part of the *Rehearsal Transpros'd*.

Finally, in his last work, Marvell completed his defence of John Howe by urging him not to continue the argument with Danson if he really had the welfare of the church at heart: 'lest, as David, for having been a man of blood, was forbid to build the temple . . . so he, as being a man of controversie' (4: 242). A great Puritan metaphor for the construction of the new church polity and doctrine was thus transferred from the *First Anniversary* celebrating Cromwell to the pacifist prose where it more properly belonged, and Marvell himself stepped lightly out of the arena, with his sense of dignity restored: 'As for myself, I expect in this litigious age, that some or other will sue me for having trespassed thus far on theological ground: but I have this for my plea, that I stepped over on no other reason than (which any man may legally do) to hinder one divine from offering violence to another' (4: 42). The Avenger or the vigilante (and the man who twice was accused of quarrelling in Parliament) reassumes the role of benevolent and law-abiding citizen.

NOTES

1. Gilbert Burnet, *History of My Own Time*, ed. O. Airy (Oxford, 1897), 1: 467.

2. Anthony à Wood, *Athenae Oxonienses* (London, 1691), p. 620.

3. See, for example, John S. Coolidge, 'Martin Marprelate, Marvell and *Decorum Personae* as a Satirical Theme', *PMLA* 74 (1959), 526–32; Raymond Anselment, 'Satiric Strategy in Marvell's *The Rehearsal Transpros'd*', *Modern Philology* 68 (1970), 137–50; and, for a serious

political analysis, John M. Wallace, *Destiny his Choice: The Loyalism of Andrew Marvell* (Cambridge, 1969), pp. 184–207.

4. See John Harrison and Peter Laslett, *The Library of John Locke* (Oxford, 1965), Nos. 1994, 2938, 1935, 1931–3.

5. D. I. B. Smith, ed., *The Rehearsal Transpros'd and The Rehearsal Transpros'd: The Second Part* (Oxford, 1971), cites from *HMC Report* 7, p. 5l8a, Lord Anglesey's message to Roger L'Estrange that the king would not have the *Rehearsal Transpros'd* suppressed 'for Parker has done him wrong, and this man has done him right' (xxii).

6. Francis Bacon, *A Wise and Moderate Discourse* (London, 1641), pp. 7–8.

7. Anon., *A Modest Confutation* (1642), p. 18.

8. John Collins, *Farewell Sermons of some of the most Eminent of the Nonconformist Ministers* (London, 1816), p. 310.

9. O. Udall, *Perez Uzza. Or. A Serious Letter sent To Master Edm. Calamy January the 17th 1663, Touching His Sermon at Aldermanbury . . . Intimating his Close Design, and dangerous Insinuation against the Publick Peace* (London, 1663), p. 29.

10. Samuel Parker, *A Discourse of Ecclesiastical Politie, Wherein The Authority of the Civil Magistrate over the Consciences of Subjects in Matters of External Religion is Asserted; The Mischiefs and Inconveniences of Toleration are Represented, And all Pretenses Pleaded in Behalf of Liberty of Conscience are Fully Answered* (London, 1669), iii–ix.

11. *The Rehearsal Transpros'd and The Rehearsal Transpros'd: The Second Part*, ed. D. I. B. Smith (Oxford, 1971), p. 22.

12. The phrase is J. P. Kenyon's, in *The Stuarts* (Glasgow, 1958, 1970), p. 121.

13. By Legouis, *Andrew Marvell* (Oxford, 1965), pp. 206–8, 221–3.

14. Marvell, *Complete Works*, ed. A. B. Grosart (1875, repr. New York, 1966), 4: 229. All the prose works except the two parts of *The Rehearsal Transpros'd* are cited from this edition.

# Chapter 6

# The naked truth of history

This last chapter deals with the two pamphlets which, though perhaps not the most famous of Marvell's works in his lifetime, had the greatest influence thereafter: the *Short Historical Essay touching General Councils, Creeds, and Imposition in Religion* that Marvell attached to *Mr. Smirke* in 1676, and the *Account of the Growth of Popery and Arbitrary Government*, published with a false 'Amsterdam' imprint early in 1678. In both these pamphlets, Marvell developed yet another (for him) new venture, the truth-telling or illusion-shattering history of events in the past whose revelation should lead to reforms in the future. In the case of the *Essay*, Marvell anticipated the radical advice of John Locke that the civil magistrate should keep his hands off religion. In the case of the *Account*, his initiative led to the identification of a distinctive kind of history-writing, soon to be labelled 'secret history',[1] though its premise, paradoxically, was that the secrets of governments *should* be exposed if citizens were to be able to exercise their citizenship responsibly.

On 1 July 1676 Marvell wrote to his friend Sir Edward Harley describing the appearance of a number of books in the tolerationist controversy, including his own. As he sometimes did for prudential reasons (and as Locke was later to do with his *Letter concerning toleration*) he talks about it and himself in protective grammatical (third-person) disguise:

> The book said to be Marvels makes what shift it can in the world but the Author walks negligently up & down as unconcerned. The Divines of our Church say it is not in the merry part so good as the Rehearsall Transpros'd, that it runns dreggs: the Essay they confesse is writ well enough to the purpose he intended it but that was a very ill purpose . . . Dr. Turner first met it at Broom's went into a Chamber & though he were to have dined which he seldome omits nor approves of Fasting yet would not come down but read it all over in consequence. The Bishop of London has carryed it in his hand at Councill severall days, showing his friends the passages he has noted but none takes notice of them . . . I

know not what to say: Marvell, if it be he, has much staggerd me in the busnesse of the Nicene & all Councills, but had better have taken a rich Presbyterians mony that before the book came out would have bought the whole Impression to burne it. Who would write?

(Poems and Letters, 2: 345–6)

Marvell's comments to Harley convey a good deal of satisfaction about the disturbance he was causing, at court and elsewhere. He particularly enjoys the fact that Turner missed his dinner, so anxious was he to find out what *Mr. Smirke* had done to his reputation; and that Henry Compton, Bishop of London, who had himself licensed Turner's attack, was carrying his book around, trying to get his fellow councillors to pay attention to particular passages. More important, however, Marvell's letter tells us what he himself thought of as the most daring part of his project – not *Mr. Smirke* itself, but rather his gunpowder plot against the Nicene Council and the other councils that followed it.

Despite Marvell's grammatical caution here (and his pseudonym Andreas Rivetus), it was common knowledge that he was the author. On 23 May Sir Christopher Hatton had written to his brother: 'I hope Andrew Marvel will likewise be made an example for his insolence in calling Dr Turner, Chaplain to His Royal Highnesse, Chaplaine to Sr Fobling Busy, as he terms in his scurrilous satyrical answer to his Animadversions on Naked Truth'.[2] But this sideways swipe at James, Duke of York, via his chaplain Turner, who would later be rewarded with the bishopric of Ely, was perhaps the least dangerous of Marvell's accomplishments. In every sense the work was subversive; published without license, by at least three underground presses, it cost the Licenser of the Press, Sir Roger L'Estrange, a good deal of time and money in an effort to suppress it officially, as the anonymous Presbyterian Marvell mentions in his letter had tried to do unofficially. At least one of the publishers was indicted, Nathaniel Ponder, who also published the *Rehearsal Transpros'd* and the works of John Owen, and who would later become John Bunyan's publisher.

## A SHORT HISTORICAL ESSAY

In *Mr. Smirke* itself, Marvell reused some of the tactics that had worked so well with Samuel Parker in the *Rehearsal Transpros'd*; but he evidently decided that the best way to argue positively for toleration in his own day was to tell his readers a continuous (and scandalous) story;

to give his own version of the founding legends, not of Christianity itself as told in the Gospels, but of the institutionalization of the early Christian church. He planned to demythologize the very notion of orthodoxy. For this he needed to convey texture, the hidden motives and the human, all-too-human tale of how the church decided what we should all believe. His sources were the early ecclesiastical historians, Eusebius, Sozomen and Socrates Scholasticus; and instead of using the readily available translation by Meredith Hanmer of the first two – a translation made in the late Elizabethan era with a strong Protestant agenda already built in[3] – Marvell decided to retranslate, working from the Latin translation by John Christopherson, whose three-volume version of Eusebius, Sozomen and Socrates Scholasticus had been published in Louvain in 1569. Retranslating allowed him, of course, to give his own interpretation of the facts, either by editorial commentary, or merely by the words that as translator he selected. It is fair to say that the events he selected, and the way he described them, did not put the ancient history of the church in a particularly admirable light.

Here is his lead up to the convening by Constantine of the epoch-making Council of Nice, which took place in 325. The trouble begins, he suggests, with Bishop Alexander and his personal relations with his subordinates:

> This Alexander was the bishop of Alexandria, and appears to have been a pious old man, but not equally prudent, nor in Divine things of the most capable, nor in conducting the affairs of the Church, very dextrous; but he *was* the bishop . . . They were used, (Sozom. l.ii.c.16) at Alexandria to keep yearly a solemn festival to the memory of Peter, one of their former bishops, upon the same day that he suffered martyrdom; which Alexander having celebrated at the Church with publick Devotion was sitting after at home, expecting some guests to dine with him (Sozom. l.ii.c.16). As he was alone and looking towards the seaside, he saw a pretty way off the boys upon the beach, at an odd Recreation, imitating it seems, the rites of the Church and office of the bishops, and was much delighted with the sight as long as it appear'd an innocent and harmless representation: but when he observed them at last how they acted the very administration of the sacred mysteries, he was much troubled, and sending for some of the chief of his clergy, caused the boys to be taken and brought before him.

By questioning, Alexander learned that 'a lad of their play-fellows, one Athanasius, had baptized some of them that were not yet initiated in those sacred mysteries';

whereupon Alexander inquired the more accurately what the bishop of the game had said, and what he did to the boys he had baptized, what they also had answered or learned from him. At last, when Alexander perceiv'd by them that his *pawn bishop* had made all his removes right, and that the whole ecclesiastical order and rites had been duely observed in their Interlude, he, by the advice of his priests about him approved of that mock-baptism, and determined that, the boys 'being once in the simplicity of their minds dipped in the divine grace', ought not to be re-baptized . . .[4]

The point of this anecdote is not only to establish the character of Alexander as an ancestor of good-hearted but simple-minded Bishop Herbert Croft,[5] but to reveal the absurdity of the claims of bishops to monopoly over the rites of the church, if children could imitate them in play and have the rituals stand as effective. For 'this good natured old Bishop Alexander, . . . was so far from anathemising, that he did not so much as whip the boys for profanation of the Sacrament against the Discipline of the Church, but without more doing, left them, for ought I see, at liberty to regenerate as many more Lads upon the next Holy day as they thought convenient' (*Complete Works*, 4: 114). And 'pawn-bishop' was a double-edged phrase, given that the precocious child in question was Athanasius, who was about to become Alexander's protégé, and eventually to have a creed attached to his name.

The next stage of the drama consisted in the appearance of Arius, whose own ambitions for a bishopric, Marvell suggests, led him to propose his controversial notions of the Trinity, which caused such disturbance among the clergy that the early church began to take rigidly opposed positions: 'Whereas truth', remarked Marvell as commentator, 'for the most part lyes in the middle, but men ordinarily look for it in the extremities' (*Complete Works*, 4: 115). Eventually Arius was excommunicated; but the controversy continued still so hotly that the emperor Constantine felt compelled to convene the first great deliberative council of the church at Nice. Once assembled – and Marvell makes much of the fact that the bishops all got their way paid to this convention, and every comfort provided – the squabbles continued:

It seemed like an ecclesiastical cock-pit, and a man might have laid wagers either way; the two parties contending in good earnest either for the truth or for the victory, but the more unconcerned, like cunning betters, sate judiciously hedging, and so ordered their matters that which side soever prevail'd, they would be sure to be the winners. They were indeed a most venerable assembly, composed of some holy, some grave, some wise, and some of them learned persons: . . . In the mean time you may imagine that *hypostasis, persona, substantia, subsistentia, essentia, coessentialis, consubstantialis, ante saecula coaeturnus*, &c. were by so many disputants pick'd to the very bones, and those too broken afterwards to come to the marrow of divinity. And never had Constantine in his life so hard a task as to bring them to any rational results . . . And thus this first, great General Council of Nice, with which the world had gone big so long, and which look'd so big upon all Christendom, at last was brought to bed, and after a very hard labour deliver'd of *homoousios*.

(*Complete Works*, 4: 118–19)

*Homoousios*, or consubstantial (with God the Father), was the term applied to Christ by the Council, in denial of the Arian heresy that Christ was merely of like substance (*homoiousos*) – as Marvell pointed out, all that struggle over a single letter of the alphabet. In other words, Arius was defeated, and his interpretation of the Trinity declared heretical; 'and whoever held the contrary was to be punish'd by deprivation and banishment, all Arrian books to be burned, and whoever should be discover'd to conceal any of Arrius his writings, to dye for it' (*Complete Works*, 4: 119).

This, then, was the beginning of persecution in the early church, persecution not of the church by its pagan enemies, but of Christians by Christians. And then Marvell summarizes his satire's more serious message, which is presented in strikingly personal terms:

as to the whole matter of the Council of Nice, I must crave liberty to say, that from one end to the other, though the best of the kind, it seems to me to have been a pityful humane business, attended with all the ill circumstances of other worldly affairs, conducted by a spirit of ambition and contention, the first and so the greatest Œcumenical blow that by Christians was given to Christianity . . . It is not their censure of Arianism, or the declaring of their opinion in a controverted point to the best of their understanding, . . . that could have moved me to tell so long a story, or bring my self within the danger and aim of any captious Reader, speaking thus with great liberty of mind but little concern for any prejudice that I may receive, of things that are by some men idolized. But it is their imposition of a new article or Creed upon the Christian world not being contained in express words of Scripture to be believed with divine faith, under spiritual & civil penalties, contrary to the priviledges of Religion, and making a precedent follow'd & improv'd by all succeeding ages for most cruel persecutions, that only could animate me. In digging thus for a new deduction they undermined the fabrick of Christianity; to frame a particular doctrine they departed from the general rule of their Religion; and for their curiosity about an article concerning

Christ, they violated our Saviour's first institution of a Church not
subject to any addition in matters of faith, nor liable to compulsion
either in belief or in practice.

(Complete Works, 4: 122–3)

Had a creed been necessary, Marvell continued dryly, it seems likely
that either Christ himself, or his Apostles when they received the gift
of tongues, or St. Paul when he was received up into heaven and
heard unspeakable things, would have seen fit to provide it. Calling
the new creed 'a gibbrish of their imposing', and insisting on the
necessity and adequacy of the Scriptures, Marvell established his
radical principle:

> it becomes every man to be able to give a reason and account of his
> faith, and to be ready to do it, without officiously gratifying those who
> demand it onely to take advantage: and the more Christians can agree in
> one confession of faith the better. But that we should believe ever the
> more for a Creed it cannot be expected. In those days when Creeds
> were most plenty and in fashion, and every one had them at their finger
> ends, 'twas the Bible that brought in the Reformation.

Once again, he could not help mixing gravity with levity, mocking
those who could easily assimilate a creed for the sake of a benefice:

> 'Tis true, a man would not stick to take two or three Creeds for a need,
> rather then want a living, and if a man have not a good swallow, 'tis but
> wrapping them up in a Liturgy, like a wafer, and the whole dose will go
> down currently; especially if he wink at the same time and give his
> 'assent and consent' without ever looking on them.

'But without jesting, for the matter is too serious', he continued
with his *own* credo, which would also become that of John Locke
and the American Constitution:

> Every man is bound to 'work out his own salvation with fear and
> trembling', [Philip.ii.12.] – and therefore to use all helps possible for his
> best satisfaction; hearing, conferring, reading, praying for the assistance of
> God's Spirit; but when he hath done this, he is his own expositor, his
> own both minister and people, bishop and diocess, his own Council; and
> his conscience excusing or condemning him, accordingly he escapes or
> incurs his own internal anathema.

(Complete Works, 4: 124–5)

That is to say – and coming from a man who spent nearly twenty
years of his life as a Member of Parliament for Hull, this was an

important distinction – there can never be representative government in spiritual matters:

> No, a good Christian will not, cannot, atturn and indenture his con-
> science over, to be represented by others. It is not as in secular matters,
> where the States of a kingdom are deputed by their fellow subjects to
> transact for them.
>
> (*Complete Works*, 4: 126–7)

By now, although I have been doing little more than selectively
quoting Marvell, who in turn was selectively and mischievously
quoting and annotating Eusebius and Socrates Scholasticus, we can
see why the *Essay* was an extremely dangerous book. First, Marvell
had gone considerably beyond the early reformers, Luther and Calvin,
who used the authority of the Council of Nice, 'the most sacred of
all' councils, as ammunition against papal claims to control over
church doctrine. Second, in this pamphlet, even more clearly than in
the *Rehearsal Transpros'd*, Marvell reveals himself to be leaning towards,
growing into, an extreme Protestant or Miltonic principle of self-
determination in religion, that self-determination to be based exclusively on individual readings of the Scriptures, not on the say-so of
either church or state. To take that position in Restoration England
was to be a Nonconformist; and Nonconformists were, of course,
forbidden to hold public office.

But third, and most dangerous, Marvell traced the history of religious
persecution back to its origins, and laid the blame for it not on the
Roman emperors, but specifically on the early Christian bishops. In
fact, Marvell reversed the verdict of ecclesiastical history on Constantine the Great, who was virtually sanctified for his care of the
church. Although he imports plenty of compliments to Constantine,
such as would transfer quite nicely into compliments to Charles II, he
makes it clear that benevolence towards the higher clergy had, and
still has, the opposite effect from what was intended. For the warm
summer provided by Constantine, after the 'long and sharp winter
under Dioclesian', produced a pestilence. 'It show'd itself first in
ambition, then in contention, next in imposition, and after these
symptoms, broke out at last like a plague-sore, in open persecution'
(*Complete Works*, 4: 104). When Constantine not only 'restored [what]
had been all confiscate under Dioclesian, but was every day adding
some new possession, priviledge, or honor, a bishoprick became very
desirable, and was not only "a good work," [I Timothy iii.1], but a
good thing' (*Complete Works*, 4: 105). And, he continued:

the arts by which Ambition climbs, are calumny, dissimulation, cruelty, bribery, adulation, all applyed in their proper places and seasons . . . They cast such crimes at one another, that a man would scarse think he were reading a history of bishops, but a legend of divels: and each took such care to blacken his adversary, that he regarded not how he smutted himself thereby and his own order, to the laughter or horror of the by-standers.

(*Complete Works*, 4: 105–6)

Needless to say, their successors were all too visible in the Anglican bishops or would-be bishops of the Restoration church, and Turner's mud-slinging at Bishop Herbert Croft, not to mention his subsequent promotion to a bishopric of his own, would make Marvell's topical point with painful exactitude.

But at least the early church had been concerned with doctrine, whereas the Restoration church was all in a dither about ceremonies, which, Marvell adds as he draws towards his peroration, 'are of much inferior consideration: faith being necessary, but ceremonies dispensable' (*Complete Works*, 4: 155). So Marvell ends with a set of positive recommendations to the higher clergy of his own day:

that they will inspect their Clergy, and cause many things to be corrected, which are far more ruinous in the consequence than the dispensing with a surplice; . . . that before they admit men to subscribe [to] the Thirty-nine Articles for a benefice, they try whether they know the[ir] meaning. That they would much recommend to them the reading of the Bible. '*Tis a very good book*, and if a man read it carefully, will make him much wiser . . . That they do not come into the pulpit too full of fustian or logick. A good life is a clergyman's best syllogism, and the quaintest oratory; and 'till they outlive 'm they will never get the better of the fanaticks.

(*Complete Works*, 4: 157–8; italics added)

Thus 'a very good book' is set demurely against the 'very good thing' of a bishopric, as indeed its opposite pole in ethical and ontological terms, however alike the simple phrases seem. And Turner and his ilk are requested to 'have some reverence at least for *The Naked Truth* of History, which either in their own times will meet them, or in the next age overtake them' (*Complete Works*, 4: 156).

The closing gestures of the *Essay* are particularly shrewd, and very characteristic. Once again Marvell invokes the authority of Richard Hooker's *Laws of Ecclesiastical Polity*, citing Hooker's pacific hope, in the preface to that work, that 'The time will come when three words, uttered with charity and meekness, shall receive a far more blessed reward, then three thousand volumes written with disdainful sharpness of wit'. But his last words were these: 'And upon this condition, "let my book also" (yea, myself, if it were needful) "be burnt by the hand of the" Animadverter' (*Complete Works*, 4: 160). Thus a genuine threat to himself, which the publication history of the *Essay* evinces, is turned into a self-sacrificial gesture, one that imagines Marvell as a late victim in the chronicle of persecution he has himself reissued.

As for the history of Marvell's *Essay*, it floated free of *Mr. Smirke*, and achieved its own distinctive set of audiences. New editions of it appeared in 1680 (a year *before* the posthumous edition of his *Miscellaneous Poems*); in 1687, the year before the Glorious Revolution, as one of the first publications of the Whig publisher Richard Baldwin; in 1703, in an intelligently corrected text almost certainly generated by the attempts of the Earl of Nottingham and his High Church faction to pass the Occasional Conformity Bill against the Dissenters; and in 1709, as part of a collection by William Stephens entitled *An Account of the Growth of Deism in England*, which probably relates to the furore generated by the High Churchman Henry Sacheverell, who on 5 November of that year, Gunpowder Plot day, preached an inflammatory sermon attacking the Dissenters and all the forms of partial toleration that had been introduced in the Williamite settlement.

## AN ACCOUNT OF THE GROWTH OF POPERY AND ARBITRARY GOVERNMENT

A year after the appearance of *Mr. Smirke* and the *Essay*, which had caused such a flurry at court and in the Licenser's office, Marvell perceived the opportunity and the necessity for turning his newly developed skills as a historian back to the political scene. The country was now embroiled in the Third Dutch War, and the stakes had risen considerably since the Second. As compared with the military incompetence, the lack of proper Intelligence, the personally motivated misconduct of the mid 1660s, the country now faced, Marvell believed, a well-organized, highly coordinated threat to its most cherished institutions, in both church and state; and in place of the isolated targets, the individually venal office holders, whom the 'Painter' poems had held up for recognition and hopefully for removal, there was now a powerful group of unknown size, with a coherent strategy of muzzling both press and Parliament, of destroying history as they gained control over its media. What was needed, therefore, was not satirical attack, the weapon of minority opinion, but a style and genre that could be readily identified with the constitutional principles and public institutions that were now at stake. The pamphlet begins with a frightful, uncompromising warning:

> There has been now for divers years a design been carried on to change the lawful Government of England into an absolute Tyranny, and to convert the established Protestant Religion into downright Popery.[6]

And in several strongly worded pages, he proceeded, first, to define the English constitution and Established church in ideal terms, and then to execrate the papacy; pausing to deliver an extremely back-handed compliment to James, Duke of York, for his honesty in revealing his Catholicism under the pressure of the Test Act.

As in his earlier pamphlets, Marvell then laid out plainly the procedures he intends to use in bringing this conspiracy to public notice:

> And now, should I enter into a particular retail of all former and latter transactions, relating to this affair, there would be sufficent for a just volume of History. But my intention is only to write a naked narrative of some of the most considerable passages in the meeting of Parliament the 15th of February 1676: such as have come to my notice, which may serve for matter to some stronger pen, and to such as have more leisure and further opportunity to discover and communicate to the publick . . . Yet, that I may not be too abrupt, and leave the reader wholly destitute of a thread to guide himself by thorow so intriguing a labyrinth; I shall summarily, as short as so copious and redundant a matter will admit, deduce the order of affairs both at home and abroad, as it led into this Session.
>
> (*Complete Works*, 4: 263–4)

Marvell's proposal, then, is to identify himself with historiography, but within certain limitations. His 'naked narrative' may be compared with the 'Naked Truth of History' invoked in his defense of Bishop Croft; but instead of 'the Historian' featured in the *Essay*, the general term for his ecclesiastical sources, the author of the *Account* is more modestly defined. He is merely a 'relator' (we would call him a reporter) of events which have come to his own 'notice', and par-ticularly of the parliamentary session which followed the Long Pro-rogation. The relator is needed to collect and preserve basic records, especially at a time when large amounts of public documentation were disappearing into the fire; but his work is seen as preparatory to a complete or 'just volume of History', to be undertaken in the future by 'some stronger pen'.

These aspects of historical method and stance reappear in the *Account*'s closing paragraphs. Having brought his narrative further than proposed, to include the third occasion on which the House of Commons was illegally adjourned without its own consent, Marvell concludes it by emphasizing the sincerity and veracity of his procedure:

> Thus far hath the conspiracy against our Religion and Government been laid open, which if true, it was more than time that it should be discovered, but if anything therein have been falsely suggested, the disproving of it in any particular will be a courtesie both to the publick and to the relator; who would be glad to have the world convinced of the contrary, though to the prejudice of his own reputation.
>
> (*Complete Works*, 4: 411)

So impersonal has he managed to be, in fact, that he expects to be reproached for obscuring the issue by those who actively oppose the Government. 'Some will expect, that the very persons should have been named; whereas he only gives evidence to the fact, and leaves the malefactors to those who have the power of inquiry. It was his design indeed to give information, but not to turn informer' (*Complete Works*, 4: 413). This provision of anonymity, not only for himself but for those 'to whom he hath only a publick enmity, no private animosity', is, of course, partly a fiction, since in most cases the conspirators could be identified by their offices; but as a fiction it is a more serious version of the notion that Thomas Danson's *Discourse* had written itself and it appears to proceed from the same generous motives. Marvell's offer to Danson to 'preserve his, whatever, former reputation, and leave him a door open to ingenuity in the future' (*Complete Works*, 4: 174), exactly corresponds to his present hope that the conspirators 'might have the privilege of statesmen, to repent at the last hour, and by one signal action to expiate all their former misdemeanours'. If they should fail to do so, and if others insist on justice, the relator has given adequate directions for their discovery; and 'if any one delight in the chase, he is an ill woodman that knows not ... the beast by the proportion of his excrement' (*Complete Works*, 4: 413). The metaphor of the satiric hunt, momentarily recalling those of the *Rehearsal Transpros'd*, underlines by its very unexpectedness that hitherto Marvell had been avoiding that brutalizing exercise.

Nevertheless, Marvell fully expects the *Account* to be treated like the 'late printed book' described in a letter to Hull in November 1675. The Lords themselves 'voted it a Libell: and to be burnt by the hands of the Hangman & to inquire out the Printer and Author' (*Complete Works*, 2: 172). Only in a perverse society, Marvell asserts, could books like these, written in the interest of open public discussion, be suppressed as libellous. In reality, it is the tyrants in the Privy Council who are 'the living libels against the government'. The *Account* should be recognized as a statement of loyalty, 'written with no other intent than of meer fidelity and service to his Majesty, and God forbid that it should have any other effect, than that "the mouth of all iniquity and flatterers may be stopped", and that his Majesty, having discerned the disease, may with his healing touch apply the remedy'. The *Account* thus concludes with the same formula of advice-to-the-king, the same fiction of the king's personal immunity from criticism, that had redirected the Dutch War satires toward constructive thinking; 'for so far is the relator himself from any sinister surmise of his Majesty . . . that he acknowledges, if it were fit for Caesar's wife to be free, much more is Caesar himself from all crime and suspicion' (*Complete Works*, 4: 414).

The *Account*, then, is offered to the public as disinterested documentary history. What Marvell claims to have done, however, and what he has actually done are not the same. This becomes evident even in the opening pages of the pamphlet, where Marvell sets out to define the institutions endangered by the conspiracy. Beginning with the threat to the state, he describes the English constitution in a long passage whose importance depends not only on its statements but also on its syntax. Unlike less fortunate nations who suffer from arbitrary monarchies, Marvell explains:

> here the subjects retain their proportion in the Legislature; the very meanest commoner of England is represented in Parliament, and is a party to those laws by which the Prince is sworn to govern himself and his people. *No money* is to be levied but by the common consent. *No man* is for life, limb, goods, or liberty, at the Soveraign's discretion: but we have the same right (modestly understood) in our propriety that the prince hath in his regality . . . His very Prerogative is *no more* than what the Law hath determined. His Broad Seal, which is the legitimate stamp of his pleasure, yet is *no longer* currant, than upon the trial it is found to be legal. He *cannot* commit any person by his particular warrant. He *cannot* himself be witness in any cause: the balance of publick justice being so delicate, that not the hand only but even the breath of the Prince would turn the scale. *Nothing* is left to the King's will, but all is subjected to his authority; by which means *it follows that he can do no wrong*; nor can he receive wrong; and a King of England keeping to these measures, may without arrogance, be said to remain the onely intelligent Ruler over a rational People.
>
> (*Complete Works*, 4: 248–9; italics added)

One can pause here, in the middle of Marvell's definition, because the rhetoric allows it, and note the following points. Firstly, that if Marvell intends to provide an orthodox description of the balance of powers in the mixed state, he has not started in the orthodox manner, by defining the scope of the king's prerogative, and then its limitations. Rather, he has begun with what the king may not and cannot do to his subjects, in an astonishing series of negative propositions which must have given Charles, if he read them, rather a start. Secondly, there is no mention of the House of Lords in the balance of power. The Commons' jealously guarded sole right over financial legislation, and the individual's rights of liberty and property, are stated and restated; but nothing is said of the judiciary powers vested in the Lords, which had recently been so sadly abused. And the effect of this omission is fortified by the sense of verbal balance between two, not three, powers, a highly serious use of alliteration and verbal balance. England has an 'intelligent Ruler' matched by a 'rational People', an exact equation of 'his regality' and 'our propriety'. Roger L'Estrange, who focused much of his attack on what he called *The Growth of Knavery* on Marvell's opening statements, was not deaf to the implications of this rhetoric. The balance between regality and propriety carried with it, he warned, 'an Innuendo, that the King may as well Forfeit his Crown, as the Subject his Free-hold'.[7] The result is an eloquent definition of the constitutional limits upon monarchy which goes far beyond the corresponding passage in the *Rehearsal Transpros'd*, where religious obligation alone was in question. The statement of the king's immunity from error and its repercussions is consistent with the previous negations: 'by which means it follows that he can do no wrong; nor can he receive wrong'. A ruler whose hands are tied cannot be blamed for arbitrary government. L'Estrange's response reveals Marvell's strategy with considerable acuteness: 'Let us suppose that this Charge of a Popish, and Arbitrary Design, does neither Intend nor Reflect any Imputation upon his Majesty; . . . It is yet a worse Libel Another Way . . . For he employs his Utmost Skill to represent his Majesty only Passive in all his Administrations' (L'Estrange, *An Account*, pp. 43–4).

In the second half of his statement, Marvell proceeds to define what remains to the king after these restrictions have been understood:

In recompense therefore, his person is most sacred and inviolable; and whatsoever excesses are committed against so high a trust . . . his ministers only are accountable for all, and must answer it at their perils. He hath a vast revenue constantly arising from the hearth of the Householder, the sweat of the Labourer, the rent of the Farmer, the industry of the

Merchant, and consequently out of the estate of the Gentleman: a large
competence to defray the ordinary expense of the Crown, and maintain
its lustre. And if any extraordinary occasion happen, or be but with any
probable decency pretended, the whole Land at whatsoever season of
the year does yield him a plentiful harvest . . . He is the fountain of all
honours, and has moreover the distribution of so many profitable offices
of the Household, of the Revenue, of State, of Law, of Religion, of the
Navy and (since his present Majestie's time) of the Army, that it seems as
if the Nation could scarce furnish honest men enow to supply all those
imployments . . . In short, there is nothing that comes nearer in Government to the Divine Perfection, than where the Monarch, as with us,
injoys a capacity of doing all the good imaginable to mankind, under a
disability to all that is evil.

(*Complete Works*, 4: 248–50)

If this description of the prerogative were to be read as acceptable
loyalism, it could only have been by some predisposition in the
audience. The *effect* of loyalty is certainly created, but with magnificent imprecision, by the use of metaphor and myth rather than legal
statement. The king's person is 'most sacred and inviolable', although
(as L'Estrange observed) Charles I had discovered the contrary. The
controversial Supply becomes a 'plentiful harvest' yielded by person-
ifications of the classes or estates. His right of appointing officers,
which was in fact balanced by Parliament's right of impeachment, is
the 'fountain of all honours'; and political idealism acquires in the
last lines a tone not unworthy of James I, who was addicted to the
analogy between kingship and the rule of God Himself. If one looks
more closely, even these abstractions become less reassuring. Nothing is said of that area of prerogative, the king's right of making war
and peace and forming alliances, which was the cause of the present
governmental stalemate. The sense of a grateful country yielding up
extra revenues for some 'extraordinary occasion', such as the war
against the Dutch, is qualified by the possibility that such occasions
might be only 'pretended'. Not long afterwards, Marvell would speak
to the 'pretended causes' of that war (*Complete Works*, 4: 282). Even
stronger is the irony informing the king's right of appointment, since
'it seems as if the Nation could scarce furnish honest men enow' to
fill all the positions he has to bestow. As Marvell was shortly to
accuse the Commons of widespread conflict of interest, approxi-
mately one-third of its members holding one of those 'profitable'
offices, his statement is patently a thinly disguised reproach.

The inference of irony here is in fact confirmed in a letter Marvell
wrote to 'a Friend in Persia' in August 1671, which describes how

'the King having, upon Pretence of the great Preparations of his Neighbours, demanded three hundred thousand Pounds for his Navy, (tho in Conclusion he hath not set out any,) . . . our House gave several Bills . . . all Men foreseeing that what was given would not be applyed to discharge the Debts, which I hear are at this Day risen to four Millions, but diverted as formerly'. The same letter explains the Commons' weakness, its agreement to the pretence, in terms of multiple bribes: 'such was the Number of the constant Courtiers, increased by the Apostate Patriots, who were bought off, for that Turn, some at six, others ten, one at fifteen, thousand Pounds in Mony, besides what offices, Lands, and Reversions, to others, that it is a Mercy they gave not away the whole Land, and Liberty, of England' (*Complete Works*, 2: 324–5).

Even without such guides to its interpretation, Marvell's constitutional statement is significantly different from the political orthodoxy. The document that best expressed the Stuart constitution was probably Charles I's answer, in June 1642, to the Nineteen Propositions of Parliament, which, even allowing for the Crown's point of view, provided a far more substantial account of the Crown's prerogative at a moment when it was about to be denied in practice.[8] In 1677, Charles's statement was quoted in full by the author of *A Second Pacquet of Advices . . . to the men of Shaftsbury*, on the grounds that 'a better Description of Kingly and Parliamentary Interest of Government cannot be had than what was described by the Pen of his Majesties Royal Father' (pp. 63–5). In Charles's speech, which really was a definition of a mixed state, too much so indeed for some of his advisers, including Clarendon, the division of power between king, Lords and Commons is stated without any equivocation. The actual government of the state, that is, 'power of treaties of war and peace, of making peers, of choosing officers and councillors for state, judges for laws, commanders for forts and castles, giving commissions for raising men, to make war abroad, or to prevent and provide against invasions and insurrections at home, benefit of confiscations, power of pardoning, and some more of the like kind are placed in the King'. By contrast, the House of Commons, 'an excellent convener of liberty, but never intended for any share in government, or the choosing of them that govern', is legally entitled to nothing more than a watchdog function. In order 'that the prince may not make use of this high and perpetual power to the hurt of those for whose good he hath it, and make use of the name of publick necessity for the gain of his private favourites and followers', the Commons is 'solely entrusted' with the powers of impeachment and of initiating financial legislation. Finally, the judicatory powers of the Lords are explicitly defined as the mediatorial factor, 'an excellent screen and bank between the prince and people, to assist each against any encroachment by the other, and by just judgments to preserve that law which ought to be the rule of every one of the three'. The total effect of Charles's speech was of actual, rather than merely rhetorical, balance. Beside it Marvell's statement is revealed as an ingenious challenge to the theory of the mixed state, at least as it is currently vulnerable to absolute government in disguise.

Marvell withholds from the definition of the Restoration State the sanction of his earlier metaphors. We do not find the images of music and building with which he had dignified Cromwell's far less balanced Instrument of Government; the king is no Amphion of constructive harmony; and we miss the positive sense of design, of workmanship and cooperation, with which Marvell had been able to describe a parliament of which he had no personal experience. In the *First Anniversary*, despite the 'resistance of opposed Minds', 'the most Equal still sustein the Height, / And they as Pillars keep the Work upright'. In the *Account*, the only building to be found is the result of our 'hacking and hewing one another, to frame an irregular figure of political incongruity' (*Complete Works*, 4: 281).

After these preliminary gestures, Marvell turned to his history of the 1677 session of Parliament and what led up to it; a tale which begins with the Second Dutch War, the signing of the Triple League between England, the United Provinces and Sweden, and the machinations of Charles II and Louis XIV to secretly undermine that alliance. The Pope's role as the focus of satirical invective is occasionally taken over by Louis XIV, whose combination of spiritual presumption and political ambition were at this point in history far more directly responsible for the 'growth of popery' in England. Marvell's characterization of Louis harks back to that of Samuel Parker, whose dangerous crusading instincts had been mocked by association with French romances. When Louis declared war on the Netherlands in 1672, giving no other reason than that the Dutch had caused a 'diminution of his glory', Marvell's question about the style of his declaration characteristically stands for bigger things: 'Was ever, in any age or nation of the world, the sword drawn upon no better allegation? a stile so far from being "Most Christian," that nothing but some vain French romance can parallel or justify the expression' (*Complete Works*, 4: 285). Similarly, Marvell claims, it was the sinister romance between Louis and Charles's ministers that best explained the Long Prorogation, from 22 November 1675 to 15 February

1677. Although it was supposedly caused by the quarrel between the
Lords and Commons over the Shirley-Fagg case, the silencing of
Parliament for so long a period allowed the French more than a clear
year to harass English ships, while being supplied with English soldiers
and ammunition. When Parliament finally met:

> that very same day the French king appointed his march for Flanders. It
> seemed that his motions were in just cadence, and that, as in a grand
> balet, he kept time with those that were tuned here to his measure. And
> he thought it a becoming gallantry to take the rest of Flanders our
> natural out-work, in the very face of the King of England and his *petites*
> *maisons* of Parliament.
>
> (*Complete Works*, 4: 319)

International conspiracy was all the more alarming for being represented as French choreography.

In contrast to this rococo villainy, the *Account* produced an ideal
of true political heroism. Since the death of Cromwell, Marvell had
found himself short of major heroes, and had had to make the best of
General Monck's slightly absurd adventures, the sacrificial gesture of
Archibald Douglas, and the scarcely disinterested victory of the Country party over the Excise. However, in the 1670s the question of
courage became associated in his mind with resistance to royal, ministerial, or clerical despotism. He admired and wrote Latin poems
about the daring of Colonel Thomas Blood, that 'most bold, and yet
sober, Fellow' (*Poems and Letters*, 2: 326) who, as a political protest,
had tried to seize the crown from the Tower, and that of James
Mitchell, who, in re-enactment of C. Mutius Scaevola's Roman
heroism, had made an attempt on the life of a tyrannical Scottish
bishop.[9] When Charles took the unprecedented step of attending
sessions of the House of Lords, thereby inhibiting the freedom of
debate, Marvell recognized the courage of those who spoke out notwithstanding: 'The Lord Lucas made a fervent bold Speech against
our Prodigality in giving, and the weak Looseness of the Government,
the King being present . . . But all this had little Encouragement, not
being seconded' (*Poems and Letters*, 2: 322–3). It was characteristic of
the general repression that Lucas' speech, delivered in February 1671,
was voted by the Lords to be libellous, and was publicly burnt by the
hangman. 'I take the last Quarrel betwixt us and the Lords', added
Marvell, 'to be as the Ashes of that Speech'. It is the ashes of burned
books and speeches which become, as we shall see, a symbol of the
irrepressibility of honest civic rhetoric, and hence of the inevitable
failure of political censorship.

The issue on which the heroic standard was now erected was the proposal of a new Test Oath to be administered to all Members of Parliament. In April 1675 Marvell had supplied his constituents with a text of the proposed oath, which differed from previous loyalty oaths by concluding 'And I do sweare that I will not at any time indevour the alteration of Government either in Church or State' (*Poems and Letters*, 2: 148–9). It was thus a blatant attempt to eradicate all political opposition or pressure for reform, and in a letter to Popple in July of the same year Marvell described it as a device of 'their Episcopal Cavalier Party' for getting rid of Parliament if it 'proved refractory' (*Poems and Letters*, 2: 341). In defiance, four members of the House of Lords – Shaftesbury, Buckingham, Salisbury and Wharton – proposed that the effect of the Long Prorogation was to render this session illegal, and Parliament therefore dissolved. This was Marvell's opportunity to define his new kind of civic heroism:

> those Lords, that were against this oath, being assured of their own loyalty and merit, stood up now for the English liberties with the same genius, virtue and courage, that their noble ancestors had formerly defended the great Charter of England, but with so much greater commendation, in that they had here a fairer field, and *a more civil way of decision*: they fought it out under all the disadvantages imaginable: they were overlaid by numbers: the noise of the House, like the wind, was against them, and if not the sun, the fire-side was always in their faces; nor being so few, could they, as their adversaries, withdraw to refresh themselves in a whole day's ingagement: yet never was there a clearer demonstration how dull a thing is humane eloquence, and greatness how little, when the *bright truth* discovers all things in their proper colours and dimensions, and shining, shoots its beams thorow all their fallacies.
>
> (*Complete Works*, 4: 309; italics added)

What we might recognize here is the unabashedly heroic resonance (and indeed some of the details) of Milton's *Areopagitica: A Speech for the Liberty of Unlicensed Printing*, the greatest (and likeliest) precedent in any discussion of freedom of opinion. Milton himself had described political debate as military action, and the activities of the censors as an offence against the chivalric code:

> When a man hath . . . drawn forth his reasons as it were a battell raung'd, scatter'd and defeated all objections in his way, calls out his adversary into the plain, offers him the advantage of wind and sun, if he please; only that he may try the matter by dint of argument, for his opponents then to sculk, to lay ambushments, to keep a narrow bridge of licencing where the challenger should passe, though it be valour

anough in shouldiership [sic], is but weaknes and cowardise in the wars of Truth.[10]

This interpretation of the debate on the Test, as a crucial battle in the defence of Truth against political repression, is confirmed by another allusion that may also connect Marvell's pamphlet with Milton's. When Marvell points out that the official records of the Lords' proceedings were burned in the next session by order of the House, he adds a significant phrase: 'but the sparks of it will eternally fly in their adversaries faces'. In so doing he is remembering one of Francis Bacon's own comments on censorship, in the *Wise and Moderate Discourse*, which Milton had himself cited in *Areopagitica* (*Prose Works*, 2: 542). 'Indeed', Bacon had warned, 'we ever see it falleth out, that the forbidden writing is thought to be a certaine Sparke of truth that flieth up in the faces of them that seeke to choke and tread it out; whereas a booke authorized, is thought to bee but *temporis voces*, the language of the time.'[11]

His standards of conduct and constitutional principles well established, Marvell could finally turn to his announced subject, the session of Parliament which followed the Long Prorogation, and to his new role as parliamentary reporter. His position was that both Houses should have declared the session illegal and forced Charles to call a new election. In a letter to Edward Thompson prior to the session, he spoke of attempts 'to make the Parliament men believe . . . they are dissolved by this Long Prorogation and that therefore it will be unsafe for them to sit. But it seems to be a Cavill and if the Parliament will not believe them they may spare their turning for Statutes and Precedents' (*Poems and Letters*, 2: 350). But apart from statutes and precedents, a common theme of Shaftesbury's pamphlets in 1675 and Buckingham's speech in 1676 was that the House of Commons had outlived its usefulness as a representative body. Marvell develops this theme into a major 'digression' on the weakness and corruption of the House. Its longevity is seen as a long-term strategy, by which the Government gradually accumulated men it could count on: 'Where the cards are so well known, they are only fit for a cheat, and no fair gamester but would throw them under the table' (*Complete Works*, 4: 331). Consciousness of its own guilt has deprived the Commons of one of its most important defences, the right of impeachment, and even those who were not actually on the king's payroll had succumbed to another, more insidious, kind of self-interest, the unwillingness of men who hold a comfortable seat to hazard it in an election.

On 1 July 1676 Marvell had described to Sir Edward Harley the arrest of one Francis Jenks for calling in public for 'a new Parliament as the Right and Remedy of the Nation', and on 17 July he reported to Popple that 'Mr. Jinks will not petition the king . . . but keeps his prison as his fort . . . & perhaps may be prisoner till michaelmas terme, noe matter he is a single brave fellow' (*Poems and Letters*, 2: 345, 348). The Commons, in contrast, when reassembled in February 1677, did nothing but haggle about procedure. The *Account* does not mention the particular demurral of Richard Temple, one of Marvell's heroes from the *Last Instructions* and now traitor to the Country party, who objected: 'Because the legality of our meeting is questioned by libels without doors, must we therefore make it a question within doors';[12] nor that on 21 February Marvell had acted as teller for the Noes against Temple's chairmanship of the Supply debate (*JHC*, 9: 386), which in taking place at all was the ultimate proof of the Commons' venality. In the Lords, however, the four main speakers, refusing to apologize for their charge that the session was illegal and the Constitution in danger, were sent to the Tower, thereby justifying Buckingham's warning that, if things continued in this manner, kings of England might 'also take away any man's estate when they please, and deprive every one of his liberty, or life, as they please'.[13] And so, Marvell comments:

> a prorogation without precedent was to be warranted by an imprisonment without example. A sad instance! . . . for nothing but Parliament can destroy Parliament. If a House shall once be felon of itself and stop its own breath, taking away that liberty of speech, which the King verbally, and of course, allows them . . . to what purpose is it coming thither?
> (*Complete Works*, 4: 322)

Marvell subsequently rebuked the Commons for failing to resent 'that breach upon the whole Parliament', as he chose to consider the imprisonment of the four peers, but in his own capacity as a Member of Parliament he had apparently adopted a similar discretion. Reporting to his constituents on the opening of the session, he remarked: 'no mention appears in the Journall of any Question of the validity of the Prorogation which tendernesse of the House you will also do well to imitate, by not propagating what I confide to you about it' (*Poems and Letters*, 2: 179). And, if we look back at Chapter 1, there is evidence that Marvell could not and did not include himself among the few good men remaining in the Commons, the 'handful of salt' (*Complete Works*, 4: 329) that he exempted from his general condemnation.

Both Houses, then, had been complicit in their own silencing, and in the repression of individual protest outside Parliament. Nothing, however, justified the extraordinary humiliation suffered by the Commons in 1677, to which Marvell devoted the last part of his pamphlet. From 5 March onwards they had been debating and formulating requests to Charles to take unequivocal action against France, and to ally with the United Provinces against the Spanish Netherlands. These debates, which are reported with remarkable fullness, reveal the care with which the addresses to the king were worded, and that the Members were fully cognizant of the delicate constitutional issue. The court party opposed the addresses as an invasion on the foreign policy prerogative; the Opposition replied:

> the prerogative is not all intrench't upon; we do not, nor do pretend to treat or make alliances; we only offer our advice about them, and leave it with the King . . . It is not more than other persons may do to the King, or doubtless the privy council may advise him in this particular, and why not his great council?
>
> (*Complete Works*, 4: 396–97)

The *Account* suddenly begins to sound like the idealizing 'advices' which concluded the Dutch War satires and begged for a more candid relationship between the king and his public advisers: 'We hope his Majesty will declare himself in earnest, and we are in earnest; having his Majestie's heart with us, let his hand rot off that is not stretcht out for this affair; we will not stick at this or that sum or thing, but we will go with his Majesty to all extremities' (*Complete Works*, 4: 367). At the same time Marvell has to admit, rather grudgingly, that in these debates the Commons has partially recovered its lost dignity. The 'little, but solid, and unbiassed party' (*Complete Works*, 4: 329), which he had formerly exempted from his general contempt, can now flourish in a context in which the self-interest of the majority happens to coincide with the interests of the nation.

Charles's response to this unexpected firmness was not in the least conciliatory. On 28 May the Commons received a sharp chastisement for their interference. The insult was completed by the Speaker in adjourning the House immediately without its own consent, an insult repeated on 16 July and again on 3 December. One further adjournment occurred after Marvell had published his pamphlet, but the others were primary evidence for his thesis. On 16 July, we are told, the Speaker made his announcement and 'in the same moment stamps down on the floor, and went forth (trampling upon, and

treading underfoot, I had almost said, the privileges and usage of
Parliament, but however) without shewing that decent respect which
is due to a multitude in order, and to whom he was a menial servant'
(*Complete Works*, 4: 408). The parenthesis and the withdrawn hyperbole are far more effective in suggesting the real meaning of such
events than any plain assertion, and shortly afterward Marvell confirms both the thesis and the structure of his pamphlet with ironical
finesse: 'if neither one prorogation, against all the laws in being, nor
three vitious adjournments, against all precedents, can dissolve them,
this Parliament is then immortal' (*Complete Works*, 4: 410). But perhaps the last straw was the management of the media in the world
outside. After the king's rebuke to them for interfering in foreign
policy,

> that which more amazed them afterwards was, that while none of their
> transactions or addresses for the public good are suffered to be printed,
> but even all written copies with the same care as libels suppressed; yet
> they found this severe speech published in the next's days news book, to
> mark them out to their own, and all other nations, as refractory disobe-
> dient persons that had lost all respect to his Majesty. Thus were they well
> rewarded for the itch of perpetual sitting and acting, the Parliament
> being grown to that height of contempt, as to be gazetted among run-
> away servants, lost dogs, strayed horses, and highway robbers.
>
> (*Complete Works*, 4: 406)

Marvell did not live to see the victory of this abused Parliament
over Danby, and the achievement on 21 April 1679 of what he had
so often argued for: Charles dismissed the Privy Council and swore
in a new group of thirty councillors, including ten peers and five
commoners, committing himself to make no more major decisions
without their advice. The last few months of his life were witness to
more of the same old stalemate. This helps to explain the tone of
Marvell's last-surviving personal letter, written to William Popple on
10 June 1678. 'There have been great Rewards offered in private,
and considerable in the Gazette', Marvell informed his nephew, to
anyone who could give information as to the author or printer of
the *Account*. Unofficially, however, the secret is out. 'Three or four
printed Books since have described, as near as it was proper to go,
the Man being a Member of Parliament, Mr. Marvell to have been
the Author; but if he had, surely he should not have escaped being
questioned in Parliament, or some other Place' (*Poems and Letters*,
2: 357). Symmetrically, then, this letter matches his account to Sir

Edward Harley about the appearance of *Mr. Smirke*. Apart from the dry indirection of the third-person approach, it is surely with a dark sense of the *mot juste* that Marvell invoked, as a possible protection against his enemies, the idea of parliamentary privilege whose undermining he had recently made apparent. Two months later he was dead, not without suspicion, as Whig historians and editors liked to repeat without any evidence, of poison.

But as the *Short Historical Essay touching General Councils, Creeds, and Imposition in Religion* stayed useful for nearly half a century after his death, so the *Account* had a long half-life. As the *Essay* was republished in 1680, in the context of the Popish Plot, and by Richard Baldwin in 1687, as 'Very Seasonable at this Time' (that is, speaking to the ecclesiastical crisis provoked by James II), so was the *Account*. In Baldwin's *Mr. Andrew Marvell's Character of Popery*, whose title page flaunted the date, 17 January 1688/9, and the licenser's 'This may be printed', we might see not defensiveness but triumphalism, the work asserting a new liberal climate for Whig publications.

Knowledge of the secret clauses in the Treaty of Dover subsequently gave credibility to Marvell's conspiracy theory and, though he did not succeed in shaming Parliament into any real confrontation with Charles on the constitutional issue, the *Account* must have contributed to the climate of opinion that led to the fall of Danby and the reconstitution of the Privy Council. Whole sections of it have earned a place in the parliamentary histories of his period, suggesting that Marvell, despite his disclaimer, had indeed written a 'just volume of History'; and from the literary historian's point of view, his discovery of the premises and purposes of 'secret history' had substantial ramifications in the later seventeenth and eighteenth centuries. In 1712 the *Secret History of Europe*, sometimes attributed to John Oldmixon, cites large sections of the *Account*, especially its heroic account of the attack on the Test Act by the four peers. Oldmixon himself explains the context of his return to Marvell as being that suggested above for the 1709 reappearance of the *Essay* – the trial of Henry Sacheverell, the bishop whose court sermon seemed to challenge the premises of the Revolution of 1688 and to destabilize the nation's commitment to moderate Protestantism. 'I wish', wrote Oldmixon, 'the Reader would make the Comparison between the year 1675, and 1710 himself; for I am very little verst in Parallels, and whatever my Imagination may furnish me with for my self, I should certainly want Words to express it; wherefore I shall be content with repeating what this Honest and Witty Author [Marvell] says on the subject' (p. 160). A few pages later the message is fully unveiled:

Never was there shewn since the Restauration, such a Spirit of Liberty, as in the Opposition to this Bill, which would for ever have put an end to any [opposition] in England. Nor has the Debate a little Resemblance with the Vigour that was lately exerted in the same Cause, on the Tryal of the Incendiary. The Temper of the Clergy was the same then, as some hot Men of 'em have shewn in the same Controversy, with this difference only, that there was more Folly in the latter, the Court being against 'em, and more Corruption in the former, the Ministry making a bold Effort to attack our Constitution.

(p. 195)

And almost at the end of the eighteenth century, in 1792, there appeared *The Secret History of the Court and Reign of Charles the Second, by A member of his privy council . . . with . . . a supplement continuing the narrative in a summary manner to The Revolution, by the Editor*. The anonymous 'editor' of this two-volume work has been subsequently identified as Charles McCormick, who turned Marvell's warnings against the encroachments of absolutism upon George III, citing especially the passage in which Marvell had described the humiliation of the Commons, their gazetting along with run-away servants and highway robbers ('Supplement', p. 73).

Given this evidence of his continued usefulness, one might even be willing to condone the fervent over-statements of Alexander Grosart, the late nineteenth-century editor of Marvell's prose, that these pamphlets constituted 'a SOURCE from which has gone the ennobling and transforming POWER that has secured to us our national liberties of speech and act, against which reaction is as impossible as of the sea against its tidal laws' (*Complete Works*, 2: xxxix). But if this seems too high-flown for contemporary taste, we might end instead with Marvell's tributes to Cromwell, which work as well for him. It is those who trouble the waters frequently that make those waters heal; and the tree when fallen shows taller than when it grew.

NOTES

1. See my *Early Modern Liberalism* (Cambridge, 1997), pp. 183–231.
2. *Poems and Letters*, 2: 394; citing *Hatton Correspondence*, 1: 128.
3. *The Auncient Ecclesiastical Histories*, trans. Meredith Hanmer (London, 1585), with a dedication to the Earl of Leicester.
4. Marvell, *Complete Works*, ed. A. B. Grosart (1875; repr. New York, 1966), 4: 113–14; italics added.
5. This seems to have been Marvell's view of Croft; but for a much more dignified account of Croft and his campaign for toleration, see

Newton Key, 'Comprehension and the Breakdown of Consensus in Restoration Hertfordshire', in *The Politics of Religion in Restoration England*, eds. Tim Harris, Paul Seaward and Mark Goldie (Oxford, 1990), pp. 191–215.

6. Marvell, *Complete Works*, ed. A. B. Grosart (1875, repr. New York, 1966), 4: 248.

7. L'Estrange, *An Account of the Growth of Knavery* (London, 1678), p. 46.

8. The centrality of the royal *Answer* in English constitutional theory thereafter is documented by Corinne Comstock Weston, 'The Theory of Mixed Monarchy under Charles I and After', *English Historical Review* 75 (1960), 426ff.

9. The poems are *Bludius et Corona* (1: 178) and *Scaevola Scoto-Britannus* (*Poems and Letters*, 1: 213–14), both of which appear in the Popple manuscript. Blood's attempt took place in May 1671, and Mitchell's punishment in January 1677.

10. Milton, *Complete Prose Works*, ed. D. M. Wolfe *et al.* (New Haven, 1953–82) 2: 562–3.

11. Bacon, *A Wise and Moderate Discourse* (London, 1641), p. 11. The aphorism originated with Seneca and Tacitus.

12. Cobbett, *Parliamentary History of England*, London, 12 vols, 1806–12, 4: 833.

13. Cobbett, *Parliamentary History*, 4: 818–20.

# Appendix

# The *second* and *third advices to a painter*

THE SECOND ADVICE TO A PAINTER FOR DRAWING
THE HISTORY OF OUR NAVALL BUSYNESS IN
Imitation of Mr Waller.

> Navim si poscat sibi peronatus arator
> Luciferi rudis exclamet Melicerta perisse
> Frontem de rebus – Pers. Sat 5

London, Aprill 1666

Nay Painter, if thou dar'st designe that Fight                    1
Which Waller only Courage had to write;
If thy bold hand can without shaking draw
What ev'n the Actors trembled at when they saw;
Enough to make thy colours change, like theirs,
And all thy Pencills bristle like their haires;
  First in fit distance of the Prospect vain,
Paint Allen[1] tilting at the coast of Spain:
Heroick act, and never heard till now
Stemming of Herc'les Pillars with his Prow.                      10
And how two Ships he left the Hills to wast[2]
And with new Sea-marks Dov'r and Calais grast.
  Next let the flaming London come in view
Like Nero's Rome, burnt to rebuilt it new.
What lesser Sacrifice then this was meet
To offer for the safety of the Fleet?
Blow one Ship up, another thence dos grow:
See what free Cityes and wise Courts can doe!
So some old Merchant, to ensure his Name
Marries afresh, and Courtiers share the Dame.                    20
So whatsoere is broke the Servants pay't;
And Glasses are more durable then Plate.

1. Commander of a squadron in the straits.
2. He ran 2 of his Ships on ground.

No May'r till now so rich a Pageant feign'd
Nor one Barge all the Companyes contain'd.
　　Then, Painter, draw cerulean Coventry,[3]
Keeper, or rather Chanc'lour of the Sea:
And more exactly to expresse his hew,
Use nothing but oltramarinish blew.
To pay his Fees the silver Trumpet spends:
And Boatswains whistle for his Place depends:　　　　　30
Pilots in vain repeat the Compasse ore
Untill of him they learn that one point more.
The constant Magnet to the Pole dos hold,
Steele to the Magnet, Coventry to Gold.
Muscovy sells us hemp and pitch and tarre;
Iron and Copper Sweden, Munster[4] Warre,
Ashley Prise (Gawden victualls) Carteret
　　　　　(Warwick Customes)
Sells pay, but Coventry dos sell the Fleet.
　　Now let our Navy stretch its canvas Wings
Swoln like his Purse, with tackling like its strings　　　40
By slow degrees of the increasing gaile,
First under Sale, and after under Saile.
Then, in kind visit unto Opdams Gout,
Hedge the Dutch in only to let them out.
(So Huntsmen faire unto the Hares give Law,
First find them, and then civilly withdraw)
That the blind Archer, when they take the Sea,
The Hamburgh Convoy may betray at ease.
(So that the fish may more securely bite
The Fisher baits the River over Night.)　　　　　　50
　　But Painter now prepare, t'inrich thy Piece
Pencill of Ermins, Oyle of Ambergris.
See where the Dutchesse, with triumphant taile
Of num'rous Coaches Harwich dos assaile.
So the Land-Crabbs at Natures kindly call,
Down to engender at the Sea doe crawle.
See then the Admirall, with Navy whole
To Harwich through the Ocean caracole.
So Swallows bury'd in the Sea, at Spring
Returne to Land with Summer in their Wing.　　　　60
　　One thrifty Ferry-boat of Mother-Pearl
Suffic'd of old the Cytherean Girle.
Yet Navys are but Properties when here,
A small Sea-mask, and built to court you, Dear.

---

3. Duke of York's Secretary.
4. Bishop of Munster who was feed by us to make warr with Holland.

Three goddesses in one; Pallas for Art,
Venus for sport, and Juno in your Heart.
  O Dutchesse if thy nuptiall Pomp were mean,
Tis payd with intrest in this navall Scene.
Never did Roman Mark, within the Nile
So feast the faire Egiptian Crocodile:                        70
Nor the Venetian Duke, with such a State,
The Adriatick marry at that rate.
  Now Painter spare thy weaker art, forbear
To draw her parting Passions and each Tear;
For Love alas has but a short delight:
The Winds, the Dutch, the King, all call to fight.
She therefore the Dukes person recommends
To Bronkard, Pen, and Coventry as Freinds:
(Pen much, more Bronkard, most to Coventry
For they, she knew, were all more 'fraid then shee).          80
  Of flying Fishes one had sav'd the finne,
And hop'd with these he through the Aire might spinn
The other thought he might avoid his Knell
In the invention of the diving Bell,
The third, had tryd it and affirm'd a Cable
Coyl'd round about men was impenetrable.
But these the Duke rejected, only chose
To keep far of, and others interpose.
  Rupert that knew not fear but health did want,
Kept State suspended in a Chais-volant.                       90
All, save his head, shut in that wooden case,
He show'd but like a broken Weather-glasse:
But arm'd in a whole Lion Cap-a-chin,
Did represent the Hercules within.
Dear shall the Dutch his twinging anguish know
And feel what Valour, whet with Pain, can doe
Curst in the meantime be the Traitress Jael
That through his Princely Temples drove the Naile.
  Rupert resolv'd to fight it like a Lyon,
But Sandwich hop'd to fight it like Arion:                    100
He, to prolong his Life in the dispute,
And charm the Holland Pirats, tun'd his Lute:
Till some judicious Dolphin might approach,
And land him safe and sound as any Roach.
  Now Painter reassume thy Pencill's care,
It hath but skirmisht yet, now Fight prepare,
And draw the Battell terribler to show
Then the last judgment was of Angelo.
  First, let our Navy scour through Silver Froath
The Oceans burthen, and the Kingdomes both:                   110

Whose ev'ry Bulk may represent its Birth
From Hide,[5] and Paston,[6] Burthens of the Earth
Hide, whose transcendent Paunch so swells of late,
That he the Rupture seems of Law, and State,
Paston, whose Belly bears more Millions
Then Indian Caricks, and contains more Tunns.
   Let sholes of Porpisses on every side
Wonder in swimming by our Oakes outvy'd:
And the Sea Fowle at gaze behold a thing
So vast, more strong, and swift then they of Wing.                          120
But with presaging Gorge yet keep in sight
And follow for the Relicks of a Fight.
   Then let the Dutch with well dissembled Fear
Or bold Despaire, more than we wish draw near.
At which our Gallants, to the Sea but tender,
And more to ffight, their easy Stomachs render:
With Breast so panting that at every stroke
You might have felt their Hearts beat through the Oake.
While one, concern'd most, in the intervall
Of straining Choler, thus did cast his Gall.                               130
"Noah be damned and all his Race accurst,
"That in Sea brine did pickle Timber first.
"What though he planted Vines! he Pines cut down,
"He taught us how to drink, and how to drown.
"He first built ships, and in the wooden Wall
"Saving but Eight, ere since indangers all.
"And thou Dutch Negromantick Fryer, [be] damn'd
"And in thine own first Mortar-piece be ram'd,
"Who first inventedst Cannon in thy Cell,
"Nitre from Earth, and Brimstone fetcht from Hell                          140
"But damn'd and treble damn'd be Clarendine
"Our Seventh Edward and his House and Line
"Who, to divert the danger of the Warre
"With Bristoll, hounds us on the Hollander.
"Foole-coated Gown-man, sells to fight with Hans
"Dunkirk, dismantling Scotland quarrells France
"And hopes he now hath bus'nesse shap't and Pow'r
"T'out last his Life or ours, and scape the Tow'r:
"And that he yet may see, ere he goe down,
"His dear Clarinda circled in a Crown."                                    150
   By this time both the fleets in reach debut[e]
And each the other mortally salute

---

5. Chancellor.
6. Parlement man for Yarmouth: He proposed in Parlament the giving the King and
  was afterwards made a Lord.

Draw pensive Neptune biting of his Thumms,
To think himself a Slave whos'ere orecomes.
The frighted Nymphs retreating to the Rocks,
Beating their blew Breasts, tearing their green Locks
Paint Echo slain, only th'alternate Sound
From the repeating Canon dos rebound.
    Opdam sailes in, plac'd in his navall Throne,
Assuming Courage greater then his own:                           160
Makes to the Duke, and threatens him from farr
To naile himself to's Board like a Petarre:
But in the vain attempt takes Fire too soon,
And flyes up in his Ship to catch the Moon.
Monsieurs like Rockets mount aloft, and crack
In thousand Sparks, then dansingly fall back.
    Yet ere this happen'd Destiny allow'd
Him his Revenge, to make his Death more proud.
A fatall Bullett from his side did range,
And batter'd Lawson.[7] O too dear Exchange!                     170
He led our Fleet that Day, too short a Space,
But lost his Knee (dy'd since) in Gloryes Race.
Lawson, whose Valour beyond Fate did goe
And still fights Opdam through the Lakes below.
    The Duke himself, though Pen did not forget,
Yet was not out of dangers rando[m] set.
Falmouth was there, I know not what to act
Some say t'was to grow Duke too by Contact.
An Untaught Bullet in its wanton Scope
Quashes him all to pieces, and his Hope.                         180
Such as his Rise such was his Fall, unprais'd,
A Chance-shot sooner took then Chance him rais'd:
His Shatterd Head the fearlesse Duke distains,
And gave the last first proof that he had Brains.
    Barkley[8] had heard it soon, and thought not good
To venture more of Royall Harding's Blood.
To be immortall he was not of Age:
(And did ev'n now the Indian Prize presage)
And judg'd it safe and decent, cost what cost,
To lose the Day, since his Dear Brother's lost.                  190
With his whole Squadron streight away he bore
And, like good Boy, promist to fight no more.
    The Dutch Aurania carelesse at us saild,
And promises to do what Opdam faild.
Smith to the Duke dos intercept her Way

7. Chief Admiral under the Duke.
8. Barkley afterwards, plunder'd a rich Duch Indian ship.

And cleavs t'her closer then the Remora.
The Captaine wonder'd, and withal disdain'd
So strongly by a thing so small detaind:
And in a raging Brav'ry to him runs.
They stab their Ships with one anothers Guns.                    200
They fight so near it seems to be on Ground.
And ev'n the Bullets meeting, Bullets wound.
The Noise, the Smoak, the Sweat, the Fire, the Blood
Is not to be exprest nor understood.
Each Captaine from the Quarter-Deck commands,
They wave their bright Swords glitt'ring in their hands
All Luxury of Warre, all Man can doe
In a Sea-fight, did passe betwixt them two
But one must conquer whosoever fight:
Smith took the Giant, and is since made Knight.                  210
     Marleburgh, that knew and dar'd too more then all
Falls undistinguisht by an Iron Ball.
Dear Lord, but born under a Starre ingrate!
No Soule so clear, and no more gloomy Fate.
Who would set up Warr's Trade that meant to thrive
Death picks the Valiant out, the Cow'rds survive.
What the Brave merit th'Impudent do vant;
And none's rewarded but the Sycophant.
Hence, all his Life he against Fortune fenc'd;
Or not well known, or not well recompens'd.                     220
But envy not this Praise to's Memory:
None more prepar'd was or lesse fit to dye.
     Rupert did others and himself excell
Holms, Teddyman, Minns bravely, Samson fell.
What others did let none omitted blame:
I shall record whos'ere brings in his Name.
But unlesse after Storyes disagree,
Nine onely came to fight, the rest to see.
     Now all conspires unto the Dutchman's Losse:
The Wind, the Fire, we, they themselves do crosse.              230
When a Sweet Sleep the Duke began to drown,
And with soft Diadem his Temples crown.
But first he orders all beside to watch;
And they the Foe while he a Nap should catch.
     But Bronkard,[9] by a secreter instinct
Slept not: nor needs it, he all Day had wink't.
The Duke in Bed he then first draws his Steele,
Whose Virtue makes the misled Compasse wheele;
So ere he wak'd both Fleets were innocent.

9. The Duke's Treasurer.

And Bronkard Member is of Parliament. 240
    And now dear Painter, after pains like those
'Twere time that thou and I too should repose.
But all our Navy scap'd so sound of Limm
That a small space ser'vd to refresh its trimm.
And a tame Fleet of their dos Convoy want,
Laden with both the Indyes and Levant.
Paint but this one Scene more. The world's our own
The Halcyon Sandwich dos command alone.
    To Bergen now with better Maw we hast,
And the sweet spoyles in Hope already tast. 250
Though Clifford in the Character appears
Of Supracargo to our Fleet and theirs:
Wearing a signet ready to clap on,
And seize all for his Master Arlington.
    R'yter whose little Squadron skim'd the Seas
And wasted our remotest Colonyes,
With Ships all foule return'd upon our Way.
Sandwich would not disperse, nor yet delay.
And therefore, like Commander grave and wise,
To scape his Sight and Fight, shuts both his Eys. 260
And, for more State and sureness, Cuttins true
The left Eye closes, the right Montague.
And even Clifford profer'd, in his Zeale
To make all safe, t'apply to both his Seale.
Ulisses so, till he the Syrens past,
Would by his Mates be pinion'd to the Mast.
    Now may our Navy view the wished Port
But there too (see the Fortune) was a Fort.
Sandwich would not be beaten, nor yet beat.
Fooles only fight, the Prudent use to treat. 270
    His Cousen Montague,[10] by Court Disaster
Dwindled into the wooden Horse's Master,
To speak of Peace seem'd among all most proper.
And Talbot then treated of nought but Copper?
Or what are Forts when void of Ammunition?
With Freind or Foe what would we more condition?
Yet we three dayes till the Dutch furnisht all
Men, Powder, Cannon, Money, treat with Wall
Then Teddy, finding that the Dane would not,
Sends in Six Captains bravely to be shot, 280

10. Montague was Master of the Hors to the Queen. One day as he led he, he
    tickled her palm; she ask'd the King what that ment: the King, by this means
    getting knowledge of it, turn'd Montague out of his place. After which disgrace
    he went to sea.

And Mountague, though drest like any Bride,
Though aboard him too, yet was reacht and dy'd.
  Sad was this Chance, and yet a deeper Care,
Wrinkles our Membranes under Forehead faire.
The Dutch Armada yet had th'Impudence
To put to Sea, to waft their Merchants hence.
For, as if all their Ships of Wall-nut were,
The more we beat them, still the more they bear.
But a good Pilot and a fav'ring Winde
Bring Sandwich back, and once again did blind.          290
  Now gentle Painter, ere we leap on Shore
With thy last strokes ruffle a Tempest ore:
As if in our Reproach, the Winds and Seas
Would undertake the Dutch while we take Ease
The Seas their Spoiles within our Hatches throw.
The Winds both Fleets into our Mouths doe blow.
Strew all their Ships along the Coast by ours,
As easy to be gather'd up as Flow'rs.
But Sandwich fears for Merchants to mistake
A Man of Warre, and among Flow'rs a Snake.              300
Two Indian Ships pregnant with Eastern Pearle
And Di'monds, sate the Officers and Earle.
Then warning of our Fleet, he it divides
Into the Ports, and he to Oxford rides,
While the Dutch reuniting, to our Shames,
Ride all insulting ore the Downs and Thames.
  Now treating Sandwich seems the fittest choice
To Spain, there to condole and to rejoyce.
He meets the French, but, to avoyd all harms,
Ships to the Groyne (Embassyes bear not Arms!)         310
There let him languish a long Quarantain,
And neer to England come till he be clean.
  Thus having fought we know not why, as yet
W'have done we know not what, nor what we get.
If to espouse the Ocean all this paines
Princes unite, and will forbid the Baines.
If to discharge Fanaticks: this makes more;
For all Fanatick turn when sick or poore.
Or if the House of Commons to repay:
Their Prize Commissions are transfer'd away.            320
But for triumphant Checkstones, if, and Shell
For Dutchesse Closet: 't has succeeded well.
If to make Parliaments all odious: passe.
If to reserve a Standing Force: alas.
Or if as just, Orange to reinstate:

Instead if that he is regenerate.
And with four Millions vainly giv'n, as spent;
And with five Millions more of detriment;
Our Summe amounts yet only to have won
A Bastard Orange,[11] for Pimp Arlington.                    330
　　Now may Historians argue Con and Pro.
Denham saith thus: though Waller alwayes So.
But he, good Man, in his long Sheet and Staffe
This Penance did for Cromwell's Epitaph.
And his next Theme must be of th'Duke's Maistresse
Advice to draw Madam Edificatresse.
　　Hence forth, O Gemini! two Dukes command:
Castor and Pollux, Aumerle, Cumberland
Since in one Ship, it had been fit they went
In Petty's double-keel'd Experiment.                        340


　　　　To the King.
　　Imperiall Prince, King of the Seas and Isles
Dear Object of our Joys and Heaven's Smiles,
What boots it that thy Light dos guild our Dayes
And we lye basking by thy milder Rayes?
While Swarms of Insects, from thy warmth begun
Our Land devour, and intercept our Sunn.
　　Thou, like Jove's Minos, rul'st a greater Crete
(And for its hundred Cittyes count thy Fleeet.)
Why wilt thou that State-Dedalus allow,
Who builds thee but a Lab'rinth and a Cow?                   350
If thou a Minos, be a Judge Severe:
And in's own Maze confine the Engineer.[12]
Or if our Sunn, since he so near presumes,
Melt the soft wax with which he imps his Plume[s]
And let him falling leave his hated Name,
Unto those Seas his Warre hath set on Flame.
From that Enchanter having clear'd thine Eyes
Thy Native Sight will pierce within the Skyes:
And view those Kingdomes calm of Joy and Light
Where's universall Triumphs but no Fight.                    360
Since both from Heav'n thy Race and Pow'r descend
Rule by its pattern, there to reascend.
Let Justice only draw: and Battell Cease.
Kings are in War but Cards: they're Gods in Peace.


11. L. Arlington maried a Duch Lady a Bastard of the Family of the Prince of
　　Orange.
12. Chancellor Hide.

THE THIRD ADVICE TO A PAINTER
London. October 1st, 1666.

Sandwich in Spain now, & the Duke in Love,
Let's with new Gen'ralls a new Painter prove.
Lilly's a Dutchman, danger in his Art:
His Pencills may intelligence impart.
Thou Gibson that among thy Navy small
Of marshall'd Shells commandest Admirall;
Thy self so slender, that thou show'st no more
Then Barnacle new hatcht of them before:
Come mix thy water colours, and expresse
Drawing in little, how we do yet lesse.                              10
    First paint me George and Rupert, ratling far
Within one box, like the two Dice of War:
And let the terrour of their linked Name
Fly through the aire like chainshot, tearing Fame.
Jove in one clowd did scarsely ever wrap
Lightning so fierce, but never such a Clap.
United Gen'ralls! sure the only spell
Wherewith United Provinces to quell.
Alas, ev'n they, though shell'd in treble Oake
Will prove an addle Egge with double Yolke.                          20
    And therefore next uncouple either Hound,
And loo them at two Hares ere one be found.
Rupert to Beaufort hollow: ay there Rupert
Like the phantastick hunting of St Hubert.
When he with airy Hounds, and Horn of aire,
Pursues by Fountainbleau the witchy Hare.
Deep Providence of State, that could so soon
Fight Beaufort here ere he had quit Toulon!
So have I seen, ere humane quarrells rise,
Foreboding Meteors combate with the Skyes.                           30
    But let the Prince to fight with rumour goe:
The Gen'rall meets a more substantiall Foe.
Ruyter he spyes, and full of youthfull heat,
Though half their Number thinks his odds too great.
The Fowler so watches the watry spot
And more the Fowle, hopes for the better shot.
Though such a Limbe were from his Navy torn
He found no weaknesse yet: like Samson shorn.
But swoln with sense of former Glory won,
Thought Monk must be by Albemarle outdon.                            40
Little he knew, with the same Arm and Sword
How far the Gentleman outcuts the Lord.

Ruyter, inferior unto none for Heart,
Superior now in Number and in Art,
Askt if he thought, (as once our rebell Nation)
To conquer theirs too by a Declaration.
And threatens, though he now so proudly saile,
He shall tread back his Iter Boreale.
This said, he the short Period, ere it ends,
With iron words from brazen mouths extends.                    50
   MONK yet prevents him ere the Navyes meet,
And charges in: himself alone a Fleet.
And with so quick and frequent motion wound
His murd'ring sides about, the Ship seem'd round.
And the Exchanges of his circling Tire
Like Whirling hoopes show'd of triumphall Fire.
Single he dos at their whole Navy aime,
And shoots them through: a Porcupine of Flame.
He play's with danger, and his Bullets trowles
As't were at Trou Madam, through all their Howles.             60
In noyse so regular his Cannon met,
You'd think that Thunder were to Musick set.
Ah, had the rest but kept a time as true,
What Age could such a Martiall Consort shew?
   The listning aire, unto the distant shoare,
Through secret Pipes conveys the tuned roare:
Till, as the Echoes vanishing abate,
Men feel a deaf sound, like the Pulse of Fate.
If Fate expire, let Monk her place supply:
His Gunns determine who shall live or dye.                     70
   But Victory dos always hate a Rant:
Valour her Brave, but Skill is her Galant.
Ruyter no lesse with virtuous envy burns,
And Prodigyes for Miracles returns.
Yet Shee observd, how still his iron Balls
Bricold in vain against our oaken Walls.
And the hard Pellets fell away, as dead,
Which our inchanted timber phillip'd.
Leave then, said she, th'invulnerable Keele:
We'l find their foible, like Achilles' heele.                  80
   He, quickly taught, powrs in continuall clowds
Of chaind Dilemmas through our sinewy Shrowds
Forrests of Masts fall with their rude embrace:
Our stiffe Sailes masht are netted into Lace.
Till our whole Navy lay their wanton Marke,
Nor any Ship could saile but as the Arke.
Shot in the wing, so, at the Powders call

The disappointed Bird dos flutt'ring fall.
Yet Monk, disabled, still such Courage shows
That none into his mortall gripe durst close.                    90
So an old Bustard, maim'd, yet loath to yeild,
Duells the Fowler in Newmarket Field.
But soon he found 'twas now in vain to fight
And imps his Plumes the best he may for Flight.
   This Painter were a noble task, to tell
What indignation his great Breast did swell.
Not vertuous Men unworthily abus'd,
Not constant Lovers without cause refus'd,
Not honest Merchant broke, not skillfull Play'r
Hist of the Stage, not Sinner in despayre,                       100
Not loosing Rookes, not Favourites disgrac't
Not Rump by Oliver or Monk displac't,
Not Kings depos'd, not Prelates ere they dye
Feele half the rage of Gen'ralls when they fly.
   Ah, rather then transmit our scorn to Fame
Draw Curtains gentle Artist ore this Shame.
Cashiere the Mem'ry of Dutell, raisd up
To tast in stead of Death's, his Highnesse Cup.
And, if the thing were true, yet paint it not
How Barclay, as he long deserv'd, was shot.                      110
Though others, that survey'd the Corps so clear,
Say he was only petrify'd with Fear
And the hard Statue, mummy'd without Gumme,
Might the Dutch Balm have spar'd & English Tombe.
Yet if thou wilt, paint Mings, turn'd all to Soule;
And the great Harman chark'd almost to coale;
And Jordan old, thy Pencills worthy paine,
Who all the way held up the Ducall Traine.
But in a dark cloud cover Askue, when
He quit the Prince t'imbarke in Loovesten.                       120
And wounded Ships, which we immortall boast
Now first led captive to an hostile Coast.
   But most, with story of his Hand or Thum,
Conceale, as honour would, his Grace's Bum.
When the rude Bullet a large Collop tore
Out of that Buttock, never turn'd before.
Fortune it seem'd would give him, by that lash,
Gentle correction for his Fight so rash.
But should the Rump perceive't, they'd say that Mars
Had now reveng'd them upon Aumarle's Arse.                       130
   The long disaster better 'ore to veile
Paint only Jonas three dayes in the Whale
Then draw the youthfull Perseus, all in hast,

From a Sea-Beast, to free the Virgin chast:
But neither riding Pegasus for speed,
Nor with the Gorgon sheilded at his need.
For no lesse time did conqu'ring Ruyter chaw
Our flying Gen'rall in his spungy Jaw.
So Rupert the Sea-dragon did invade:
But to save George himself, and not the Maid.            140
And so, arriving late, he quickly mist
Ev'n Sailes to fly, unable to resist.
   Not Greenland Seamen, that survive the fright
Of the cold Chaos, and half-eternall Night,
So gladly the returning Sun adore,
Or run to spy their next years Fleet from Shoar
Hoping, yet once, within the oyly side
Of the fat Whale againe their Spears to hide:
As our glad Fleet, with universall shout
Salute the Prince, and wish the second bout.            150
Nor Winds, long Pris'ners in Earth's hollow Vault
The fallow Seas so eagerly assault;
As firy Rupert, with revengefull Joy,
Dos on the Dutch his hungry Courage cloy.
But soon unrigg'd, lay like a uselesse board:
As wounded in the wrist men drop the Sword.
When a propitious Clowd betwixt us stept
And in our aid did Ruyter intercept.
Old Homer yet did never introduce
To save his Heroes, Mist of better use.                 160
Worship the Sun, who dwell where he dos rise:
This Mist dos more deserve our Sacrifice.
   Now joyfull Fires, and the exalted Bell
And Court-gazets our empty Triumph tell,
Alas: the time draws near when overturn'd
The lying Bells shall through the tongue be burn'd
Paper shall want to print that Lye of State
And our false Fires true Fires shall expiate.
   Stay Painter here a while, and I will stay:
Nor vex the future Times with nice survey.              170
See'st not the Monky Dutchesse, all undrest?
Paint thou but her, and she will paint the rest.
   The sad Tale found her in her outer Roome
Nailing up Hangings, not of Persian Loome:
Like chast Penelope, that ne'er did rome,
But made all fine against her George came home.
Upon a Ladder, in her coat most shorter,
She stood, with Groome and Porter for Supporter.
And carelesse what they saw, or what they thought

With Hony pensy, honestly she wrought.                          180
For in She-Gen'ralls Britch, none could (she knows)
Carry away the piece; with Eys or Nose.
One Tenter drove, to lose no time nor place,
At once the Ladder they remove and Grace.
While thus they her translate, from North to East,
In posture [just] of a foure-footed Beast,
She heard the News: but alter'd yet no more
Then that what was behind she turn'd before.
Nor would come down; but with an hankercher,
Which pocket foule did to her necke prefer,                      190
She dry'd no Tears, for she was too viraginous.
But only snuffing her Trunk cartilaginous,
From scaling Ladder she began a Story,
Worthy to be had in me(mento) mory.
Arraigning past, and present, and futury;
With a prophetick, (if not spirit,) Fury.
Her Haire began to creep, her Belly sound,
Her Eys to startle, and her Udder bound.
Half Witch, half Prophet, thus she-Albemarle,
Like Presbyterian Sibyll, out did Snarle.                       200
'Traytors both to my Lord and to the King,
Nay now it grows beyond all suffering.
One valiant Man on Land, and he must be
Commanded out to stop their leaks at Sea.
Yet send him Rupert, as an helper meet:
First the command dividing, ere the Fleet.
One may, if they be beat, or both be hit
Or if they overcome, yet Honours split
But reck'ning George already knockt o' th'head,
They cut him out like Beef, ere he be dead.                     210
Each for a quarter hopes: the first dos skip,
But shall snap short tho, at the Gen'ralship:
Next they for Master of the Horse agree:
A third the Cockpit begs: not any mee.
But they shall know, ay, marry shall they doe
That, who the Cockpit has, shall have mee too.
    I told George first, as Calamy did me,
If the King these brought over, how 'twould be.
Men, that there pickt his Pocket, to his Face,
To sell intelligence, or buy a Place.                           220
That their Religion pawn'd for Clothes; nor care
'Thas run so long, now to redeem't, nor dare.
O what egregious Loyalty to cheat!
O what Fidelity it was to eat!

While Langdales, Hoptons, Glenhams starv'd abroad,
And here, true Roylists sunk beneath the load.
Men that did there affront, defame, betray
The King, and do so here, now who but they?
What say I Men? nay rather Monsters: Men
Only in Bed, nor, (to my knowledge), then.                    230
   See how they home return, in revell rout,
With the same Measures that they first went out.
Nor better grown, nor wiser all this while;
Renew the causes of their first Exile.
As if (to show you Fooles what 'tis I mean)
I chose a foule Smock, when I might have clean.
   First, they, for Fear, disband the Army tame
And leave good George a Gen'ralls empty Name
Then Bishops must revive, and all unfix
With discontent for Consents twenty six.                      240
The Lords House drains the Houses of the Lord
For Bishops voices silencing the Word
O Bartlemew, Saint of their Calender!
What's worse? thy Ejection or thy Massacre?
Then Culp'per, Gloster, ere the Princesse, dy'd:
Nothing can live that interrupts an Hide.
O more then human Gloster! Fate did shew
Thee but to Earth, and back againe withdrew.
Then the fat Scriv'ner durst begin to think
'Twas time to mix the royal Blood with ink.                   250
Barclay, that swore, as oft as she had Toes
Dos, kneeling, now her chastity depose.
Just, as the first French Card'nall could restore
A Maidenhead to his Widdow-Niece and Whore.
For Portion, if she should prove light when weigh'd
Four Millions shall within three years be paid.
To raise it, we must have a Navall War:
As if't were nothing but Tara-tan-tar.
Abroad all Princes disobliging first,
At home, all Partyes but the very worst.                      260
   To tell of Ireland, Scotland, Dunkirk's sad,
Or the Kings Marriage; but he thinks I'm mad.
And sweeter creature never saw the Sun,
If we the King wisht Monk, or Queen a Nun.
But a Dutch war shall all these rumours still,
Bleed out these Humours, and our Purses spill.
Yet, after one Dayes trembling Fight, they saw
'Twas too much danger for a Son-in-Law.
Hire him to leave with six score thousand pound;

As with the Kings Drumms men for sleep compound.                    270
Then modest Sandwich thought it might agree
With the State-prudence, to do lesse then he.
And to excuse their timorousnesse and sloth,
They've found how George might now do lesse then both.
    First, Smith must for Leghorn, with force enow
To venture back againe, but not go through.
Beaufort is there, and, to their dazeling Eys,
The distance more the object magnifyes.
Yet this they gain, that Smith his time shall lose
And for my Duke, too, can not interpose.                            280
    But fearing that our Navy, George to break,
Might yet not be sufficiently weake;
The Secretary that had never yet
Intelligence but from his own gazett,
Discovers a great secret, fit to sell:
And pays himself for't ere he would it tell.
Beaufort is in the Chanell, hixy, here:
Doxy, Toulon: Beaufort is ev'ry where.
Herewith assembles the supream Divan,
Where enters none but Devill, Ned, & Nan:                           290
And, upon this pretence, they streight design'd
The Fleet to sep'rate, and the world to blind.
Monk to the Dutch, and Rupert (here the Wench
Could not but smile) is destined to the French.
To write the order Bristoll's Clerke they chose;
(One's slit in Pen, another in his Nose)
For he first brought the News; and 'tis his Place:
He'le see the Fleet devided like his Face.
And through that cranny in his gristly part,
To the Dutch chink, intelligence may start.                         300
The Plot succeeds: the Dutch in hast prepare
And poore pilgarlick George's Arse they share.
And now, presuming of his certaine wrack,
To help him, late, they write for Rupert back.
Officious Will seems fittest, as afraid
Lest George should looke too far into his Trade.
On the first draught they pause with Statesmen's care
Then write it faire, then copy't out as faire
Then they compare them, when at last 'tis sign'd
Will soon his purstrings, but no seale could find.                  310
At night he sends it by the common Post
To save the King of an Expresse the cost.
Lord what adoe to pack one letter hence!
Some Patents passe with lesse circumference.

Well George, in spight of them thou safe dost ride,
Lessn'd, I hope, in nought but thy Back-side.
For as to reputation, this retreat
Of thine exceeds their Victoryes so great.
Nor shalt thou stirre from thence, by my consent,
Till thou hast made the Dutch and them repent.                    320
'Tis true I want so long the nuptiall guift,
But as I oft have don, I'le make a Shift.
Nor with vain Pomp will I accoast the Shore,
To try thy Valour, at the Buoy-i'th'nore.
Fall to thy worke there, George, as I do here:
Cherish the valiant up, the cow'rd cashiere.
See that the Men have Pay, & Beef, & Beere;
Find out the cheats of the four-millioneer.
Out of the very Beer they steale the Malt,
Powd'r out of Powder, powder'd Beef the Salt.                    330
Put thy hand to the Tub: instead of Ox,
They victuall with French Pork that has the Pox.
Never such Cotqueans by small arts to wring:
Ne'r such ill Huswives in the managing.
Pursers at Sea know fewer cheats then they:
Mar'ners on Shore lesse madly spend their Pay.
See that thou hast new Sailes thy self, and spoyle
All their Sea-market and their cable-coyle.
Tell the King all; how him they countermine
Trust not, till don, him with thy own designe.                    340
Looke that good Chaplains on each Ship do wait,
Nor the Sea-Diocesse be impropriate.
Looke to the Pris'ners, sick, and wounded, all
Is Prize, they rob even the Hospitall.
Recover back the Prizes too: in vain
Wee fight if all be taken that is ta'ne.
    Now by our coast the Dutchmen, like a flight
Of feeding Ducks, morning and ev'ning light.
How our Land Hectors tremble, voyd of sense!
As if they came streight to transport them hence.                    350
Some Sheep are stoln, the Kingdome's all array'd:
And ev'n Presbit'ry's now call'd out for aid.
They wish ev'n George divided; to command
One half of him the Sea, and one the Land.
    What's that I see? Ha: 'tis my George agen:
It seems they in sev'n weeks have rigg'd him then.
The curious Heav'n with Lightning him surrounds,
To view him, and his Name in Thunder sounds:
But with the same shaft gores their Navy near,

As ere we hunt, the Keeper shoots the Deere.                    360
Stay Heav'n a while, and thou shalt see him saile;
And how George too can lighten, thunder, haile.
Happy that time that I thee wedded, George,
The Sword of England, and of Holland scourge.
Avant Rotterdam-dog, Ruyter, avant,
Thou water-rat, thou shark, thou Cormorant:
I'le teach thee to shoot scizzers. I'le repaire
Each rope thou loosest, George, out of this haire.
Ere thou shalt lack a saile and lye a drift,
'Tis strong and course enough, I'le cut this Shift.             370
Bring home the old ones, I again will sew,
And darn them up to be as good as new.
What twice disabled? never such a thing:
Now, Souveraigne, help him that brought in the King
Guart thy Posteriours left, lest all be gone:
Though Jury-masts, th'hast Jury-buttocks none.
Courage. How bravely whet with this disgrace,
He turns, and Bullets spits in Ruyter's Face!
They fly, they fly. Their Fleet dos now divide:
But they discard their Trump; our Trump is Hide.               380
    Where are you now De Ruyter with your bears?
See how your Merchants burn about your ears.
Fire out the wasps George from their hollow trees,
Cramm'd with the honey of our English Bees.
Ay, now they'r paid for Guiny: ere they steere
To the gold coast, they find it hotter here.
Turn theyr ships all to stoves, ere they set forth
To warm their traffick in the frozen North.
Ah Sandwich, had thy conduct been the same,
Bergen had seen a lesse, but richer Flame.                      390
Nor Ruyter liv'd new Battel to repeat,
And oftner beaten be then we can beat.
    Scarse has George leisure, after all this pain,
To tye his Briches: Ruyter's out againe.
Thrice in one year! why sure the man is wood:
Beat him like Stockfish, or he'le ne'r be good.
I see them both prepar'd againe to try:
They first shoot through each other with the Eye;
Then – But that ruling Providence, that must
With humane Projects play as Winds with dust,                   400
Raises a Storm, (so Constables a fray
Knock down) and sends them both well cuft away.
Plant now Virginian Firrs in English Oke,
Build your Ship-ribbs proof to the Cannon's stroke,

To get a Fleet to Sea, exhaust the Land,
Let longing Princes pine for the Command:
Strong Marchpanes! Wafers tight! so thin a puffe
Of angry aire can ruine all that huffe!
So Champions having shar'd the Lists and Sun,
The Judge throws down his Warder & they've done.                410
For shame come home George: 'tis for thee, too much
To fight at once with Heaven and the Dutch.
   Woe's me, what see I next? Alas the Fate
I see of England, and its utmost date.
These flames of theirs, at which we fondly smile,
Kindled, like Torches, our Sepulchrall Pile.
Warre, Fire and Plague against us all conspire:
We the Warre, God the Plague, Who rais'd the Fire?
See how Men all, like Ghosts, while London burns,
Wander and each over his ashes mourns.                          420
Dear George, sad Fate, vain Mind that me did'st please
To meet thine with far other Flames then these.
Curst be the Man that first begot this Warrre,
In an ill houre, under a blazing Starre.
For other's sport, two Nations fight a Prize:
Between them both Religion wounded dyes.
So of first Troy, the angry Gods unpaid,
Ras'd the foundations, which themselves had layd.
   Welcome, though late, dear George: here had'st thou been,
We'd scap'd (let Rupert bring the Navy in.)                     430
Thou still must help them out when in the mire:
Gen'rall at Land, at Sea, at Plague, at Fire.
Now thou art gone, see, Beaufort dares approach:
And our whole Fleet, angling, has catch't a Roach.
   Gibson farewell, till next we put to Sea:
Faith thou has drawn her in effigie.


        To the King.
   Great Prince, and so much greater as more wise,
Sweet as our Life, and dearer then our Eyes:
What Servants will conceale, and Couns'lours spare
To tell, the Painter and the Poet dare.                         440
And the assistance of an heav'nly Muse
And Pencill, represents the crimes abstruse.
Here needs no Sword, no Fleet, no foraine Foe
Only let Vice be damm'd, and Justice flow.
Shake but, like Jove, thy locks divine, & frowne;
Thy Scepter will suffice to guard thy Crowne.
Hark to Cassandra's Song, ere Fate destroy,

By thy own Navy's wooden horse, thy Troy.
Us our Apollo, from the Tumult's wave,
And gentle gales,though but in Oares, will save.                    450
   So Philomel her sad embroyd'ry strung,
And vocall silks tun'd with her Needle's tongue.
(The Picture dumbe, in colours lowd, reveal'd
The tragedy's of Court, so long conceal'd.)
But, when restor'd to voice, increas'd with Wings,
To Woods and Groves, what once she painted, sings.

# Bibliography

SIGNIFICANT EARLY EDITIONS

*Miscellaneous Poems. By Andrew Marvell, Esq; Late Member of the Honourable House of Commons.* London: Robert Boulter, 1681.

*The Works of Andrew Marvell Esq.* Ed. Thomas Cooke. 2 vols. London, 1726; reissued 1772. Contains the poems of 1681, reordered; some Restoration satires, a short Life and a few letters.

*The Works of Andrew Marvell Esq. Poetical, controversial and political. Containing many original letters, poems and tracts, never before printed, with a new life of the author.* Ed. Captain Edward Thompson. 3 vols. London, 1776. Contains all the contents of Cooke's edition, with some new poems and satires; the bulk of the Corporation letters and a few private ones; and 5 of the 6 prose tracts.

*The Complete Works in Verse and Prose of Andrew Marvell M.P.* Ed. Alexander B. Grosart. 4 vols. Privately printed, 1872–75. Repr. AMS Press, 1966. Adds to prose tracts the *Remarks upon a Late Disingenuous Discourse*; includes translations of Latin poems.


PROSE PAMPHLETS

*The Rehearsal Transpros'd: Or, Animadversions Upon a late Book, Intituled, A Preface Shewing What Grounds there are of Fears and Jealousies of Popery.* London. Printed by A. B. for the Assigns of John Calvin and Theodore Beza, 1672.

*The Rehearsal Transpros'd: The Second Part.* London: Nathaniel Ponder, 1673.

*Mr. Smirke: Or, The Divine in Mode: Being Certain Annotations, upon the Animadversions on the Naked Truth. Together with a Short Historical Essay, concerning General Councils, Creeds, and Impositions, in Matters of Religion . . . By Andreas Rivetus, Junior.*

*An Account Of the Growth of Popery, and Arbitrary Government in England.* 'Amsterdam', 1677.

*Remarks Upon a Late Disingenuous Discourse, Writ by one T.D. Under the pretence De Causa Dei . . . By a Protestant.* London: Christopher Hussey, 1678.

## 180   Bibliography

IMPORTANT OR USEFUL MODERN EDITIONS

*Poems and Letters.* Ed. H. M. Margoliouth. 2 vols. Oxford: Clarendon, 1927,
1952; Rev. Pierre Legouis, 1971. The definitive modern edition.
*Miscellaneous Poems* (1681), facsimile reprint. Menston: Scolar Press, 1973.
An appendix reproduces corrections and additions made in Bodleian MS.
Eng. Poet. d. 49.
*Complete Poems.* Ed. E. S. Donno. Harmondsworth: Penguin, 1972.
*Complete Poetry.* Ed. George de F. Lord. New York: Modern Library, 1968;
repr. 1984. Includes *Second* and *Third Advices to a Painter.*
*The Rehearsal Transpros'd and the Rehearsal Transpros'd: The Second Part.* Ed.
D. I. B. Smith. Oxford: Clarendon, 1971.
*An Account of the Growth of Popery and Arbitrary Government*, facsimile. Ed. G.
Salgado. Farnborough: Heppenheim, 1971.

CRITICAL WORKS

Abraham, Lyndy (1990) *Marvell and Alchemy.* Aldershot: Scolar Press.
Allen, D. C. (1960, 1968) *Image and Meaning: Metaphoric Traditions in Renais-
sance Poetry.* Baltimore: Johns Hopkins University Press.
Berger, Harry (1988) *Second World and Green World: Studies in Renaissance
Fiction Making.* Berkeley, Los Angeles and London: University of Cali-
fornia Press.
Brooks, Cleanth (1947) 'Criticism and Literary History: Marvell's "Horatian
Ode"', *Sewanee Review* 55: 199–222.
Bush, Douglas (1952) 'Marvell's "Horatian Ode"', *Sewanee Review* 60: 362–76.
Chambers, A. B. (1991) *Andrew Marvell and Edmund Waller: Seventeenth
Century Praise and Restoration Satire.* University Park and London: Penn-
sylvania State University Press.
Chernaik, W. L. (1983) *The Poet's Time: Politics and Religion in the Work of
Andrew Marvell.* Cambridge: Cambridge University Press.
Chernaik, W. L. and Martin Dzelzainis (eds.) (1999) *Marvell and Liberty.*
London: Macmillan.
Colie, R. L. (1970) *'My Ecchoing Song': Andrew Marvell's Poetry of Criticism.*
Princeton: Princeton University Press.
Condren, C., and A. D. Cousins (eds.) (1990) *The Political Identity of Andrew
Marvell.* Aldershot: Scolar Press.
Cullen, Patrick (1970) *Spenser, Marvell and Renaissance Pastoral.* Cambridge,
MA: Harvard University Press.
Datta, Kitty Scoular (1969) 'New Light on Marvell's "A Dialogue between
the Soul and Body"', *Renaissance Quarterly* 22: 242–55.
Dixon Hunt, J. (1978) *Andrew Marvell: His Life and Writings.* Ithaca: Cornell
University Press.
Eliot, T. S. (1921) 'Andrew Marvell', *Times Literary Supplement*, 31 March,
pp. 201–3; repr. in *Andrew Marvell, 1621: Tercentenary Tributes.* London:
Oxford University Press.

Bibliography **181**

Empson, William (1930) *Seven Types of Ambiguity*. London: Chatto and Windus.

Empson, William (1935) *Some Versions of Pastoral*. London: Chatto and Windus.

Everett, Barbara (1979) 'The Shooting of the Bears: Poetry and Politics in Andrew Marvell', in *Andrew Marvell: Essays on the Tercentenary of his Death*, ed. R. L. Brett. Oxford: Oxford University Press.

Farley-Hills, D. (1974) *The Benevolence of Laughter: Comic Poetry of the Commonwealth and Restoration*. London and Basingstoke: Macmillan.

Friedman, D. M. (1970) *Marvell's Pastoral Art*. Berkeley: University of California Press.

Gearin-Tosh, Michael (1972) 'The Structure of Marvell's *Last Instructions to a Painter*', *Essays in Criticism* 22: 48–57.

Goldie, Mark (1990) 'Danby, the Bishops and the Whigs', in *The Politics of Religion in Restoration England*, eds. Tim Harris, Paul Seaward and Mark Goldie. Oxford: Blackwell, pp. 75–105.

Griffin, Patsy (1995) *The Modest Ambition of Andrew Marvell*. London: Associated University Presses.

Haley, K. H. D. (1953) *William of Orange and the English Opposition, 1672–74*. Oxford: Oxford University Press.

Hirst, Derek, and Steven Zwicker (1993) 'High Summer at Nun Appleton, 1651: Andrew Marvell and Lord Fairfax's Occasions', *Historical Journal* 36: 247–69.

Kelliher, H. (1978) *Andrew Marvell: Poet and Politician, 1621–78*. London: British Library.

Key, Newton (1990) 'Comprehension and the Breakdown of Consensus in Restoration Herefordshire', in *The Politics of Religion*, pp. 191–215.

Klause, J. (1983) *The Unfortunate Fall. Theodicy and the Moral Imagination of Andrew Marvell*. Hamden, CT: Archon.

Legouis, Pierre (1965) *Andrew Marvell, Poet, Puritan, Patriot, 1621–78*. Oxford: Clarendon.

Leishman, J. B. (1966) *The Art of Marvell's Poetry*. London: Hutchinson.

Lord, George de F. (1966) 'Two New Poems by Marvell', in *Evidence for Authorship: Essays on Problems of Attribution*, eds. D. V. Erdman and E. G. Fogel. Ithaca: Cornell University Press.

Lord, George de F. (1967) 'From Contemplation to Action: Marvell's Poetical Career', *Philological Quarterly* 46: 207–24.

Lord, George de F. (1963–75) Poems on Affairs of State 1660–1678, 7 vols., New Haven.

Loxley, James (1995) ' "Prepared at Last to Strike in with the Tyde?": Andrew Marvell and Royalist Verse', *Seventeenth Century* 10: 39–62.

Nevo, Ruth (1963) *The Dial of Virtue: A Study of Poems on Affairs of State in the Seventeenth Century*. Princeton: Princeton University Press.

Patterson, Annabel (forthcoming) 'The *Advices to a Painter* in Marvell's canon', *Studies in English Literature*.

Pritchard, Allan (1983) 'Marvell's "The Garden": A Restoration Poem?' *Studies in English Literature* 23: 371–88.

Rivers, Isabel (1973) *The Poetry of Conservativism 1600–1745: A Study of Poets and Public Affairs from Jonson to Pope*. Cambridge: Cambridge University Press.

Shifflet, Andrew (1998) *Stoicism, Politics and Literature in the Age of Milton*. Cambridge: Cambridge University Press.

Syfret, R. H. (1961) 'Marvell's Horatian Ode', *Review of English Studies* 12: 160–72.

Wallace, J. M. (1968) *Destiny his Choice: The Loyalism of Andrew Marvell*. Cambridge: Cambridge University Press.

Worden, B. (1987) 'Andrew Marvell, Oliver Cromwell, and the Horatian Ode', in *Politics of Discourse: The Literature and History of Seventeenth-Century England*, eds. Kevin Sharpe and Steven Zwicker. Berkeley and Los Angeles: University of California Press.

# Index

For Product Safety Concerns and Information please contact our EU
representative GPSR@taylorandfrancis.com Taylor & Francis Verlag GmbH,
Kaufingerstraße 24, 80331 München, Germany

Printed and bound by CPI Group (UK) Ltd, Croydon, CR0 4YY
11/04/2025
01844012-0001